# Entering
# Hekate's Cauldron

# Entering Hekate's Cauldron

## Spells, Spirits, Rites, and Rituals

### CYNDI BRANNEN

WEISER BOOKS

This edition first published in 2025 by Weiser Books, an imprint of
Red Wheel/Weiser, LLC

With offices at:
65 Parker Street, Suite 7
Newburyport, MA 01950
*www.redwheelweiser.com*

ISBN: 978-1-57863-881-9

Library of Congress Cataloging-in-Publication Data available upon request

Cover by Sky Peck Design
Interior photos by Cyndi Brannen
Interior by Debby Dutton
Typeset in Adobe Garamond Pro and Incognito Pro

Printed in the United States of America
IBI
10 9 8 7 6 5 4 3 2 1

*Hail Hekate, Witch Queen,*
*Mistress of the Moon,*
*That rises and sets in her Cave,*
*Home of her eternal*
*Cauldron.*

*Dark Mother, grant me entrance*
*Into your secret lair.*
*Shine your torchlight*
*To the inner chamber*
*Where your Cauldron*
*resides.*

*I come, as your witches have*
*since before time,*
*Seeking the keys*
*Of Knowledge.*
*Of the Craft.*
*Of Mystery.*
*To enter Hekate's Cauldron,*
*To be reborn*
*Into the Witch*
*I have always been.*

# Contents

# Practica

## Rites, Rituals, Spells, and Spirits

# Introduction

## *The Keys of the Cauldron*

*Just below the surface floats a key
Unlocking Magick and Mystery,
Medicine for the Witch's Soul.
Plunging in to claim it,
I feel the spirits swirling.
Within my grasp, the key
Unfurls countless secrets,
Now seeping into my skin,
Healing, transforming, empowering.*

This is an incantation that can bring your personal cauldron into view. Pause for a moment to allow the image of the key floating in a cauldron to take form. Connect with your breath and let it fill your body's cauldron—your belly. Slow down your breathing; let the image become clear. Make some notes or draw some quick sketches. What does the key look like? What about the cauldron? What else is in the cauldron? What emotions come through? What messages are revealed?

However you perceive your cauldron, trust that it is how you are meant to see it. Explore the images; ask them what they would have you to know. Allow them to develop into their own spirits and become helpmates for your witchery. Now link these images to one area on which you are working—a problem, a situation, a goal, or an aspect of your personal development. Let your intuition tell you what is most important, even if it isn't necessarily what's top of mind. Write down what your intuition tells you beside your notes and sketches. Then craft an intention—a short powerful statement that declares that your desired outcome is already in progress and links the symbols in your images to it—something like this:

*With this Key, this Cauldron,*
*And the Spirits revealed.*
*I so declare that* [desired outcome].
*As it is written,*
*So it becomes.*

The final lines in this example transform your intention into an incantation, creating a spell. Refine it until it feels right for you, then allow it to come to life. Craft your own written talisman out of the incantation and connect with it to boost your efforts to manifest the spell. Hekate's Wheel, also known as the strophalos, is a symbol that evokes momentum for any spell. Envision it spiralling outward, releasing your incantation.

### This is the essence of witchcraft.

Emotions are typically the compelling force flowing through all witchcraft. When we perform spells, rituals, and rites, we are seeking a desired state of being. As you craft your spell, pay attention to the emotions that come up as you create your incantation; notice any emotions that arise when you work with your written talisman. Observe how your spell is supported by your card readings, your dreams, synchronicities and unusual events, your experiences, and any messages you receive. This is how you cast your own magick circle, and within your circle is the book.

Hekate beckons us into the mysteries of her cauldron, from whence the essence of witchcraft flows. We feel its touch in our intuition, in the tingle in our fingers when we craft spells, and in the knowing that abides in every witch's soul. To enter her cauldron is to be reborn, built anew from her mysteries. Within the cauldron, knowledge and spirits and spells abide. Gather round the cauldron with me as I share a compendium of rituals, rites, spells, and spirits.

## Hekate's Cauldron

This book is in the tradition of a Book of Shadows. You'll find tried and true rites, rituals, and spells focusing on witchcraft that is rooted in history yet abides in modern life. This is a goddess witchcraft that spirals out from a deep alignment to not only Hekate but also to her companions. It is a system of witchcraft focused on healing and empowerment designed to help us live magickal lives that reflect deep personal authenticity. Consider it for what it is—shared practices from a well-established coven of which I am so blessed to be the High Priestess.

My perspective is what I call Modern Hekatean Witchcraft. I am inspired by ancient texts—from spells to myths—and merge them with solid modern personal-development methods and magickal techniques. To me, there is no symbol more evocative, no tool more powerful than the cauldron. It is the epicenter of witchcraft. Whether I am burning leaves to banish heartache, or brewing a botanical infusion, or storing witchy treasures, or taking a ritual bath, the cauldron lies at the heart of my craft. Yet although the cauldron can take diverse forms and has countless uses, it is much more than a symbol or a tool. It is a portal to a deeper world and a connector with the spirits—and even with great Hekate herself. In the center of my personal etheric inner temple, there abides a cauldron from which flows the pure potential of witchcraft.

The cauldron, like Hekate, has a rich tale to tell. Indeed, it embodies the wisdom of the ages that comes from both bane and blessing. To enter her cauldron is to immerse ourselves in Hekate's magick and mystery. From the Wyrd Sisters to ancient stories of Medea rebirthing powerful men via her cauldron, the connection between witches and simmering pots of mysterious ingredients has been told innumerable times, and Hekate resides at the center of all these tales. For witches, the cauldron is the essential tool for brewing magick, medicine, and mystery.

Stories from around the globe and across the ages have recounted the potency of the cauldron—from tales of Cerridwen, the Welsh goddess who immersed Taliesin in her cauldron, to the mythology of the king of the Norse gods, Odin. Throughout history, the cauldron has stood as a font of mystery, a source of healing and transformation, and an invitation to the world of spirits and spells.

*The Witch seeks Wisdom,*
*Practices the Craft,*
*And unlocks the Mystery.*

## The Personal Cauldron

Envision the personal cauldron that you envisioned during the earlier incantation as the container for all your witchcraft, a sort of sacred space. If you are fortunate enough to have a room you can dedicate as sacred space, see this as your cauldron. Should your witchcraft consist of a small collection of objects and books tucked away in a corner, that is your cauldron as well. The cauldron is simply a circle rendered into three dimensions and fueled by the Sacred

Flame, from which rises smoke and steam. In chapter 1, you'll learn how to enchant your personal cauldron with a ritual. For now, just begin to see your witchcraft as a cauldron and connect with the vision that came through to you as you crafted your spell.

## The Book of Shadows

A Book of Shadows can take many forms, and its contents are very individual. My personal Book of Shadows is full of rites, rituals, spells, and spirits. The pages are filled with a wholistic sort of witchery that heals, empowers, and transforms and is drawn from ancient wisdom, including correspondences from astrology, stones, and alignment with the deeper world. The spirits that inhabit the pages come in numerous shapes and sizes, from plant allies to ascended beings. Much of my personal Book of Shadows becomes part of my coven's official record, which we call a "grimoire." There's a long history of magickal texts that can inspire us, especially what's known as the *Greek Magical Papyri*. Several of the entries from there have found their way into our grimoire.

There are loads of ways to create your own Book of Shadows. You can keep your witchy records in an elaborate notebook or in myriad less traditional digital formats. Personally, I use a combination of methods that merges my writing in my beloved books with computer-based information-management tools. I take photos of anything that lends itself to being recorded visually—although I believe that some practices, like ceremonial rituals, are not meant to be captured in this way. Develop a system that works best for you. This can take time. Whether you use paper or digital media, be sure to perform a spell to enchant your Book of Shadows to ensure that it is protected and connected to you and to its contents. I do this by creating a talisman on the title page, typically one that features an incantation, correspondences, and a sigil. I also recommend that you keep your Book of Shadows separate from your everyday journaling. My Book of Shadows is a structured, formal record that draws from the more free-form notes in my journals.

## The Structure of This Book

The components of witchcraft are keys that unlock magick and mystery. Sometimes they are easily accessible, floating near the cauldron's surface; you just have to roll up your sleeve and reach in. At other times, you may need to dive deep into the waters to retrieve them. Some of us are natural spellcasters; others are skilled at divination. The contents of any specific cauldron are thus individual. My personal cauldron contains plants, spirits, goddesses, astrology, the cards, mythology, and other tools. These components are then filtered through my psycho-spiritual lens. Part of immersing yourself in Hekate's Cauldron is discovering what your individual keys are.

The major keys of witchcraft are *foundations, knowledge, spellcraft, and mystery,* and I've organized the coming pages around these keys. In part 1, I give you what I consider to be the foundations of witchcraft. Part 2 addresses the knowledge Hekate embodies; part 3 explores spellcraft; and part 4 delves into the deeper mystery of magick.

### The Foundation
Part 1, "The Foundation," reviews ways to get started with your craft. Beginning with connecting to the cauldron as the center point of witchcraft. Since the altar is so important, I share some tips for creating one in this section. This section concludes with a discussion about the realms and includes a ritual bath and tarot card–reading technique.

### The Knowledge
Part 2 focuses on knowledge about Hekate—from her origins to her symbols. Here you'll learn ways to honor her, as well as how to connect to her diverse aspects. The final chapter in part 2 explores Hekate's companions, from her close associations with ancient goddesses to her connections with other dark goddesses and male deities.

### The Craft
Part 3, "The Craft," is all about spellcraft. Starting with some of the keys for practicing witchcraft that I've developed over the years. I offer tips for creating your own apothecary, including tools and supplies. You'll also find an extensive discussion of correspondences, which are typically physical objects that have deeper properties—like plants, colors, and stones. This is followed by an examination of how to incorporate numbers, which are thought forms with physical representations, into your witchery. There's a selection of spells that you can use "as is" or to provide inspiration for creating your own.

## The Mystery

In part 4, "The Mystery," spirits emerge from the cauldron. Discover beings from animals to ancestors through rituals and other mystical experiences.

## Practica: Doing Witchcraft

Throughout the coming chapters, you'll find ways to practice Modern Hekatean Witchcraft, including meditation journeys, spells, rituals, and other techniques that you can use as they are written or as a source of inspiration for developing your own personal workings. My hope is that you will use them as opportunities to immerse yourself in the energy of Hekate and her cauldron.

## Meditation and Transcendence

Meditation is the shifting of awareness to being present within yourself while opening up to the mysteries of Hekate and her deeper world. When we become aware of our thoughts through contemplation (which is the beginning of meditation), we peer into our own mysteries. Meditation is not emptying the mind; it's expanding it to see beyond the ordinary. A contemplative walk, a ritual bath, or even our beauty regimen can become mindful when we enter into these activities with intention and presence. Meditation moves us from being controlled by our thought spirals to being the creator of our thoughts.

You may find that it helps to record yourself reading the meditations in this book and then playing them back when you are ready for the experience. Some of the meditations can be found on the *Keeping Her Keys* podcast, too.

## The Cauldron of "Good Enough"

Allow your magick to be a bit messy. What is real is often not flawless. Whether it's a sigil with less than perfect symmetry, an incantation written on a scrap of paper, or a talisman that may not be ready to make its debut on social media, these little flaws actually render your magick more powerful. Go gently, with purpose, following what feels true in your soul.

*I am Good.*
*I am Enough.*
*I abide in the Cauldron of Good Enough.*

YOURS IN HEKATE'S CAULDRON, CYNDI

# Part I

## *The Foundation*

# Chapter 4

## *Entering Hekate's Cauldron—Starting the Journey of Magick and Mystery*

*Round, round, round*
*Swirl the sacred waters.*
*Becoming elixir,*
*Enchanting potion,*
*A potent Witches Brew,*
*Drawing me into*
*the Magick and Mystery.*

There are three primary ways that witches generally work with cauldrons, but they all relate to the central function of a cauldron serving as a sacred vessel that unlocks witchery. Cauldrons can act as containers for liquid-based formulations—for instance, adding botanicals to water and then heating the mixture to release their essence, whether we consume the brew or use it for another purpose. I keep a large cast-iron cauldron atop my woodstove for this, although I use others just for liquids as well. I have medium-sized cauldrons that I use for burning botanicals and others that I use for storing magickal supplies.

Traditional cauldrons are made from sturdy metal or pottery and usually have three legs. I have quite a few triple-legged cauldron mugs. But symbolic cauldrons can be any container you use for witchery—from a censor for burning incense to a tub where you do your ritual bathing.

Cauldrons can be used for all manner of witchcraft. A favorite with my students is what we dubbed the "Chthauldron," a combination of Hekate's epithet Chthonia (of the Underworld) and the word "cauldron." We use the Chthauldron to contain anything we need to release or banish, writing simple intentions on scraps of paper.

## Choosing a Cauldron

For liquids that are meant to be consumed, choose one that is food safe. For burning objects or incense, cast iron or another strong metal is best. There's absolutely nothing more witchy than the traditional three-legged black cast-iron cauldron. As a storage vessel, you can buy ceramic vessels or even craft your own. In the coven, we've made them from air-dry and polymer clays. No matter what form they take, your cauldrons will make themselves known to you—whether they are modern kitchen pots or more traditional vessels.

## Cauldron Khernips / Triformis Ritual

Khernips is an ancient rite of purification through the blending of the three realms (land, sea, and sky) with the Sacred Flame and pure water. Whether you've acquired a new cauldron or are rededicating an existing one, enchanting it ensures that it is attuned to witchery and to you personally. The primary method I teach for cleansing, protecting, and connecting with a cauldron is known as the Triformis ritual. Triformis is an ancient title of Hekate that refers to her three forms and her governance over the three realms. You can use this ritual not just for your cauldron but also as part of your daily ritual, for cleansing your home, and so on. It is truly an all-purpose ceremony.

If you have separate cauldrons dedicated to the three realms, begin this ritual with the cauldron of the sea, then anoint the other two following the steps outlined. (See more on the specific cauldrons in chapter 3.)

### Supplies

- A nonporous cauldron

- Pure water of your choice. I like a blend of land, sea, and sky—well water, ocean, and rain—but any pure water will be excellent. To level it up, charge it by leaving it outside overnight during a full moon.

- A "torch" (matches or a lighter)

- A dried sprig of a suitable botanical, big enough that you can set it alight but not so big that you can't safely hold on to it. Some of the tried-and-true ones are mugwort, rosemary, and thyme. My personal favorite is the wormwood that grows abundantly on my property. If you get the fresh rosemary or thyme from the supermarket, allow it to air-dry for about three days so that it will burn easily. You can certainly combine botanicals into a bundle, which is what I often do. To do this, gather them and tightly wrap one end with cotton cording.

● The spell talisman you made at the beginning of this book

**Process**

Start by filling your cauldron with the water. Light the botanical sprig and allow the flame to develop, then plunge it into the water and stir it counter-clockwise, while saying:

*I banish all that blocks and binds.*

Using either three fingers of your left hand or the sprig, asperge yourself and your space by anointing your body with the water and sprinkling it around you. Then stir the sprig clockwise, saying:

*All is protected from harm.*

With either the sprig or three fingers of your right hand, asperge yourself and your space. Then place the sprig totally in the water and hold up the cauldron, saying:

*I am connected to all that makes me healthy and whole.*

Feel free to customize the incantation as you feel led, perhaps even naming your cauldron.

For a deeper experience, you can find the formula for Circe's Philter in *Entering Hekate's Garden*. This is a favorite of mine and my students.

# Chapter 2

## Creating an Altar—Cauldrons, Sacred Flame, Icons, and More

*Treasures found and given,*
*Round the cauldron,*
*Sacred Flame burning bright,*
*The altar emerges.*
*With each piece I place,*
*The spirits awaken*
*And Great Hekate smiles.*

Altars are meant to be expressions of how we connect to Hekate and her deeper world. There are countless ways to create them. I generally use some sort of tray as the foundation of my altar. This is based on ancient altars known as "eschara" that were associated with Hekate. You can also use an altar cloth instead of a tray, or you can use both.

I have several altars throughout my home. In my witching room, I have what I call a formal altar and a working altar. The formal altar, which is more structured, is where I place offerings and perform rituals. The working altar is where I do my witchcraft. This space is always changing and transforming as I organize spell components, do readings, and creatively explore spirits. You can prepare your altar spaces using the ritual given at the end of chapter 1.

Almost any object can be enchanted and, because creativity is essential in witchcraft, I encourage you to express yourself freely in your altar design. That being said, there are some fundamental items you need, such as cauldrons, candles, and statues. We have talked about cauldrons, but now I want to focus on candles—the physical representation of the Sacred Flame. Then we'll look at other altar components such as statues, images, and icons.

# Hekate's Sacred Flame

The flame is a key feature of any witch's altar. Whether you are rendering spirited liquids or igniting botanicals into sacred smoke, the connection between fire and our cauldrons runs deep. Hekate's iconic twin torches symbolize the essential power of fire as dual forces of creation and destruction. Using traditional methods, such as burning botanicals and lighting wax candles, are fabulous, but oil warmers and LED lights can also attune you to Hekate's Sacred Flame.

You can enchant "blank" candles with botanicals, empower them with sigils, and anoint them with sacred oils to support you in your magick. For instance, you can make an *Oleum Spirita* (spirited oil) by mixing botanicals with high-quality olive oil and letting the mixture rest for a few days, then anointing a candle by rubbing the oil sparingly around the candle in a clockwise motion. Alternatively, you can create a base around a candle with botanicals, stones, and charms.

## Oleum Spirita: Crafting Spirited Oil

*Oleum Spirita*, which translates from Latin as "oil of spirits," is a foundational mixture that can be worked with in countless ways. It is meant to be personally connected to the practitioner, so develop yours as you feel led. Alternatively, you can craft yours using this tried-and-true formula.

### Supplies

- A cauldron, pot, or other warming appliance
- Seven botanicals, covering a spectrum of magickal properties, so they can be adapted for any working
- Two to three cups of high-quality olive oil
- Strainer
- Glass storage container for completed oil
- Parchment paper
- An eye dropper for working with the oil

I recommend having at least one botanical that is a bit challenging to acquire, one that you find in the natural world to represent the wildness. The rest can be cultivated, especially those you grow yourself. They can be fresh, dried, or already in oil. Generally, triple the amount for fresh compared to dried, and use only a few drops of an oil. Use intuitive amounts of each, or about one teaspoon of each.

The traditional Oleum Spirita botanicals, all of which are sacred to Hekate, we use in the coven include:

- *Aster* for the wild, since they are not easily cultivated; for their properties of agape, the universal love; and for the deeper world and spirits

- *Benzoin* for mysticism and gentleness; ground resin or the oil can be used.

- *Juniper* for cleansing, especially for removing barriers to the deeper world. Berries, sprigs, or the oil can be used.

- *Lavender* lends clarity and calm. Oil, fresh, or dried all work well.

- *Mugwort* unlocks our power, aligns with spirits, and protects during our etheric explorations.

- *Poppy,* seeds or flowers, for visions and messages from beyond

- *Rose* petals, hips, buds, or leaves; preferably ones that are not chemically treated, as many commercially available ones are

If you use these ingredients, the oil will have a lovely earthy smell.

**Process**

This is a lovely oil to make as part of your devotional work during the Dark Moon to reinforce your commitment to Hekate and the craft.

You can recite the following incantation throughout the creation process—when adding the botanicals to the cauldron, when heating and stirring, and when straining and pouring into the final container.

1. Place the botanicals in your warming appliance.

2. Pour the olive oil over the botanicals, stirring to coat them all well. The oil sets the foundation for cleansing, protection, and well-being.

3. Gently heat on low, stirring occasionally.

4. Let it simmer for several hours until the oil takes on an earthy smell and you "feel" that it is ready.

5. Allow the completed oil to cool, then strain to remove the botanicals and funnel the oil into a glass storage container.

6. Squeeze the excess oil from the botanicals and dry them on parchment paper. You can later use them in spells and as fire starters.

7. Add the date, any astrological notes, your sacred name, and sigil to the container.

8. Adorn with charms, especially keys.

To make a cold-infused oil, blend the botanicals and oil and let it rest, covered, for several days in a cool, dark place before straining into the storage container.

### Incantation

*In the Name of Hekate,*
*In the Name of Plant Spirits,*
*I now call forth Oleum Spirita,*
*As Helpmate and Companion.*
*Pasikratea, the Universal Queen, and Olive,*
*Burning bright liquid, add your fire and power, bringing together all spirits.*
*Pantrophos, the Nurturer, and Aster, lend your protection and connection to*
*    the spirits.*
*Propylaia, the Threshold, and Benzoin, add your ease and mysticism.*
*Triformis, the Transformer, and Juniper, banisher extraordinaire, clear the*
*    way to truth and sacredness.*
*Aregos, the Helper, and Lavender, bring clarity and calm to this potion.*
*Kleidoukhos, the Keeper of Keys, and Mugwort, Witches best friend, open me*
*    to the mysteries and protection grant.*
*Aidonaea, the Depths, and Poppy, bring the visions and messages from beyond.*
*Anima Mundi, the Soul of the Universe, and Rose, sacred flower, awakener of*
*    bane and blessing.*
*I now render these spirits into this oil,*
*Calling them together,*

*Crafting it whole.*
*As I create, so it becomes.*
*This oil is consecrated for all my work.*
*Oleum Spirita,*
*Helpmate,*
*Guide.*
*Protector,*
*Connector,*
*Sacred Medicine of Hekate's Garden.*

Add this sigil of Oleum Spirita to finish enchanting your oil.

## Applications

Oleum Spirita can be used to enchant just about anything, but be mindful of any objects whose appearance may be impacted by the application of oil, such as wood. Also, before applying liberally to the skin, test a small patch for sensitivities. Here are some examples of use:

- After the object is cleansed, consecrate and revivify statues, cauldrons, the Cista Mystica, tools, and more. Generally, apply with a clockwise motion.

- Add to other magickal mixtures, especially glues and paints. Just a few drops does the trick.

- Apply to spell bags, talismans, and such.

- Anoint yourself to encourage transcendent experiences during meditations and rituals. Apply a few drops in a clockwise motion at the root, heart, and crown centers.

- Apply as a healing balm; work a bit into the afflicted area.

Oleum Spirita will keep for several months, even a couple of years, if stored in a dark bottle in a cool, dark place.

## Threefold Candle Ritual: Igniting the Sacred Flame

To perform this candle-based version of the Triformis ritual, all you need is a candle of your choosing, a "torch" (a lighter or match), a cauldron(s), and a spell talisman. You may have seen me perform this ritual on my podcast.

Start by lighting the candle, while saying:

> *As I ignite this candle, I am connecting to Hekate's Sacred Flame, illuminating her magick and mysteries.*

Holding the candle in your left hand, move it in a counterclockwise circle three times, saying:

> *I banish all that blocks this connection and all that which harms.*

With the candle in your right hand, move it in a clockwise circle three times, saying:

> *I am protected by Hekate's Sacred Flame, casting the circle round me and all I care for.*

Hold the candle with both hands at your heart center and say:

> *This flame burns within me. Hail Hekate and her Sacred Flame.*

Set the candle down on your altar and say:

> *This altar is enlivened with the Sacred Flame and is dedicated to Hekate, her magick, and her mysteries.*

I recommend softening your gaze while looking at the flame, gently focusing on the flickering, to access messages and visions.

## Statues, Images, and Icons

Our statues, images, and symbols of the goddess are means of veneration and conduits for connecting to her. Traditionally, these images and icons were set up at boundaries, thresholds, and crossroads and were called *Hekataion* (singular) and *Hekataia* (plural). Statues, images, symbols, and other representations of deities are beautiful, but their power is much more than aesthetic. Icons were often offered as signs of veneration, but they are also beacons for connecting with the deeper world. Properly activated, they serve as a means of two-way communication.

Iconic objects can become depleted of their power over time, so I recommend cleansing them then recharging them by anointing them with a sacred oil, such as Oleum Spirita, or passing them through sacred smoke from finely ground dried botanicals, such as mugwort, or resins, such as frankincense or myrrh. These objects can also be protected and enchanted to amplify their power as portals of alignment.

If anointing with oil, I recommend using Oleum Spirita, which is specifically made for sacred work. Soil, salt, and smoke can be used to vivify objects not amenable to liquid anointing. Alternatively, you can heat oil in a diffuser—simply a different type of cauldron—to create sacred vapor. When anointing representations of Hekate, start at her head and work down to the feet, representing her chthonic (Underworld) aspects. Make three passes down the object—the first to remove negative energies, the second to gain its blessing, and the third to activate the object.

If burning botanicals or resins, always line the bottom of a heat-proof cauldron with a layer of sand or small pebbles to create a foundation. For botanicals that burn well, like mugwort and wormwood, place them directly on the foundation. For items that are harder to ignite, use a charcoal disk as a base. The disks can be broken into smaller pieces, if necessary. To create sacred ash, let the remnants of these burnings accumulate in your cauldron, then store them in a glass container. You can learn more about sacred smoke and ash in *Entering Hekate's Garden*.

Through vivification an object becomes attuned to the energy of the deity. Some traditions believe that part of a spirit's energy actually becomes "ensouled" within the object during vivification. Others believe that the object serves merely as a conduit for its power. Either way, vivification links an object to its spirit and directs the energy of the spirit into it. When you activate a Hekatean icon, you are calling upon the goddess to bless you as the caretaker of the icon and petitioning her to create a portal of connection or to apotheosize (deify) an object, leaving her imprint on it. Be sure to prepare an appropriate offering to make as you ask for her blessing.

### Ritual of Vivification: Enlivening and Renewing Sacred Objects

This brief ritual is suitable for anointing and activating any sacred object—sometimes called *materia sacris*. The oil you choose should be made of a fixative (base oil) and botanicals that are sacred to the deity you are petitioning. You can use the Oleum Spirita described above, or you can craft your own personal oil. You can revivify an existing icon or use a new one.

I always light a candle before beginning this ritual because I like to anoint icons with the oil while reciting an incantation and then pass them through sacred smoke. If the icon you are activating is not suitable for anointing with a liquid, use only sacred smoke. Make three passes with either the oil or the smoke—one for cleansing, one for protection, and one for activation. As you make each of the three passes, hold the icon at your heart center and say a brief incantation—either this one or one you create yourself.

> Hail [icon].
> I honor you with this [oil].
> Attend me now.

Anoint the object in a counterclockwise direction, while saying:

> Cleanse this [icon], removing all barriers between me and you.

Anoint the object in a clockwise direction, while saying:

> I call upon you to protect this [icon], creating a circle of connection between me and you.

Anoint the feet, heart, and crown of the object (adapt as necessary), while saying:

> I call upon you to bless this [icon], rendering it and me sacred.
> I pledge to honor you.

You can adorn statues and images of your deities with offerings such as botanicals, ribbons, bones, charms, and other items. You can keep offering bowls or plates on your altar, or you can create a cauldron that is specifically dedicated to offerings. In chapter 5, you'll learn about a traditional food offering known as a Hekate's Supper. But if you want to give her a food offering now, choose something that is valuable to you—cakes, or cheese and nuts. Botanicals, especially roses, make wonderful offerings. Let your intuition guide you toward items that seem appropriate, beginning with what you already have.

I like to offer some words of gratitude, without expecting anything in return. When making an offering, recite something like this:

*Hail Hekate,*
*I give you this* [icon] *as offering and as a token of my sincerity.*
*I am grateful.*

## Enchanted Objects for the Altar

Add objects to your altar that speak to you of magick and mystery, be they conventional items or something that is uniquely yours. There are many lovely things you can have on your altar, including:

- Cauldron(s)

- Icons: any image or object that is evocative of Hekate for you

- Candles: adorned with botanicals and charms, inscribed with symbols and sigils to amplify the magick

- Trays: traditional on Hekatean altars and inspired by ancient practices

- Correspondences: botanicals, stones, colors, and animals that help you connect with Hekate and her deeper world

- Symbols: keys, torches, the special wheel labyrinth known as the *strophalos*, and any other symbols you associate with Hekate

- Personal items: trinkets, photos, art you've created, found treasures (from leaves to bones), anything that amplifies your connection to Hekate and her deeper world

# Chapter 3

# The Eternal Cauldrons of
# Land, Sea, and Sky

*The eternal cauldrons I now call,*
*Land for the earth and the world around me.*
*Sea for the water and the down below.*
*Sky for the air and the up above.*
*Flowing through all the*
*Power of the Sacred Flame,*
*Rendering spirit into all.*

In ancient texts, such as Hesiod's *Theogony*, Hekate held governance over the three realms of land, sea, and sky. Her essence is woven into these realms—which are both separate and one—creating the cosmic cauldron from which her magick emanates. And the three ways in which we perform our own cauldron witchery align with these realms as well.

## The Realms of the Cauldrons

In Hekatean magick, these three realms are symbolized by three eternal cauldrons, with the Sacred Flame running through all.

**The Cauldron of Land** acts as a vessel for earthly treasures and provides the strong roots and foundations of knowledge. This is where we formulate our intentions. Symbolized by a layer of earth (sand, pebbles) that lies at the bottom of the cauldron, forming a protective layer.

**The Cauldron of Sea** is the vessel used for containing our liquid concoctions. This cauldron governs our emotions, our intuition, and our witchcraft. This is where the mystery awakens.

**The Cauldron of Sky** pertains to the celestial and the element of air. The smoke and vapor rising from the cauldron is symbolic of this realm.

Fire, the spirit of witchcraft that is symbolized by Hekate's torches, ignites all three of these cauldrons, running throughout as the essence of creation and destruction. It is fire that creates and burns land, fire that warms the sea, and fire that awakens the sacred smoke to send it floating skyward. Having a separate cauldron for each of these realms can make your witchery more effective and more transforming.

## Hekate and the Three Realms

As said above, Hekate embodies the three realms. The realm of land references her presence as a guide throughout our earthly journey, particularly her prominence at crossroads and thresholds. These may be physical junctures—such as where roads intersect, a stream, a hedge—as well as personal transitions. The realm of sea evokes her depths and primordial power, while the realm of sky connects to Hekate's more transcendent side, offering keys to the greater mysteries.

## The Cauldrons Within: The Three Selves

Mapping onto the three realms, we, too, have a trinity of core aspects. The lower self, represented by the root center, inhabits the energetic epicenter deep within our bones. This aligns with our emotions, our intuition, and our magick. The middle self, energetically located at our heart center, is the crossroads between our interior lives and the external world. It's associated with our actions, how we show ourselves to others, our relationships, and our material reality. The higher self, while connected at its base to our regular consciousness, climbs high into the intellectual and mystical. This is where the third eye is located; its symbol is a crown stretching up to the world of spirit.

## The Cauldrons Three Ritual Bath

My favorite way to connect to the three cauldrons is with this simple ritual. While soaking in my bathtub (cauldron of land), I ignite botanicals (cauldron of sky) and connect to the sacred smoke. At the end of the ritual or bath, I pour water (cauldron of sea) over the burning botanicals (usually moon water). Fire—the spirit of witchcraft and the foundation of all three cauldrons—empowers the entire ritual. If getting into a tub isn't an option for you, the shower works just as well, as does wrapping yourself in blankets.

## Method

Begin by making an infusion. Immerse rose petals plus about half a teaspoon each of mugwort and yarrow in a cup of boiling water. Let it steep for five minutes. Strain out the plant matter and pour the infusion into your tub as it fills with water.

If possible, arrange a cauldron and a candle in the tub area. Ignite the botanicals (yarrow and mugwort again) in the cauldron to create a sacred smoke that will enhance your connection to the eternal cauldrons. Just use a pinch of each, either lit directly or placed on a small piece of burning charcoal.

You can also anoint yourself with sacred oil while in the tub (see chapter 10). Including stones, such as moonstone or selenite, can enhance your journey.

## Invocation

Once you have completed the previous steps but before entering the tub, envision it as Hekate's Eternal Cauldron. When you are ready, invoke the experience with these words (or ones of your own):

> I am entering Hekate's Cauldron. I am a witch born of the cauldron, and to the cauldron I now return.

Immerse yourself in the water, continuing to speak the incantation. Close your eyes and deepen your breathing. Pull your breath all the way down, filling your belly and gently expanding your core. Do this until you feel your roots stretching down into the depths.

## Meditation

Direct your breath to your heart center, opening up to the magick and mysteries of Hekate's Cauldron. Connect your root, the seat of your intuition, to your heart center, the intersection of your internal and external worlds. Shorten your breath so it stops at your throat, then let it float upward, cleansing your mind and connecting to your heart and root so that all is aligned. Rest in that energy of alignment, noticing anything that comes to the surface. Your physical self is well tended, and now it is time to journey to the deeper world of Hekate.

Your deeper sight, your soul vision, your third eye, opens, and you see a gate. Stepping through the gate, you enter Hekate's Garden. The path before you is lit with torches that seem to beckon you. As you walk the path, take in the sights of the garden. The plants, animals, and spirits are being revealed as you are meant to see them.

You come to a great cauldron illuminated by torches, the moon's reflection shimmering on its surface. An offering appears in your hands; you add it to the cauldron. You contemplate whether to take a sip from the cauldron, or splash your hand in it, or fully immerse yourself there. The choice is yours. Whatever you choose, notice the images and sensations that arise. You may receive a gift. Abide here for a few moments until you feel satiated, then return to the garden entrance.

Gently come back into your physical self, returning your attention to your breath. Take in the sensation of the water on your body; explore the boundary between your physical self and the water. Reflect upon your experiences during the journey.

When you are ready, get out of the tub and end the experience with words such as:

*I have entered Hekate's Cauldron and been transformed.*

Record your experiences in your journal, including sketches of anything you saw.

## The Cauldrons Oracle Reading

Follow up the ritual bath with this reading to help you process your experience. Tarot and oracle cards reveal messages from Hekate, your spirit guides, and other allies, giving you guidance and insight into where you are on your journey and providing answers to specific questions you ask. Tarot decks are based on a centuries-old system of divination, while oracle decks are based on a variety of different systems—everything from animals to goddesses. Work with a deck that feels right for you. Generally, I ignite sacred smoke in my cauldron and pass the deck through it before beginning a reading.

If you are using a new deck, connect to it by having a conversation with it; interact with the deck just as you would when getting to know someone new in your life. If the deck feels a bit unsettled, cleanse it by passing it through sacred smoke to align it with you. The deck can also rest on a bed of sea salt prior to use to drain impurities.

Begin by connecting with Hekate and seek her presence for your reading with an invocation:

*Great Hekate, reveal your wisdom through these cards.*

## Card #1: The Significator

*I call forth the card that is who I am or am becoming.*

Connect to the spirit of fire, calling forward your significator, or personal power card. This is the card with which you are most aligned; it is the fire that fuels the other cards in the reading. It can indicate a rather permanent relationship, or it may be a card that comes forward as a short-term guide. You can either ask the cards to reveal your significator or you can intentionally select the one that feels best to you. If you are working with a traditional tarot deck, the Minor Arcana (the numerical cards that are divided into suits) can be challenging as significators, so you may want to remove them before you begin. When you are ready, draw or choose your first card and place it in the center of your reading area. This is your personal significator.

## Card #2: The Cauldron of Land

*I seek guidance for my middle self, actions, and interactions with the external world.*

Focus on this intention while holding and shuffling your cards, drawing when ready. This card represents the cauldron of land, pertaining to the intersection of who we are on the inside with our external environment.

## Card #3: The Cauldron of Sea

*I seek guidance for my deeper self, emotions, and intuition.*

Focus on the energy of the cauldron of sea—emotions, intuition, and magick— while holding and shuffling your deck. When you are ready, draw the second card and place it below your significator.

## Card #4: The Cauldron of Sky

*I seek guidance for my higher self, the mind, and the mysteries.*

Connect with this statement while holding and shuffling your cards, drawing the one that feels right. This card will speak to the higher self and the celestial and also to the energy of attitudes and beliefs.

**Interpretation**

When you have finished drawing cards, ask Hekate to help you understand the meaning. Your intuitive interpretation will be based on the immediate emotions and thoughts that come to mind when you focus on a card. Look at the symbols, images, and colors. What do they mean to you?

Once you have considered your intuitive response, you can refer to the book that accompanied your deck or go deeper with a resource like the classic *78 Degrees of Wisdom.* How does the established meaning of the card align with your own intuitive understanding? Every reading has a story to tell. Explore the connections between the cards and discover the narrative they are sharing with you.

When you are done interpreting the cards, thank Hekate as your guide and the cards for their revelations.

# Part II

## *The Knowledge*

# Chapter 4

## The Calling and the Crossroads

*Without darkness, there is no light.*
*Without death, there is no life.*
*Without the ending, there is no beginning.*
*Without the cut, there is no growth.*
*Without the gate, there is no key.*
*Without the three, there is no one.*
*Without the crossroads, there is no way.*

Crossroads are the most sacred sites for Hekate's witches. I've met her there, along with her accompanying spirits, each and every time. Sometimes I sense her presence. Sometimes she sends an animal messenger. Sometimes I meet a stranger through whom she speaks. I know she is there because I sense a feeling of the sacred and become aware of the alertness this energy instills. To the ancients, crossroads were places where the restless dead abided. Hekate as Enodia (Guide) ruled these places and the paths leading to them. And we continue to meet her there, following the light of her pale torches.

There are diverse types of crossroads; some are literal, and some are symbolic places of liminal energy. These in-between spaces can also be sensed at dawn and dusk, at the end of driveways, at the thresholds of homes, and at graveyards. When we stand at our own sacred crossroads, our three selves are aligned. This is where the energies of land, sea, and sky meet. This is the threshold between the physical world and the realm of spirits. This is the domain of Hekate.

You can evoke the liminal power of the crossroads by constructing a symbol for one on your altar. You can make a tripod of twigs with correspondences that resonate with you. Or you can gather dirt at a three-way crossroads and place it on your altar to create the same energy. Add representations of land, sea, and sky to call in the energies of the three worlds and three selves. Place a candle to call in fire. You can also place offerings at these symbolic crossroads.

## Meeting Hekate at the Crossroads

Hekate meets us at the crossroads, inviting us to cross the threshold into her deeper world. This happens when your old ways of being no longer seem to fit. This summoning call can take countless forms—a beautiful image, a book that cries out for your attention, internet searches that lead you to Hekate, finding an unknown key. She takes up residency in your dreams and in your waking mind. Her cauldron beckons you into the mysteries.

**Entering Encounters with Hekate into Your Book of Shadows**
Creating a record of your first encounter with Hekate is an excellent way to preserve those memories. Keeping a journal that contains your personal reflections on how and when Hekate called you is also an offering to the goddess.

Here are some questions that can help you explore your experience:

- How did Hekate show herself? By stirring strong emotions? By connecting you with an image? By allowing you to hear her voice?

- What was going on in your life in that moment? Were you at a personal crossroads? Were you experiencing major stressors or health issues?

- What thoughts and feelings did you experience? Were you jolted out of stasis? Did this cause strong emotions in you? Did you experience radical changes in mindset?

- Hekate's presence often comes with gifts. Did she give you anything? Did a physical object show up unexpectedly? Did you have a dream vision of her deeper world? Did you gain any insights during meditation or ritual? Did you experience persistent images or sensations?

When you record your first encounter in your journal, you create a map of your journey that can help keep you on your path. Sketch out how the goddess appeared. Describe any gifts you received. Make notes of everything you remember about your first encounter.

Three-way crossroads are particularly associated with Hekate, linking to her triform nature. The three paths leading to this juncture can be interpreted in diverse ways. When we map them onto the modern version of the triple goddess as maiden, mother, and crone, we can orient our personal journey toward them, or we can dwell at the place where all three come together.

The three roads are also pathways to the three worlds. In the Underworld, the realm of sea, Hekate walks among the spirits and lights the way through dark nights of the soul. In the middle world of everyday life, the realm of land, Hekate guides us through the troubles and joys of existence. In the heights of the upper world, the realm of sky, she unlocks the mysteries of transcendence beyond our mortal existence.

And, as explained previously, we embody these three worlds as well. Intuition, emotions, and magick constitute the lower self. Our actions in the realm of everyday life reflect the middle self. As seekers of what lies beyond, we follow the higher self. All we experience is filtered through the main energies of these three selves—the feelings of the lower self, the actions of the middle self, and the thoughts of the higher self. These selves are symbolized through the root, the heart, and the crown, bringing our tripartite nature into alignment with the spirit of the crossroads that lies within. It is our triple nature that helps us attune to the eternal essence of Hekate. The flame is the unified wholeness of spirit.

**Mapping Your Personal Crossroads**
Using the invocation at the beginning of this chapter as your inspiration, explore the crossroads you've experienced in your life. Consider your different identities, giving special attention to how Hekate may have been guiding you without you even being aware of it. I've witnessed so many students who, as they deepen their connection with Hekate, discover that she has always been with them.

**Aligning with Hekate Affirmation**
This affirmation brings into your consciousness the fact that you are aligning to Hekate so that you can perceive what she is transmitting. Circumstances may dictate that you can't do as she says at the present moment. But you can reply with: "*Yes, I know. Thank you. And I am working toward it.*" When you open to Hekate's wisdom, you will be on the path of healing and empowerment every time.

*Great Hekate, Crossroads Queen.*
*Standing in the juncture*
*Of all I am*
*And all your ways,*
*I am in the thick.*
*I am listening.*
*I am paying attention.*
*I am able to receive.*

## Unifying the Three Selves Meditation

Begin by lighting your sacred flame and connecting with it and your altar. As you start to deepen the connection, slow your breathing. You can gaze softly at the flame or close your eyes, bringing the image of the cauldron with the Sacred Flame into your mind's eye.

Draw in a deep breath, all the way down to your sitting bones, and hold it for about three seconds. Feel your lower self, which may appear as a cauldron, and start to stir. Envision roots flowing down from your body into the earth, grounding you. Allow the nurturing energy from the earth to travel up through those roots, while at the same time releasing anything that is no longer needed into the ground.

Shift your breath toward your heart center—the intersection between your interior life and the external world. Open your heart, inviting in all that blesses, and feel the strength of your spine. The roots you sent down into the earth naturally accept your heart energy, merging it with the root energy.

Now shorten your breath so that it stops at your throat, then allow it to float up into your mind and open your higher self. Your thoughts become smaller, lighter, temporary. They clear away everyday perceptions and reveal visions and insights. Your heart stretches up, joining with your crown, and your three selves flow together in harmony.

Remain in this flow state until you feel a sense of completion. Then gently bring yourself back to regular consciousness, open your eyes, and stretch. Notice any shifts that may have occurred due to this attunement.

## Beyond the Cauldron—The Flame, the Key, and the Wheel

Hekate communicates in diverse—and sometimes surprising—ways, including dreams and synchronicities. Her language is often symbolic. Trust that what you are receiving is valid and meaningful. Hekate has many other symbols besides the cauldron that carry her messages and insights—such as swords, whips, gates, locks, botanicals, and animals. She may also gift you with *personal* connecting symbols, so be sure to pay heed to any objects that hold special resonance for you.

Her most important symbols, however, are the flame, the key, and the wheel. In the three worlds / three selves paradigm, the lower realms are symbolized by the flame, as Hekate is both the light in the darkness and the darkness itself. The key unlocks the mysteries of the upper world, calling us to transcend and perceive beyond the surface to the deeper reality. The wheel evokes the middle world / middle self with its momentum and connection to the natural cycles. Hekate's Wheel is depicted as a spinning labyrinth, known in antiquity as the *iynx*.

I also add her crown as an iconic symbol. Depicted as having seven rays in ancient portrayals, it corresponds to the original celestials in astrology known as the Sacred Seven. This septagram (also called a heptagram), evokes Hekate's totality as Anima Mundi (World Soul), attuning with the convergence of the three realms and the four elements. Thus it is a symbol of the esoteric and the occult, aligning it with magick and the mysteries.

I encourage you to focus on the symbol that holds the greatest potency for you at this time. If you can't choose, ask Hekate to send you a sign about which one is right. Add your primary symbol to your altar, wear it as a talisman, write about it and sketch it as you contemplate your practice. This will help messages come through more easily. You can even get a tattoo of your symbol.

# Chapter 5

## *Honoring Hekate on the Dark Moon*

*I set out alone,*
*Walking barefoot along the path.*
*I think of Hekate,*
*And the earth beneath my feet.*
*Torch-bearing guardian,*
*Guide along the path,*
*And gatekeeper of the mysteries.*
*To her I make this monthly quest.*
*At the crossroads, I place my offerings.*
*She meets me there,*
*Always.*

Honoring Hekate on the dark moon is a beautiful way of connecting with her and is key to our crooked journey—whether done as a few whispered words said in a dark room or a courageous trek to leave offerings at a crossroads.

There is a distinction between the dark moon (the astronomical new moon) and what the ancients called *Noumenia,* which means "new moon." Noumenia was the spiritual start of a new lunar month—the earliest waxing crescent phase of the moon when it first becomes visible again. To the ancients, the day began at sundown rather than sunrise, contrary to the system we're used to. We are now able to calculate the precise timing of each astronomical new moon, even if the moon is not physically visible. If the astronomical new moon occurs after sundown, perform your rituals before the next sundown.

## Ancient Origins of Honoring Hekate on the Dark Moon

In areas of the ancient Mediterranean, food was left at crossroads for Hekate on the dark moon to honor her and petition her for protection and guidance. This ritual dates back over 2,000 years and was called Hekate's deipnon. The term *deipnon* translates to "supper," but there was much more to this ritual than just making food offerings.

The ritual began with the purification of the home and its occupants, with a sacrificial animal (usually a black puppy) playing a central role in the process. Although animal sacrifice was common in ancient times, using black puppies was unique to Hekatean rituals. As upsetting as this sounds, it was culturally normative back then. Through this "scape puppy," the toxic energies of the home and its occupants, which they called *miasma*, were transferred to the dog and then released through the sacrifice. A kinder version of the sacrifice can be accomplished through cleansing with eggs (see page 32). Although it is unknown whether those engaging in ancient Hekate's suppers used this method, some scholars believe they may have.

When the purification was complete, the house was well cleaned and swept, and all residue from the sacrifice and the sweeping (known as *oxuthumia*) was removed and set aside for later disposal.

After the home was cleansed, an elaborate meal was prepared. It typically included eggs, fish, cheese, bread, garlic, vegetables, fruit, cakes, and probably nuts. If you are called to recreate an ancient Hekate's supper as accurately as possible, the eggs should be raw, the fish should be mullet and sprat, the cheese should freshly made, and the cake should be a sort of cheesecake upon which, according to some references, a candle burns. The ancient Greeks didn't have wax candles, however, so they used pine resin. The bread component of the feast probably resembled flatbreads or a type of savory pancakes, known as *tiganites*, that were common in ancient Greece. Fruits that were common 2,000 years ago include grapes and dates.

The completed meal and the ritual waste would then be taken to a crossroads. The whole point of the ritual was to gain Hekate's favor and to protect against unsavory spirits and negative energies. Given that it would have been known to those undertaking this ritual that the feast would likely be consumed by outcasts, we can be inspired to make offerings to the vulnerable in our own society through charitable acts and donations. Supporting at-risk dogs, the unhoused, children, women, and those rejected by the mainstream are all in keeping with the spirit of this ancient meal. While our cultural norms may be different, the theme of propitiating Hekate through both personal veneration and service to others is a tradition we can continue.

**Preparing to Honor Hekate on the Dark Moon**
Whether you are planning to create a Hekate's supper inspired by this ancient ritual or scheduling a few moments of quiet veneration, make honoring Hekate on the dark moon a priority. Your veneration can be as simple as making an offering to the goddess while petitioning her for guidance and protection. Use this invocation or create one yourself.

> *Great Hekate.*
> *Mysterious Moon.*
> *Stars above.*
> *Earth surrounds.*
> *Water below.*
> *Guide me along my way.*
> *Protect my journey,*
> *And bless my path.*
> *These offerings are reflections of my devotion.*

Many witches, including myself, have "Hekate trees," either on their own property or nearby, where they journey each month on the dark moon to honor the goddess. However you choose to honor Hekate at this time, I do recommend some preparation. Begin by creating a plan to guide you throughout your rite. Here are some items to consider as you plan:

● *Timing*: Plan your ritual for a time when you will have no distractions.

● *Location*: Whether you are embarking on a pilgrimage to a real crossroads or visiting a symbolic crossroads on your own property or honoring the goddess at a crossroads altar on the floor in your room, select a location that works best for you and make sure that it is a safe space. There are bears and wildcats where I live, as well as other troublesome night creatures, like the restless dead and porcupines. I make a lot of noise when I venture out during the dark moon, and I erect energetic shields around myself and the location to protect from unwelcome intruders. A counterclockwise circular movement with my left arm, repeated in groups of three, while reciting "I am protected from all harm, and I do no harm," is a habitual practice for when I am out in the wild. Salt sprinkled in a counterclockwise circle on the ground is also helpful for this kind of protection.

- **Moon sign**: The astrological sign in which the new moon will occur can help you determine the type of energy to highlight during your ritual. Give special attention to the sign as it relates to your personal astrology.

- **Focus**: Consider whether there is a particular aspect of Hekate that you want to express.

- **Intention**: Write a short statement establishing your focus for the ritual.

- **Daily practice**: Use your practice to enhance your plans and to attune to the focus of your ritual.

- **Offerings**: These can be either personal or traditional, as long as they are meaningfully linked to your focus.

- **Altar**: Create an altar connected to your focus that includes crossroads energy, using physical symbols, botanicals, soil retrieved from an actual intersection, images, and any items that evoke the energy of crossroads for you—for instance, two crossed keys.

- **Cauldron**: Attune your cauldron to the focus of your ritual; perhaps even have a special one in which to place your offerings.

- **Sacred flame**: Have a candle, a backyard fire, or a fire in your fireplace—anything suitable to ignite as a sacred flame at the beginning of the ritual process.

- **Cleansing**: Refer to the "Khernips/Triformis Ritual" in chapter 1, perform the egg purification ritual on the following page, and plan a good general cleaning of your home.

- **Animara**: This term, which derives from the word "soul," refers to rituals, meditations, written words, and other practices that awaken us to the mysteries and take us beyond our physical selves.

Make sure to record any dreams, synchronicities, encounters, visions, and other messages you may receive while you are planning your ritual and also during and after it.

## Lustral Egg Cleansing Ritual

The ancients used "lustral eggs" to cleanse themselves before rituals. The basic technique involves passing a raw egg (still in its shell) down the body, starting at the crown and sweeping downward, lightly touching the egg to the body. The ritual is best done naked, prior to bathing. It can be done as part of honoring Hekate on the dark moon or anytime your home or personal energy field needs cleansing. When toxins are present, they generally show up as distress and unsettled feelings within ourselves, our relations, or in the atmosphere of our homes.

### Supplies

All you need to perform this ritual is a candle and a raw egg. Place the egg in your cauldron, perhaps on a bed of cleansing botanicals and stones to amplify the purifying power. Leave the egg there for at least a few hours if it was in the refrigerator so that it reaches room temperature.

### Process

Light your candle and, with the egg in your left hand (the side of purification and banishing), proclaim your intention through a simple incantation—for example:

> *Through this egg, I am cleansed of all that blocks and binds, removing all toxins and miasma.*

Beginning at your crown, sweep the egg slowly downward toward the floor while reciting the incantation, either aloud or in your head. Be sure to scan your entire body, focusing on any parts that react to the ritual—such as registering sensations of heat or cold, feelings of numbness, or awakening emotions. Envision the egg drawing out the toxins and being sent to the earth, where they will be recycled into beneficial energy. Pay attention to any visions or messages that surface during the process.

Keep the egg outside if you intend to include it in a Hekate's supper or else dispose of it. Adding it to a Hekate's supper is inspired by the ancient practice of including household and ritual waste as part of the "meal." To cleanse a person, use one egg . To cleanse an entire home, you can walk through with an egg while reciting an incantation adapted for the purpose. Once the egg is full of miasma, it will feel heavier. When this happens, switch to a fresh egg.

# Offerings to Hekate: From Ancient to Contemporary

There will be times when you may want to merge traditional components of a Hekate's supper with personally meaningful elements, just as there may be months when honoring the goddess on the dark moon is difficult because life has other plans for you. Rest assured that Hekate understands your capacities and will never reject any sincere offerings, however humble they may be. Whether you are honoring her by offering your continued devotion through a spontaneous ritual or having a purely internal dialogue with her or going all out with your version of a Hekate's supper, trust that your veneration will be more than welcome.

For a lengthy devotional project, choose one aspect of an ancient Hekate's supper and explore it deeply each month. Connect to the meaning of the food item and make it yourself from scratch. In my coven, we often focus on one type of offering each month, creating a shared devotional experience. Include words, art, and other items that reflect commitment and devotion to the goddess in your ritual. I recommend using a dedicated tray, plate, or even cauldron to hold your offerings, like something decorated with the symbol of Hekate's Wheel or an antique platter that feels just right to you. An alternative is to wrap food offerings in a natural material, like compostable paper or corn husks, so that they won't harm the environment, and you won't need to retrieve a container.

In *Entering Hekate's Garden*, I share numerous recipes inspired by ancient Hekate's suppers, including the almost-a-ritual-in-itself "Dark Goddess Cheesecake," simple "Goat Cheese Crescents," and "Bread of the Goddess." Here are some other food items that are appropriate as offerings.

- *Cakes and breads*: Especially cheesecakes and flatbreads. *Savillum*, favored by ancient Romans, is made from simple ingredients and is in the spirit of the traditional cheesecakes included in Hekate's suppers.

- *Libations*: From a good red wine to pomegranate juice—use anything special to you.

- *Eggs*: Usually raw, although I've offered a piece of frittata, which combines the "cheesecake" with the egg.

- *Fish*: While the traditional mullet may not be readily available, similar local species make excellent substitutions. I live where scallops and lobster are the most prized local seafood, so I use those.

- *Cheese*: Especially fresh cheeses like fresh mozzarella. Or you can make your own, which is easier than you may think (see the recipe below).

- *Fruits, nuts, and vegetables*: Figs, almonds, garlic, and olives (including olive oil)

- *Botanicals*: Flowers but especially roses, bay laurel, and even resins. These can be placed on the offering tray and burned as sacred smoke.

- *Intuitive offerings*: Use objects that just seem to "appear" and emanate their desire to become involved, like natural items found when walking (leaves, rocks, seashells, etc.).

- *Corporeal evidence of devotion*: Including jewelry and bodily "waste" such as hair, nail clippings, and even blood. Whenever I cut myself, I try to add the blood to my offerings.

- *Personal evidence of devotion*: Whatever you are personally working on is appropriate, such as releasing the past or giving up something that blocks and binds, such as a "bad" habit.

- *Animal spirits*: Items that represent a living animal; anything from pet hair to bones work well.

- *Service in Hekate's name*: Working in a coven or other group dedicated to her, sharing posts on social media, making charitable donations, and volunteering, particularly with organizations supporting vulnerable people and dogs, make good offerings to the goddess.

## Making Cheese for Hekate

Some of the most transcendent experiences I've ever had are when I'm creating a Hekate's supper inspired by ancient recipes. When I'm preparing these dishes, I connect to spiritual ancestors, channeling their wisdom and generally going far beyond the physical task of cooking. Here is a recipe from my own collection that is in keeping with the type of cheese that was likely included in ancient Hekate's suppers. It is inspired by Columella's recipe for making fresh cheese in his *De Re Rustica*. Preparing this cheese opened me up to Hekate in such a profound way that I cannot find the right words to describe it.

## Supplies

- 2-gallon (8-liter) stock pot with lid
- rubber or wooden spatula for stirring
- food-grade cheesecloth
- colander
- kitchen twine or string
- parchment paper
- weight for pressing (a stone, a heavy mortar, or a weighty can)

## Ingredients

1 gallon (4 liters) of whole (4 percent fat) goat's or cow's milk (*not* ultra-pasteurized)

rennet of choice—fig, thistle, vegetable, lemon juice, or vinegar (Refer to the rennet's instructions for the amount needed based on the volume of milk. Rennet can be purchased online or in specialty stores.)

## Instructions

Pour all the milk into the stock pot. Bring the milk to a boil over medium-high heat, while stirring constantly so that it doesn't stick or burn. This will take between 15 and 20 minutes. When the milk starts to boil, keep stirring, stopping occasionally to test the height of the froth. Once the froth is about double the height of the milk, remove the pot from the heat.

Let the milk cool for about 15 minutes, then add the rennet. For vegetable rennet tablets, use half of one for soft chevre or a whole one for a mozzarella-type cheese. Let the milk separate into curds and whey for about 30 minutes.

While the rennet is rendering, line the colander with cheesecloth. Place the colander in the sink. Once the curds and whey have formed, pour the contents of the pot into the colander.

Cover the curds with the cheesecloth as the whey drains, gently pressing down to help the process.

Once most of the whey has drained, invert the colander so that the curds are in the cloth and twist the cloth to push out any remaining liquid. Put the bundle back in the colander and add the weight on top, placing a piece of parchment in between the weight and the cloth. Let the curds drain for an additional 30 minutes.

Remove the weight and place the wrapped curds in a bowl or on a plate to catch any remaining moisture. Let rest in the fridge for several hours or overnight. Remove the cheese and wrap it in paper or plastic. If stored in the refrigerator, this cheese will keep for several days.

Congratulations! You've made cheese like that used in traditional Hekate's suppers. Offer all or part of it to Hekate. You can enjoy it as a snack with fruits, nuts, and crackers or add it to eggs, pasta, or pizza. If you like, you can garnish it with a traditional botanical, such as basil or pomegranates. Drizzle it with honey or sprinkle it with bee pollen. Make a dark moon by forming the cheese into a sphere and coating it with poppy seeds. Dust it with garlic powder or rest it on a bed of bay leaves and rose petals. Experiment, and do what you feel drawn to do.

## Dark Moon Crossroads Pilgrimage
I wholeheartedly recommend making a pilgrimage to your chosen crossroads a monthly event on each dark moon. If this isn't possible, work with the energy of the crossroads on your altar. Here are some tips to consider as you venture forth on this sacred pilgrimage.

## Immediately Prior to Your Journey
Prepare your offerings and bring along a cauldron for burning sacred smoke and a candle to represent the Sacred Flame. If you are at all concerned for safety, let someone know you are setting out or take someone with you. My sons are well accustomed to me vanishing and know the spots in the wildwood and along the shore that I frequent. I recommend wearing a headlamp so that you can keep your hands free.

## Wildlife Considerations
When leaving offerings in a locale where animals are present, consider their safety when choosing the items. I once left poppets that contained mugwort, mayapple, and pennyroyal as an offering. They had vanished by the next morning.

### Incantations and Recitations

While walking, connect with Hekate through words. I like to review the previous month, highlighting what I've done to honor her and reciting an incantation or verse—even a simple chant.

### Placing the Offerings

When you arrive at the crossroads, arrange your offerings, light the candle, and burn the sacred smoke; then pledge your offerings to Hekate. You can use the pledge in the section on honoring Hekate on the dark moon, although I always recommend choosing your own words. In keeping with ancient custom, once the ritual at the crossroads is complete, pack up and walk away without looking back.

### Consuming Offerings

Whether or not you eat your offerings is up to you. Do what feels right to you. If an offering is something special that you feel is just for Hekate, then don't eat it. But if you feel as if you have connected with her by just creating the offering, then eating it can be a deeply transcendent experience. For me, cooking for Hekate is a profoundly sacred.

If, however, you have left your offerings at the crossroads and need to retrieve them after a few days, you can just put the remains in your compost bin. One of the coven's favorite aspects of Hekate is *Borborophorba*, which translates as "filth-eating goddess."

### Dark Moon Meditative Journey

This journey can be done in conjunction with a pilgrimage or on its own. Adapt the text so that it aligns with your focus.

> Light a candle and burn sacred smoke. When you are comfortable, journey to your inner crossroads, where the cauldron will reveal a special gift for you. Soften your gaze and take a deep breath, releasing all tension. If you created a physical offering, allow it to come into focus in your consciousness.
>
> Focus on yourself and feel that place deep within your core relax. Feel roots extending down from your body and grounding you, tethering you to the earth. Release anything that needs to be returned to the earth and draw up nourishment through these roots. Feel the energy of Hekate Chthonia and the awakening of intuition, feelings, and witchcraft.

Turn your attention to your heart center—the intersection of your inner self and the external world. Connect to Hekate Enodia, goddess of the crossroads, who is very much about guiding us through everyday life.

Draw your breath into your throat, then allow it to float upward, clearing away mental clutter. This is the realm of Hekate Kleidoukhos, keeper of keys to the mysteries, the greater wisdom, the infinite. This is your third eye.

Through this soul vision, see a beautiful gate. As you exhale, step through the gate into Hekate's deeper world and enter her beautiful garden. There is no moon, but the torches are lit and the pathway is clear. Ahead, you see a beautiful altar in the center of which a great flame burns, surrounded by water.

Approach the altar and let it appear to you however it wishes. Place your offering on the altar and let the experience wash over you. You may encounter Hekate. You may see one of her allies or her animals. You may even receive a token, a symbol, a key. Peer into the cauldron and see the truth revealed through symbols and objects. Reach in and retrieve yours.

As you expand your gaze out from the altar, you realize it stands at a three-way crossroads. One path goes down to Hekate's Cave; one goes up to her temple; one leads straight ahead, deeper into her garden. Does one path call to you more than another? Can you feel the liminal space of the crossroads?

When you are ready, journey back along the pathway to your regular consciousness. Step through the gate and come all the way back into your physical self, bringing with you any impressions you have. What did you see in the garden? What was your experience of the crossroads? Bring that experience into your consciousness so you can engage with it. What does it all mean for you? How does it show up in the coming days? In dreams? In visions? In meditation?

You can do a reading for guidance like the one in chapter 3, or you can stay in the presence of Hekate and dialogue with her. Draw a picture; make a collage—whatever comes through. Just enjoy the experience of honoring Hekate on the dark moon in a deeply personal and intimate way. You can make this meditative journey very simple or very elaborate. The dark moon is a sacred special time, and I hope that you find great nourishment and connection there.

# Chapter 6

## *Unlocking Hekate's History*

*Guardian of Thresholds,*
*Mistress of Life and Death.*
*Goddess of Land, Sea, and Sky.*
*Guide through the Underworld,*
*Queen of Crossroads,*
*Presiding over spirits.*
*Mother of witches,*
*Keeper of Keys.*

Hekate's history is as complex as our personal experiences of her. She is a cauldron of shadows and light. Her iconic three-bodied image hints at her multiplicities. From the Neolithic cave of the Great Mother to Shakespeare's depiction of her as the queen of witches to our contemporary connection of her to personal shadow healing, Hekate has traveled throughout the centuries, leaving a trail of mystery and magick in her wake. Common throughout all these interpretations is her association with the Underworld journey, thresholds, magick, and the mysteries.

Hekate was known to the Greeks, and, in certain parts of the ancient Greek world, she was incredibly important. Yet her origins lie deep in the mists of the past, well before Greek culture adopted her. Most scholars believe she was originally an Anatolian goddess whose origins lay in the area today known as Türkiye. In fact, the only surviving ancient temple dedicated singularly to Hekate is there. With the rise of Rome, she became known to the ancient Romans as Hecate and was then transformed in different ways as the Roman Empire spread throughout Europe.

## The Meaning of Hekate's Name

Like her historical origins, the meaning of Hekate's name is shrouded in the mists of the past. It is commonly interpreted as meaning "one from afar." To complicate matters, however, there are other possibilities: "far reaching" or "shooting" or "one of great renown" or "one who sees all." The first part of her name—*hek* or *heka*—means "one hundred" in Greek, so it can literally mean "she of one hundred," which certainly makes sense, given her multifaceted nature.

The Great Mother goddess was known by countless other names, such as Cybele, Demeter, and Isis (also called "she of ten thousand names"). The Egyptian word *heka* means "magick," and the Egyptian pantheon included a goddess named Heqet, who was associated with midwifery and other roles. There was also a god named Heka. Given the similarity in these names, it is reasonable to see a connection between these deities. In fact, Hekate was a common feminine name across the ancient Mediterranean, lending credence to her being a benevolent goddess, since children aren't typically named after nefarious spirits. Indeed, her name survives today in various versions of "Kate."

As with all words of power, there is great potency in sincerely speaking Hekate's name. Sitting in a darkened room with a lit candle and saying her name is enough to invoke her, as long as it comes from your heart. You can deepen this practice and add power to your voice by chanting in rounds of three.

## Hekate as the Great Mother Goddess

Hekate's history stretches back at least three thousand years. She flowed out of the Neolithic Great Mother who was both light and dark, death and birth, and all the spaces in between. The earliest source that specifically discusses Hekate at length is Hesiod's *Theogony*, in which she is described as a goddess who oversees the world of humans. Zeus acknowledged her governance of land, sea, and sky. In this tripartite role, she oversaw civic life, cities, and harbors. As an expression of the Great Mother, she granted boons and favors and acted as the guardian of children. Three dates in the calendar of ancient Greek festivals support this role.

## Hekate as Triple Formed

Some of the oldest known Hekatean artifacts depict her as triple formed. Surviving statues and etched charms indicate her special association with three-way crossroads, a role that was unusual among Greek and Roman deities, shared only by Hermes. The statues, known as Hekataia, were placed at boundaries, crossroads, and thresholds, perhaps indicating that her three heads allowed her to look in all directions to identify threats to those she protected. Statues of Hermes, her frequent companion, were also placed in these places.

## Hekate as Underworld Guide

The next major mention is in the Homeric *Hymn to Demeter*. In this story, an innocent young Persephone was violated by Hades, who had made an agreement with her father, Zeus, without the knowledge of her mother, Demeter. Persephone was understandably bereft. As she cried, Hekate emerged from her cave to give her succor. As the story progresses, Hekate continues to play the mediator. Ultimately, she brokered a deal in which Persephone spent the fallow season with Hades, then emerged from the Underworld to invigorate the growing season. Hekate assumed the task of guiding her back and forth between these two worlds.

## Hekate as Torchbearer

In works of art illustrating Persephone's story, and in various other examples, Hekate is shown bearing two torches. One frieze that depicts the family of older gods, the Titans, unsuccessfully warring with insurgent newer gods, the Olympians, shows her brandishing torches instead of another weapon. In fact, numerous ancient deities carried torches, especially goddesses that were often linked to Hekate, such as Persephone, Demeter, and Artemis.

Torches were thought to be symbols of the Underworld and chthonic forces, and deities that carried them were associated with the night and bringing the light into darkness. Because they were linked to the Underworld, which was lorded over by Hades, torches were sometimes referred to as his fire. Thus, Hekate carries Hades's fire. Going back even farther, fire is shown in even the earliest records as sacred to the Great Mother, and, to the ancients, it represented the dual powers of creation and destruction.

## Hekate as Transformer

In the story of Troy, Hekate transformed Hecuba (Hekabe), the desperate dethroned queen, into a dog-priestess while the conquering forces were stoning her to death. When the mystic Gale was threatened for speaking truth to power, Hekate turned her into a polecat, an animal similar to a ferret. And there are other similar tales in which Hekate transforms a desperate female into an animal. The ancient authors recording these narratives may have perceived this transformation as reflective of the "savage" nature of women. To me, these women were liberated from untenable circumstances.

## Hekate as Threshold Guardian

Hekate assumes an interesting position in the *Orphic Hymns*, an evocative collection of verses written to various deities. One of the two opening hymns is addressed to her, while the other is addressed to the gatekeeping goddess Prothyraea, a feminine spirit who watches over thresholds, including physical boundaries and the liminal space between life and death, especially during childbirth. Hekate was strongly associated with this role in several other ancient sources. The fact that the hymn to Hekate was placed first in the *Orphic Hymns* shows that she was considered the spirit who watched over the gate to the other deities.

## Hekate as Keeper of Keys

In *Orphic Hymns,* Hekate is referred to as the "keeper of keys," reinforcing her role as the divine gatekeeper. In the second hymn, as Prothyraea, the role of gatekeeper is emphasized but also divine midwife. This role was also connected to the role of psychopomp, who guided souls between the physical world and the "other side." Hekate thus presides over all thresholds, from physical boundaries to the entrance to the deeper world.

The most compelling evidence of Hekate as keeper of keys comes from the remains of the ancient temple dedicated to her at Lagina, in modern-day Türkiye, where extensive written records have been found. One inscription depicts a particularly beautiful ceremony in which a girl on the cusp of adolescence carries a key and leads a procession. This connects Hekate with keys and youth.

In the ancient Mediterranean cultures, when a woman married she was given the key to the home, even though the husband maintained ownership. This parallels Hekate's role as gatekeeper to the mysteries. The placement of

Hekatean statues at the entrance to temples of the popular Olympians supports her role as "wife" to "property-owning husbands"—the Olympian gods.

## Hekate, Crossroads, and Journeys

The ancient shrines and icons that were placed at boundaries, crossroads, and thresholds made it clear that Hekate presided over them. To the ancients, these places were not merely physical junctures; they also represented the intersection between the visible world and the deeper world. Spirits inhabited these liminal spaces, including malevolent beings.

In a region north of Athens, Hekate became intertwined with a Thessalonian goddess named Enodia, whose name translates as "in the road." This goddess governed numerous aspects of life, including roadways, and was seen as a spirit associated with safe travels, protection of homes and public buildings, and matters of civic life. As Hekate's attributes evolved, she became more strongly associated with journeys, which merely enhanced her older connection to thresholds. Getting from one place to another was often perilous, and having Hekate Enodia protecting travelers from the dangers of both humans and spirits was imperative.

## Hekate and Magick

Hekate's association with magick is demonstrated in myths and artifacts throughout antiquity. Circe, Medea, and others called upon her assistance in stories and plays. Magical coins, ancient charms, and curse tablets invoked her help. The *Greek Magical Papyri*, a collection of spells and rituals that was found in Egypt and dates back about two thousand years, is chockfull of invocations and incantations involving her. Rituals to Hekate in her roles as guardian of children and divine midwife survive as well. She is both healer and banisher—and a driving force behind what we call witchcraft today.

However, the ancient understanding of those who invoked her help in workings was very different from our contemporary view. In the ancient world, magick was a part of everyday life. Curse tablets were the ancient equivalent of venting on social media. Over the centuries, as Christianity was institutionalized and spread throughout Europe, magick associated with older pagan practices was vilified—and, along with it, Hekate. The phantasmagoric Hecate in Shakespeare's *Macbeth* and numerous artistic depictions reinforced the image of Hekate as a dangerous, maleficent spirit. Even today, she is viewed this way by some, especially in popular media.

## Hekate and the Moon

Astrology was well known to the ancients, and the association of the moon with the feminine, with intuition and emotions, and with magick and the mysteries solidified Hekate's role as a lunar goddess. Her depiction with bull's horns, which were representative of the crescent moon, was seen as symbolic of this lunar connection. As we have seen, the night of the dark moon was sacred to her, and the deipnon, her sacred supper, was included in the religious calendar. Through our modern lens, we can map her triform nature onto the three major visible phases of the moon, with the invisible dark moon representing the mysteries.

## Hekate as World Soul

Perhaps because of her triform nature—her governance over thresholds, her association with magick, and her role as a guide of souls to and from the Underworld—some Neoplatonist philosophers viewed Hekate as a force that mediated between the physical world and the deeper realms. One such was Proclus, who lived just as Christianity was taking hold. He experienced visions of Hekate and wrote about Hekate as a mediator. And the esoteric text *The Chaldean Oracles* gives a detailed description of Hekate as world soul and the fiery flower of all creation. Like the moon, she was seen as a sort of membrane that separated higher forces from life on earth, emphasizing her role as a generatrix—the source, a primal force, and the spark of vitality in all things.

## Hekate's Shadow

Studying how the ancients viewed Hekate can feel contradictory and confusing. In some ancient tales, like Ovid's *Metamorphoses* and the plays of Euripides, she's very clearly associated with what we now call witchcraft. She was venerated on the dark moon for protection, especially against evil spirits and toxic energies and forces. Many ancient rites—from the sacrifice of puppies to evoking her on curse tablets to take vengeance on troublesome neighbors—

appear nefarious by our contemporary standards. But the cultural norms surrounding these practices were very different from those that govern the way we engage with Hekate today.

## Goddess of the Eclipse and the Rise of Christianity

*Hekate, Goddess of the Eclipse.*
*Ruler of the Moon.*
*Realm of magick and mystery.*
*Land of emotions and intuition.*
*Keeper of the Keys of the universe.*
*Behold how the natural cycle of your Wheel*
*Brings dark to light,*
*Ushering in a new era.*

Before the nature of eclipses was understood, they were viewed as acts of the Divine. Hekate, so associated with the dark moon, the Underworld, and the celestial, is a goddess of the eclipse. Eclipses are special times to connect with the power of Hekate's moon to override the sun. However, as the cults of sun gods like the Greek Apollo and the Roman Sol Invictus grew increasingly powerful, they began to overshadow goddesses linked to the Underworld. Indeed, these pagan deities were especially vilified. Yet Hekate is a goddess of the eclipse; thus she has the power to defy those who try to dishonor her using solar forces. Throughout history, she and other expressions of the dark moon have maintained their presence, no matter how hard the dominant sun-god worshippers tried to marginalize them.

With the institutionalization of Christianity, Jesus was enthroned as the new sun god. As the Romans expanded their empire throughout Europe, they took with them both their pagan deities and the new Christian God, spreading them as far as what we now know as the United Kingdom and probably beyond. This focus on solar associations—with an emphasis on progress, civilization, the acquisition of wealth, and the rise of cities—grew, replacing earlier mythologies associated with the dark. As these solar associations became more entrenched, lunar associations representing the sacred feminine and manifestations of the dark goddess were devalued, and Hekate and similar dark goddesses were relabeled as dangerous, evil, scary, and off limits. Nonetheless, these powerful deities persisted in forms like the Black Madonna.

As Christianity increased its grip on the Western mind, its doctrines were often forced upon the common people, and those who didn't conform were labeled as heretics. This eventually culminated in witch trials that were used as tools of the establishment against those they didn't like. Hekate and other pagan deities were demonized, along with the practice of magick. And this is the cultural environment in which Shakespeare immortalized the nefarious view of Hekate and witches that still survives today. *Macbeth's* Hecate is a queen of witches who presides over the Wyrd Sisters, inspiring and delighting in dark deeds.

The rise of Romanticism, however, brought a renewed interest in all things Greek and Roman, including myths, art, deities, and ideas. William Blake and others from this period explored Hekate through art—in some ways restoring her image but in others reenforcing Shakespeare's archetype. Nevertheless, the increased prominence of Greek and Roman culture created an environment that inspired others, especially occultists, to reach back to earlier beliefs. By the late 19th century, although Hekate still languished in the shadow of Christianity, the misogynist characterization of powerful females as savage, dangerous, and associated with witchcraft was beginning to change. This ushered in an "acceptable" version of the sacred feminine as a pure "white goddess," much in the same way that the Virgin Mary was viewed.

## Hekate in the 20th Century and Beyond

Well into the 20th century, certain authors depicted Hekate as a hellish figure, completely disconnected from most ancient depictions of her and totally ignoring her benevolent aspects. She was defined as a "dark" goddess, in contrast to the "white" one. The latter half of the 20th century saw the rise of what's known as second-wave feminism. In 1978, psychologist Charlene Spretnak published *Lost Goddesses of Ancient Greece*, in which she reimagined Hekate as a complex moon goddess who presided over a coven of witches concerned with understanding life and death. This encouraged a new blossoming of the sacred feminine, resurrecting it from its former neglected state.

There followed a lot of serious scholarship that examined Hekate's origins and distant history and tried to be less biased—although, of course, even this work was filtered through problematic views. Then in 1990, Sarah Iles Johnston presented a view of Hekate that went well beyond hell hounds. In her doctoral dissertation, she dove into sources like *The Chaldean Oracles*, which had been translated into English, and examined Hekate as keeper of keys and world soul.

Concurrently, depth psychologist James Hillman, in his seminal *The Dream and the Underworld*, positioned Hekate as the spirit of the depths, claiming that dreams were her sacred realm. Former monk, writer, and therapist Thomas Moore, with whom Hillman was closely associated, then published his book *Dark Nights of the Soul*, in which Hekate plays a major role. With these two works, Hekatean scholarship moved into the purely psychological. Hekate came to be viewed as a psychological spirit—a goddess with whom we could connect. In *Goddesses in Older Women: Archetypes in Women over Fifty*, Jean Shinoda Bolen presents a view of Hekate as the wise crone—an interpretation that had been growing in popularity among neo-Pagans as well. Hekate was being restored as an important goddess who was associated with transitions, magick, and the deeper world.

Hekate's resurgence was entwined with a redefinition of witchcraft that moved it from the margins into the mainstream culture. With the help of the internet, what began with the Wicca movement has evolved into an explosion of witchcraft. Hekate has returned, and the cauldron is once again a sacred vessel.

Only now—spurred by a global pandemic, political upheaval, and climate change—are we starting to grapple seriously with the challenges of shifting away from a predominantly solar world, in which everything is about money, capitalism, unrestricted growth, and rationality. The goddess of the dark moon and eclipses is being restored. We are starting to see the devastating consequences of denying the sacred feminine. We are starting to understand that there must be balance between darkness and light. Without that balance, we become too immersed in the solar forces that are destroying the earth and us along with it. This resurgence is part of a larger kind of global correction—one that is reflected in our own need to recover from all of this artificial light that is drowning us.

## Crafting an Artifex Vita

Like Hekate's journey through history, our personal paths transform over time. There are times when the road is easy, and there are the dark times when we feel as if we've lost our way. Hekate often comes to us during these difficult times, shining her guiding torch so that we can get back on the path she has ordained for us. When I look back, I see how my experiences led me to this crossroads I call home—the convergence of modern life and the deeper world of Hekate. This exercise maps your own journey back to where Hekate is leading you. In it, you create a collage talisman called an "Artifex Vita" that connects her with your own personal path. *Artifex vita* is a Latin term that means "artistic life." There's no one way to create this talisman. In the coven, we've made everything from collages painted on canvas to collages created with digital tools. The first time I made an Artifex Vita, I cut up old journals and affixed them right to a canvas, along with bay leaves inscribed with different epithets that reflected both Hekate's history and my own. When I was happy with it, I used the scraps to start a fire in honor of Hekate, something I often do with ritual and magickal leftovers.

## Supplies

- A foundation, such as a 12 x 12 black canvas
- Acrylic paint or markers
- Glue, add a few drops of Oleum Spirita to make it magickal
- Bay leaves or paper
- A piece of cord

## Method

Begin by contemplating key events in your life, especially when Hekate first called you. Review your journals; look through your photos; use any resources that bring your journey to life. Ask Hekate to guide you as you do these explorations.

Create a draft of your collage on a separate piece of paper, with a crossroads as the focal point. The crossroads can be represented by Hekate's Wheel (see chapter 3). Be sure to leave enough space for what you will leave unmapped—the future. Consider the roads you have traveled, the experiences you've had, the identities you have assumed, the roles you have played. Draw in these roads leading to the crossroads.

Paint the canvas with a background of colors that feel right to you. Once the canvas is dry, place Hekate's Wheel (either drawn or a cutout) in the center. Then with a pencil, copy your drafted map onto the canvas. Select snippets from your journals, your photos, and other souvenirs of your life, layering them onto the roads you have penciled in and gluing them around the cross-roads. Group them by the themes that the roads represent. Leave room for a channeled message that will surface as you complete the talisman. This is a sep-arate space from the unmapped empty area you are leaving for future events.

Using magickal glue, secure a cord through the group for each road in whatever way it works for your design, connecting them to one another and leading to the crossroads. Add epithets to bay leaves or paper that are reflective of each of your roads and attach them to your road groups.

Anoint the canvas with Oleum Spirita, speaking this incantation (or some-thing like it that you've written yourself):

> *This talisman is testimony that I walk Hekate's road. She has always been with me, and she has created the map I follow.*

Ask Hekate to send you the inscription for the talisman, saying:

> *Hekate, what is your message for my journey?*

Add whatever message you receive in the empty space you have left.

When you are finished, thank Hekate for always guiding you, and turn the energy toward the unmapped territory, saying:

> *I walk your road into the future, which will always lead me back to your crossroads.*

# Chapter 7

## Connecting with Hekate's Characteristics, Roles, and Titles

*Great Hekate,*
*Queen of Witches,*
*Of limitless power,*
*And countless names.*
*The boundless one,*
*Force running through all.*
*Triformis, Three-Formed Shapeshifter.*
*Kleidoukhos, Keeper of Keys to the Mysteries.*
*Chthonia, Goddess of the Depths.*
*Enodia, She of the Crossroads.*
*Propylaia, Gatekeeper of the Realms.*
*Dadophoros, Illuminating Torchbearer.*
*Hieros Pyr, Sacred Source Fire.*
*Nykhia Mene, Night and the Moon.*
*Paionios, Healer of Shadows.*
*Geneteira, Primal Mother.*
*Anima Mundi, Soul of the World.*
*Guardian, Guide, and Gatekeeper.*
*Attend your epithets,*
*Be with me evermore.*

Epithets are titles that evoke specific aspects of Hekate—her characteristics, traits, and abilities. There are over one hundred epithets, which are listed in the appendix, that are used to describe Hekate in ancient and contemporary sources. One way to make sense of all these epithets is to see Hekate as a cauldron that contains all these aspects; as you ask a question or need specific guidance, different characteristics will surface with her messages.

There will always be certain epithets that resonate more for you. As you read the invocation above, which names call out to you? She arrives as Kleidoukhos (Keeper of Keys) offering access to places we may need, from Underworld healing to the higher mysteries. You may experience her as Geneteira (Great Mother), who can help you heal deep wounds of the past. She can come through as Paionios (Healer), along with Underworld and nocturnal titles, such as Chthonia (Of the Earth) and Nykhia (Of the Night), to assist with our shadow work. When in the midst of transformations, call upon her as Triformis (Three-Formed or Triple Goddess). If you long for direction or seek illumination, Dadophoros (Torch Bearer) may light up, accompanied by Hieros Pyr (a masculine epithet meaning "sacred fire"). When you are at thresholds, Propylaia (Gatekeeper) may come, often with the spirit of Enodia (Of the Road), who also watches over everyday life. When you open to her totality, she becomes Anima Mundi (World Soul), the very essence of the universe.

Hekate is arguably most widely known as the Queen of Witches, although this role has no specific ancient epithets associated with it. Nor are there any titles from antiquity that refer to her as aged, although she is often depicted as the crone. The trinity of maiden, mother, and crone is, in fact, a modern understanding of the triple goddess. Likewise, Guardian, Guide, and Gatekeeper are synthesized epithets that combine her primary roles in ancient sources into an expression of her aspect as Triformis. These roles are all interconnected, as illustrated by her triple form, although one may be more prominent than the others at different times. Today, she may resonate as Guardian; tomorrow, as Gatekeeper.

As Guardian, Hekate protects from harm and lights the way with her symbolic torches. This epithet may be especially relevant when we are exploring our shadows, feeling unsafe, or navigating complex circumstances. Related aspects include ancient epithets such as Chthonia, Nykhia, and Mene, which are associated with the Underworld, with darkness, and with the moon, respectively.

Hekate as Guide steers us along our crooked path, especially the intersection between everyday life and the practice of witchcraft. We abide at the crossroads with her, and this juncture always brings us back to her and what we know to be true. Epithets linked to this role include Enodia, as well as any of personal importance to us for that point in our lives. The symbol of Hekate's Wheel, also called the strophalos, can also be worked with as an aspect.

Hekate as Gatekeeper encompasses her governance over thresholds, including the higher mysteries of transcendence and mysticism, as well as personal transitions. Kleidoukhos and Propylaia are suitable epithets here, and keys and gates are representative symbols.

## Discovering Your Primary Epithets

Working with the list of epithets in the appendix, select the ones that resonate most with you. Explore why they are important to you. Create a record of each one in your journal, giving both the ancient title and its modern translation. Then make a note of these key points of connection:

- What does the epithet unlock for you?

- What emotions does the epithet awaken in you?

- What correspondences do you connect with the epithet (e.g., cards, astrology, colors, plants, animals, stones)?

- What symbols do you associate with the epithet (e.g., key, torch, flame, cauldron, broom, knife)?

- How can you become more aligned with the energy conveyed through the epithet?

- What messages do you receive that relate to the epithet (e.g., dreams, intuitions, synchronicities)?

### Working with Epithets

There are three main ways to work with epithets: by connecting with primary epithets; by calling on certain aspects for a specific purpose; and by focusing on learning the epithets and integrating them into your general knowledge. Because the list of Hekate's epithets is so long, however, developing a deep understanding of a few at a time, rather than trying to memorize them all, may yield a stronger bond with the goddess. Here are a few examples of ways to explore Hekate's epithets:

- Write verses, like invocations or poems, that explore the epithets.

- Choose cards from tarot and oracle decks that are evocative of the epithets.

- Create works of art, like collages (digital or paper), paintings, or statues.

- Consider images and statues that depict aspects of the goddess.

- Create an altar that focuses on the epithets.

- Create a set of oracular tiles—for instance, by writing epithets on bay leaves.

- Attune your dark moon rituals to the astrological signatures (energies) of a particular new moon.

- Unlock a sacred name that includes one or more epithets.

- Work with the epithets for self-healing and personal development.

In my book *Keeping Her Keys*, I connected Hekate's epithets to the Wheel of the Year by developing a system for linking the natural cycle with specific epithets. This is also the method I use for leading the coven through the year, with each lunar month dedicated to one aspect. You can do the same thing by attuning the epithets that call out to you with where you are in the Wheel of the Year, then coupling that with an in-depth exploration of one epithet for each lunar cycle. Generally, autumn and winter are connected to Hekate's Underworld and nocturnal aspects, while spring evokes her energizing side. Summer, with its verdant abundance, its wildfires, and its heat, resonates with her aspect as Great Mother or as Keeper of Keys. Her crossroads and threshold powers are particularly in evidence during sabbats and seasonal transitions and midpoints.

Because epithets are attuned to the aspects evoked through them, they are ideal for crafting oracle sets. The following example was inspired by the ancient rite of writing messages on bay laurel leaves and divination using symbols inscribed on tiles, which has become popular today in the form of runes. Using this oracle set is a favorite method in the coven because it yields highly accurate readings. The tiles or leaves (which I call *laurelia*) act as keys that attune to Hekate's guidance.

No matter what language an epithet is in and no matter whether it consists of words, symbols, or sigils, writing it onto a chosen medium (in this case, leaves or tiles) infuses the leaf/tile with the powers associated with the epithet. I recommend working in multiples of three, or with other sacred numbers like seven or thirteen, because it adds an additional layer of enchantment, but any number of leaves or tiles that feels right to you is fine. Examples of sigils associated with specific epithets can be found at the beginning of each chapter in *Entering Hekate's Cave*.

## Creating an Epithet Oracle Set

To create this oracle set, you will need either bay laurel leaves or objects that can be used as tiles, such as little clay charms, pieces of wood, flat stones, or even heavy paper.

## Supplies

- Bay laurel leaves are easily accessible and have been connected to divinatory practices since ancient times. Fresh leaves that have been dried for a few days work best for adding words and symbols, although the dried leaves work as well.

- If you are using tiles, choose a medium that feels right to you.

- Acrylic paint markers work well for writing epithets and symbols on the leaves or tiles.

- I recommend keeping your finished set in a dedicated cauldron or bag.

## Process

Once you have chosen your epithets and your medium, develop keywords for each one. If you're assigning a cauldron to the oracle set, be sure to cleanse and enchant it before reciting the incantation below. You can also place stones and botanicals within the prepared cauldron to augment its divinatory potential.

Determine how you'll represent each epithet—through words, symbols, or sigils. You can also choose to allow their representation to come through during the enchantment phase. Then craft an incantation that evokes them, being sure to include both the epithet and its meaning. Here's an example that you can use as inspiration for crafting your own unique incantation. Change the epithets and meanings to the ones you have chosen:

*Great Hekate,*
*Queen of Witches,*
*I call upon your blessing for this set,*
*Attuning to your guidance and truth.*
*Kleidoukhos, Keeper of Keys, the Key of Wisdom.*
*Chthonia, the Depths, the Key of Revelation.*
*Enodia, the Crossroads, the Key of Possibility.*
*Propylaia, Gatekeeper, the Key of Transitions.*
*Dadophoros, Torchbearer, the Key of Illumination.*

*Hieros Pyr, Sacred Source Fire, the Key of the Sacred.*
*Nykhia Mene, Night and the Moon, the Key of Intuition.*
*Paionios, Healer of Shadows, the Key of Healing.*
*Geneteira, Primal Mother, the Key of Nurturance.*
*Anima Mundi, Soul of the World, the Key of Transcendence.*
*Guardian, Guide, and Gatekeeper.*
*Attend your epithets.*
*Render these* [leaves/tiles] *your divine oracle.*
*As it is spoken,*
*So it becomes.*
*Hail Hekate.*

Once you are satisfied with your incantation, you can begin reciting it while inscribing the leaves or tiles.

Begin with the opening lines, then add each epithet to the leaf or tile as you speak the associated line. You can pass each leaf or tile through a suitable sacred smoke, such as mugwort, to amplify the power of the set, but it's not required. Place each completed leaf or tile in the cauldron or bag. When all the leaves/tiles are complete, hold your chosen container and repeat the closing lines of your incantation, rotating the container clockwise for as many turns as you have epithets.

**Working with the Epithet Oracle**

You can hold specific questions in your mind or write them on a piece of paper and add them to the leaves or tiles in the cauldron or bag. You can use this set in your daily reading to unlock overarching themes and advice, or you can reserve it for special lunar phases like a full or new moon. I recommend drawing one or two leaves or tiles for each reading, using the first to discern a general message and the second to expand upon it. Work with the keywords to discover their meaning. You can carry your oracle set with you or keep it on your altar.

This is a great project to do with a partner or with your coven, exchanging readings for one another.

## Hekate in the Signs: Epithets and Practices for the Dark Moon

Connecting to the astrological meaning of each new moon deepens the experience of honoring Hekate on the dark moon. Below you'll find a selection of epithets, meanings, and themes you can use for each new moon, but I encourage you to develop your own as a way to unlock both Hekate's numerous aspects and their connection to astrology.

## Aries

- *Epithets*: Ergatis (Energizer); Rixipyle (Breaker of Barriers); Agriope (Fierce)

- *Meaning*: Brash, courageous, present-focused, and independent. Hekate in Aries amplifies assertiveness, bravery, motivation, and the quest for personal freedom.

- *Themes*: As the first sign of the zodiac, Aries is excellent for rebirth. Aries can bring up conflict, yet also courage. Petition Hekate in Aries for help with both.

## Taurus

- *Epithets*: Alkimos (Strong); Enodia (of the Road); Tauropolos (Straightforward)

- *Meaning*: The bull is closely associated with Hekate because the ancients viewed horns as symbolic of the crescent moon. Bulls, in general, corresponded with the Great Mother and fertility. Taurus is a sign of endurance and the everyday. Enodia in relation to Taurus evokes steady progress for all earthly endeavors. Turn to Hekate in Taurus for assistance with earthly productivity, from work to personal pursuits.

- *Themes*: Taurus assists with earthly concerns like work, home, and possessions. Petition Hekate in Taurus for increasing endurance and tenacity, as well as releasing it.

## Gemini

- *Epithets*: Amphiprosopos (Looking Both Ways); Phaenno (Brilliant); Triformis (Triple Goddess)

- *Meaning*: Like Hekate's all-seeing, evolving multiple forms, the intelligent twin is always transforming. Focused on creativity, driven by curiosity, appeal to Hekate in Gemini for support with matters of communication and creativity.

- *Themes*: The ever-mercurial Gemini during the new moon is all about shapeshifting, making this an ideal time for transformation. Call upon Hekate in Gemini for help with communication, education, and technology.

## Cancer

- *Epithets*: Pammetor (Mother of All); Geneteira (Great Mother); Mene (Moon); Phos (Light); Atala (Tender)

- *Meaning*: Governed by the moon, and very maternal, Cancer is focused on nurturing self and others, emotions, and intuition. Call upon Hekate in Cancer to heal from past wounds and get some mothering.

- *Themes*: Healing the mother wound and opening up to Hekate as the Great Mother is an ideal focus for the Cancer new moon. Petition Hekate in Cancer for guidance on how to nurture yourself and others, whether that involves a desire to take care of yourself better or letting go of codependency.

## Leo

- *Epithets*: Therobromon (Roaring One); Leaina (Lioness); Polykleitos (Renowned)

- *Meaning*: Roaring, bold, and center stage, Leo loves the fire of self-expression. Proud Leo is lovely to be near as you bask in your personal sunshine. Hekate in Leo is the brilliant light of the summer sun, linking to abundance and harvest.

- *Themes*: Hekate during the Leo new moon can be quite boisterous, calling you forth to take center stage in your own life. Invoke the spirit of Leo wherever it is in your personal chart and petition the leonine aspects of Hekate to help you roar over your own life.

## Virgo

- *Epithets*: Aregos (Helper); Alexeatis (Destroyer of Evil); Phosphoros (Light Bearer)

*Meaning*: Concerned with comfort and order, as well as deeply sensitive, Virgo is a helpful sign that bids us to tend to hearth and home. Hekate in Virgo teaches us to take care of what matters, with attention to the small things.

*Themes*: If chaos and clutter are taking hold, the Virgo new moon is the perfect time to call upon Alexeatis to get rid of this particular evil. This is an opportune time to pretty up your witchy space, adding flowers as offerings, comforting scents, and more. Petition Hekate on the Virgo new moon to discover joy through beautiful things.

## Libra

*Epithets*: Kalliste (Fairest); Eukoline (Good Tempered); Lampadios (Torchbearer)

*Meaning*: Ruled by air, this sign craves balance and interpersonal closeness. The illuminated side of Libra is a steady burning light that guides others. But shadowy Libra also veers into self-sacrifice in the name of love. Hekate in Libra speaks to the crossroads of self-identity and the need to be accepted.

*Themes*: Because of the emphasis on commitment inherent in Libra, coupled with the initiatory energy of the new moon, rituals of both are recommended. Seek Hekate's guidance for navigating the complexities of your personal relationships and perhaps even appeal to her for a deepening of yours with her.

## Scorpio

*Epithets*: Borborophorba (Filth Eater); Erototokos (Bringer of Desire); Skotia (Darkness)

*Meaning*: Intense and always wanting it darker, Scorpio abides in the mysteries of the deeper world, including the depths of desire. Hekate as Borborophorba enables catharsis.

*Themes*: As Scorpio encourages you to peer into your own shadows, this is an excellent time for shadow healing, especially rituals of catharsis. If sex magick is your thing, or if you are curious about it, the Scorpio new moon can free you from inhibitions. For a beautiful ritual experience, offer sacred sex to Hekate, whether by yourself or with others.

## Sagittarius

- *Epithets*: Iokheaira (Archer); Ouresiphoites (Mountain Wanderer); Podarke (Fleet Footed)

- *Meaning*: Truth and adventure are the all-consuming passions of Sagittarius, whether that involves traveling the world or journeying through the realm of knowledge. Hekate in Sagittarius bespeaks the longing for exploration that leads to self-awareness.

- *Themes*: Hekate as the Archer is associated with this side of Artemis and evokes her straight-shooting nature. This is an ideal time to seek assistance with all matters associated with following your bliss, through both internal and external adventuring.

## Capricorn

- *Epithets*: Prothyraea (Gatekeeper); Stratelatis (Leader); Tartaroukhos (Ruler)

- *Meaning*: Determined, traditional, and wise, Hekate as gatekeeper of physical locations is connected to Capricorn. When you are concerned with middle-world affairs, turn to Hekate in this sign for assistance with becoming the ruler over your personal realm.

- *Themes*: Perhaps because the Capricorn new moon comes near the end of the year, and because this sign is governed by Saturn, a sign that is evocative of the ancient, this is a time when Hekate as crone often shows up. Petition Hekate in Capricorn for help in focusing on groups and covens and on tradition and governance.

## Aquarius

- *Epithets*: Astrodia (Star Walker); Promethikos (Visionary); Psychopomp (Soul Guide)

- **Meaning**: The star-born water bearer pours perspective onto earthy dwellers, offering insight into your own soul and encouraging you to break away from tradition and appreciate your own uniqueness.

- **Themes**: Soul retrieval and past-life explorations are ideally suited for the Aquarius new moon. Hekate's celestial aspects—like those associated with the higher mysteries, channeling, and astral travel—open up during this time. When troubled by the confines of everyday life, connect with Hekate in Aquarius to awaken your personal truth.

### Pisces

- **Epithets**: Einalia (Of the Sea); Phileremos (Lover of Solitude); Ambrotos (Eternal)

- **Meaning**: Otherworldly and oceanic, Pisces longs for the interior world of imagination and mysticism. Chronological time and daily life are foreign to this sign. Hekate Einalia is the sea itself—mysterious, eternal, and primordial—just like Pisces.

- **Themes**: Ritual bathing with sacred smoke and all the accoutrements for transcendent shamanic journeying is appropriate for this new moon. Make a pilgrimage to the sea and place offerings suitable for the wildlife or cleanse yourself in the ocean air. Call on Hekate's Piscean aspects to connect with her primordial essence.

## The Asteroid Hekate

The asteroid Hekate—appropriately numbered 100 in keeping with the meaning of *hek*—can be found in the birth chart online at websites that feature advanced chart selection, such as *astro.com*. After you select "Extended chart selection" from the "Horoscopes" pull-down menu, either scroll to find the asteroid Hekate in the list of options or enter the number of the asteroid ("100") in the text box. (You will need to register on the site and possibly get a subscription to access this feature.) Once you have your chart, apply the meanings to interpret where Hekate is in your personal astrology.

# Unlocking Your Sacred Name

Your *nomine sacris*, "sacred name," is the appellation by which Hekate calls you. Yours may be based on her epithets, or it may be unique to you. This is how you are known in the deeper world. Use this name when casting spells and performing rituals or anytime you need to reconnect to your own sacredness. Speaking your sacred name at the beginning of rituals and spells attunes you to your deeper nature and quiets your surface self.

If you already have a sacred name that continues to feel right, stick with it. On the other hand, Hekate may communicate that it is time to transition to a new name—a time for change, a time for spiritual growth. You may have had a name assigned to you at birth that doesn't fit you anymore, and your sacred name may heal the pain associated with it. If this is your first experience with your sacred name, trust in the process. It can be surprising what name comes through, but rest assured that it will always unlock deep truths. Whether you keep your sacred name private or share it with others is your choice.

Your inner temple contains your etheric cauldron, the place where you dive into the mysteries. It is important to be aware of the condition and appearance of your temple and your cauldron, because it will contain messages that you need to correctly interpret your sacred name, which is outlined below as part of opening your inner temple.

## Opening Your Inner Temple

Prepare for the journey to your inner temple by cleansing yourself. A ritual bath works best, but you can also just lie down comfortably and center yourself to induce an altered state of consciousness, which is the key to successful journeying. These states, often referred to as trance states, are the portals through which you enter the deeper world. Botanicals, stones, and other objects can help you achieve these altered states.

One way to induce the calm state of awareness necessary for entering a trance state is through breath control. A regular meditation practice can also help you gain control over your busy mind. These skills both draw on the same neural connections that lead to calm awareness, and this can improve your ability to induce a trance. When you focus on your breath, it takes you away from everyday life and aligns your neural networks with the world of spirits.

There are many ways to use the breath to induce trance. Counting down is a simple but effective method. Count down from thirteen at the beginning of the ritual, then count back up to twelve at the end. This leaves one strand of connection to the world of force, a technique that works very well. The procedure is explained in more detail below.

The use of botanicals to open your inner temple is another important technique, although the plant medicines that are right for each person vary greatly because we all have unique physiologies and energetic fields. In addition, your diet and medications can also interact with botanicals. Go gently into the world of botanical witchcraft. Do your own research and make the decisions that are right for you. Each person's comfort level using these substances will be different.

If you are comfortable and it is safe for you to use trance-inducing botanicals, go ahead. Mugwort, when consumed in an infusion or burned as sacred smoke, always works well for this sort of journeying. Heating essential oils and releasing their powers in a diffuser is wonderful. If this is your preferred method, I recommend a combination of eucalyptus and frankincense. Start the diffuser about fifteen minutes before your ritual journey so that the air molecules in your ritual space have been sufficiently charged.

Eucalyptus is a powerful opener that is ruled by Pluto, and some think Mars as well, making it very transformative and purifying. It also stimulates psychic abilities, so you can better connect with the mysteries within. I really like it as a stand-alone for inner-temple work, but you can also add frankincense, which is great for activating personal agency. Either way, these botanicals will enhance your ability to go deeply within yourself and prepare you for the journey described in the next section.

### Inner Temple Meditation

When you are cleansed and ready to begin your journey, ignite any candle or sacred smoke that feels right to you and get comfortable.

> Begin by acknowledging your physical surroundings. Notice the furniture, the floor, the walls—everything that surrounds you. Then disconnect from each one. Close your eyes and draw all your attention inward. Observe your thoughts. One by one, release them out into the world from which you are disconnecting. Like your material surroundings, your thoughts will be there when you return from your inner temple.
>
> Start to count down, picturing a set of stairs deep with you. With each number, descend one step. Beginning with thirteen, breathe in deeply and slowly fill your lungs. Feel your chest expand, then exhale.

Count down to twelve and pull that slow, deep breath into your belly, then exhale. On eleven, repeat that same belly breath, noticing any thoughts or images that arise from the material world. On ten, dismiss them. On nine, pull your breath deep into your lower torso, then exhale, releasing any tension there. On eight, pull your breath down through your legs to the tips of your toes, disconnecting them from the material world and wrapping them in a protective shroud. Breathe out any tension you feel.

On seven, still descending the stairs, bring your breath back up into your torso, encasing it in protection and feeling safe and secure. On six, move your breath up into your chest and your heart center. On five, draw that powerful breath down into your right arm, right to your fingertips. On four, repeat this for your left arm. On three, let your breath travel up to your shoulders and neck. Your thoughts are now completely still. On two, let your breath activate your mind and open to your inner temple. On your final breath, leave the stairs and cross over into Hekate's deeper world.

The key to your inner temple lies entirely within you. It is a gift from Hekate, placed there long before your birth into this life. You are among her chosen, and only you possess this unique key. You can feel its weight in your left hand. See the key. When you look up from it, you find yourself before the path to your inner temple.

Begin your walk toward the temple, taking note of your surroundings. Approach the entrance and open the door with your key. Once inside, you see a cauldron, illuminated by countless torches. Approach it and gaze into its depths, taking note of what surfaces. Call forth your sacred name, saying:

*Great Hekate, this cauldron flows from your eternal one, connecting me to you and your deeper world. By what name do you call me?*

Your sacred name emerges—perhaps on the surface of the cauldron, perhaps spoken to you, perhaps coming through as both symbols and words. However it comes to you, reach out to retrieve it. Hold it at your heart center and allow it to infuse you. Claim your name by proclaiming it aloud:

*I am proud to be known by Great Hekate as* [name].

Take some time to receive any additional messages, words, or symbols that are offered. When the time is right, depart the temple.

To cross back into regular awareness, return to the stairs. Count up from one to twelve, climbing up one step to the middle world with each number. On one, notice your feet reconnect to their physical form. On two, feel your legs return to the material world, released from their protective shell. On three, release the shield up through your torso. On four, your left arm returns to the material world; on five, your right arm does the same. On six, your chest reconnects to your physical heart and lungs, and the eternal fire of your inner temple warms them both. On seven, you sense your voice coming back to your embodied self. Release your crown on eight and, on nine, feel your thoughts begin to return. On ten, you begin to hear the material world once again. On eleven, bring your breath back to the middle world and begin to notice smells. On twelve, open your eyes.

Give thanks to Hekate for your sacred name and begin to look for reinforcing signs about it in your dreams and your experiences. Whether or not you create a physical representation of your name is entirely up to you.

## Offering What You Are Not: Making Negative Confessions

Negative confessions, a type of offering inspired by ancient after-life rituals associated with the Egyptian goddess Ma'at, are a way to acknowledge and release what you are *not*. They consist of statements that purify you from what blocks and binds. This deeply personal process, which invokes the spirit of Hekate Rixipyle, the barrier-smashing, chain-breaking goddess, can be very liberating. Hidden shame is the driving force behind false beliefs, whether these are based in your own misperceptions or those that others have thrust upon you. In fact, our misconceptions about ourselves are almost always rooted in the actions and opinions of others. Making these confessions can also become a kind of offering to the goddess.

Be gentle with yourself when doing this work. Ask Hekate to guide you through a personal inquiry into the harmful beliefs that are holding you back. Linking negative confessions with one of Hekate's many epithets associated with release—like Borborophorba (Filth Eater) and Anassa Eneroi (Queen of the Dead)—and offering them to the goddess is a favorite practice in the coven.

By associating your declarations of what you are *not* with specific epithets, you connect to those epithets and amplify the release. The Chthauldron discussed in chapter 1 (see page 3) is a great vessel to use for this kind of work. This method involves transmutation, the process of taking potent negative energy and reversing it to its polar opposite. Beliefs have a great deal of energy, and transmuting harmful ones through negative confessions can be a truly freeing experience.

In the coven, we write our negative confessions on paper petals and craft them into flowers, rendering what was ugly into something beautiful. You can create negative confessions in whatever way feels right to you, but working within the three-selves paradigm can give you a framework that can guide your explorations. Here are some examples.

- *"Shame in my root is like heaviness, anxiety, and fear."* Transmute this to: *"I am not heavy; I am not anxious; I am not afraid."*

- *"Shame in my heart is like disconnection, avoidance, and controlling others."* Call upon an epithet to transmute this to: *"I am not disconnected; I am not avoidant; I do not control others."*

- *"Shame in my crown is like harmful self-talk, ruminating on the past, and catastrophizing."* Transmute this to: *"I do not engage in harmful self-talk; I do not dwell in the past; I do not catastrophize."*

When you are ready with your negative confessions, write them on individual pieces of paper and place them in your cauldron.

Working with the list of epithets in the appendix, connect your declarations to epithets that seem appropriate for reversal. If you've created an oracle set, you can recite each confession and then pull a leaf or tile to divine which ones best reflect the statement. You can use the following incantation for your personal negative confessions in whole or in part or use it as inspiration for crafting your own.

> *Anima Mundi, World Soul, I have not forsaken mine.*
> *Chthonia, Guardian, I am not alone.*
> *Enodia, Guide, I am not lost.*
> *Ergatis, Energizer, I am not lazy.*
> *Kleidoukhos, Keeper of Keys, I have not rejected my truth.*
> *Klothaie, Spinner of Time, I am not possessed by the past.*
> *Kyria, Supreme, I am not weak.*

*Lampadios, Torchbearer, I will not deny my inner light.*
*Nykhia, Night, I am not afraid of my darkness.*
*Paionios, Healer, I am not a victim.*
*Phoebe, Bright One, I am not stupid.*
*Rixipyle, Breaker of Barriers, I am not imprisoned.*

On the dark moon, offer your negative confession to Hekate. The preparations you usually do before performing a ritual—refreshing the altar and cleansing—are especially important here, given that this is a ritual of release.

When you are ready to make your offering, speak this incantation (or one of your own making):

*Great Hekate,*
*I offer to you these negative confessions,*
*Releasing myself of what blocks and binds,*
*Banishing them, transmuting them into power.*

Recite your negative confessions one by one, holding the "petal" on which you wrote it at the appropriate center (root, heart, crown), and then return it to the cauldron. When you have completed this process, craft the pieces whole, either into a flower or a collage, rendering a true talisman of rebirth.

# Chapter 8

## Hekate's Companions—Goddesses and the Divine Masculine

*To Hekate, She Who Lights the Way,*
*Illuminating her companions,*
*Those of the Moon's Mysteries,*
*The Illuminating Torchbearers,*
*The Ancient Witches of Lore,*
*The Soul Guides,*
*And Mistresses of Shadows,*
*Guardians, Guides, and Gatekeepers.*
*Be with me now,*
*Lead me on my crooked journey.*

As in the tale of Persephone, Hekate is often a meditator, connecting us to other goddesses and gods. Hekate has been linked to not only Persephone but also Demeter, Persephone's mother. Hekate's lunar companions are Artemis and Selene, along with her witchy "daughters," Circe and Medea. At times, particularly in ancient spells, Hekate is evoked alongside Aphrodite (Venus to the Romans), who often is a companion for modern witches. Hekate is also connected to other dark goddesses, from the Cailleach to Kali Ma, through her associations with shadows, being uncontrollable, and her fierceness. The Morrigan and Lilith are frequently companions for many practitioners today, as may be expressions of the dark gods.

Regarding the divine masculine, while Hekate was certainly connected to the Underworld lord Hades (Pluto), she is perhaps most closely coupled with Hermes (Mercury), who shared her role as Psychopomp (Soul Guide), an association found in historical writings. In other texts, such as Hesiod's *Theogony*, her relationship with Zeus (Jupiter) is explained, citing his very different view of her compared to other goddesses. Zeus acknowledged Hekate's dominion over land, sea, and sky. She did as she pleased, in other words. There are references to her being partnered with Kronos (Saturn), hinting at how ancient her origins are. This also fits within her family tree, wherein she was related to both Kronos and Zeus.

Hekate as a Titan was the only child born to Asteria and Perses. Asteria is a goddess of the stars, whereas Perses was described as a wiseman, although his name means "destroyer." In her parentage, the roots of Hekate's association with the night and wisdom were formed. Hekate was also related to her frequent companion, Selene, another Titan goddess, whose work was as overseer of the moon.

## Working with Multiple Deities

As the divine Gatekeeper of the Mysteries, it is natural for Hekate to be accompanied by other deities, often those historically linked to her and those with whom she has much in common. She may also introduce us to goddesses, gods, and spirits that she knows will greatly benefit us, much in the same manner depicted in Persephone's story as a mediator who guides and connects.

Other deities may, in turn, lead us to her. The spirits we are close to may evolve over time. Some come for short periods, leaving us with only memories. Others are like good friends whom we may not talk to all the time, but when we do, it's always wonderful. Then there are our closest relationships with the divine, built upon a foundation of serious devotion. Yet even these bonds transform. Often, our spirit guides are revealed as personalized expressions of the divine. I've heard many accounts of how people were guided by a rather mysterious woman in their dreams, and even personal encounters, which are later understood as visitations from Hekate or other goddesses.

Our personal gods, goddesses, and other spirits create a sort of council of advisors. Some may always be present; others come and go. As with any group, sometimes they may not get along. Fundamentally, as long as Hekate and her companions are met with sincerity, our association with them, be it brief or enduring, will be beneficial. It is when we slide into shadowy expectations, calling upon them as favor-granting devices, as though pressing buttons on a vending machine, that they become troublesome. Goddess-centered witchcraft allows for the divine feminine to appear as she wills; rather than putting rigid expectations on her, we must acknowledge that she is mysterious and magical, following her own rules that we are not privy to. She often undoes conditioning we have about her and witchcraft. When you become aware of an expression of the divine feminine, or the divine masculine, meet it with curiosity, creativity, and trust.

## Gender and the Divine Feminine and Masculine

We are fortunate to live in a time when traditional gender roles are being challenged. That being said, it can be helpful to examine the historical differences between the divine feminine and masculine as a means of better understanding our own relationships with them, and perhaps even our own gender.

The divine feminine represents all matters to do with the home, family, intuition, and emotions. For goddesses associated with the moon, add magick and resisting mainstream expectations. The divine masculine was generally viewed as outward focused, more assertive, and concerned with public life. But there are numerous variations and exceptions.

Hekate was frequently partnered with Hermes in ancient sources, wherein they both typically played roles as mediators, messengers, and psychopomps. Hekate, who doesn't usually have children in the historical records, can be seen as a maiden. Hermes had sexual relations with all genders and had a child with Aphrodite, whose name inspired the former term for intersexed individuals. Through our modern lens, Hermes could easily be described as "gender fluid." These are just a few examples of the complexities of gender when relating to the divine and as reflected in our own lives.

I recommend having some sort of dedicated space for any deity that you are working with, including images and symbols representing how you experience them, along with a candle that is connected to them. Offerings can be made to them individually or as a group.

If you choose to honor them as a group, you can set up something called a Cauldron Council. Having a representation of each member is helpful. A method many in the coven use is inscribing the names and symbols of each of their council on a bay leaf or tile and keeping them in a cauldron or other container. If you choose this method, ask who has guidance to offer, then draw a name.

# Communicating with the Divine

The divine communicates with us through dreams, inner knowings, and synchronicities. It is our task to pay attention and watch out for these things. We can intentionally connect with them through rituals, readings, and even exchanging letters with them, one of my personal favorite practices. (This is explained a little later in the section called "Voces Deae.")

Although just about any deity can become part of our personal council, there are some goddesses who are more likely to take up residency. Specifically, other moon goddesses, such as Artemis and Selene, are prone to arrive when we need mystery and rewilding. Hekate's partners in the Underworld journey of healing, Persephone and Demeter, frequently show up when we are working on healing, especially wounds from the past. As we awaken to our own witch power, Circe and Medea may arrive, teaching us much about the craft and helping us resist the temptation to misuse it.

## Artemis: The Wild Mysteries

*It is nights like tonight,*
*She comes to me,*
*Gliding on pale moonbeams,*
*Shooting the wild back into me.*

Hekate and Artemis share several attributes related to their presentation as expressions of the Great Mother and also as maidens who resist conformity. Fundamentally, they are goddesses who resist the status quo, favoring the liminal and able to open the way to the mysteries. They share a special emphasis on all things related to pregnancy, childbirth, children, and the vulnerable. Hekate's affinity with magick, found in ancient plays and other texts, was sometimes shared with Artemis. It was only Artemis's later evolution into the Roman Diana that she assumed her role as a huntress. Hekate and Artemis and their interwoven nature, both in history and personal experiences, is complex. It is their nature to resist pigeonholing. Ultimately, they invite us into the mysteries of the moon and the wild.

## Themes

The Artemis that is popular today reflects her role as the maiden-huntress, the wild one who delights in freedom and all things connected to the moon.

Sometimes depicted as the maiden in the triple-goddess three stages of life model, she can thus be associated with the waxing moon. Artemis in this form is vigorous, bearing an energy similar to the sign of Sagittarius. She wanders freely into our lives, typically calling us to return to our own wild nature.

## History

While the Artemis as we know her today was found in ancient times, in some areas she was known as a Great Mother—a specific example being her worship at Eleusis. She was incredibly popular, as evidenced by numerous temples, writings, and art.

Much like how we view today's pop culture figures through our own biases, the ways Artemis and Hekate were perceived varied greatly in ancient times. Back then, of course, geography was a limiting factor, and each region would develop its own myths and histories. I feel a kinship with these ancients who were grappling with faces of the sacred feminine and using different names for it. Today we may chant, "Hekate, Cerridwen, come to us, let us be reborn"— not viewing the goddesses as disconnected beings but recognizing the different emanations of the same goddess. Artemis may be the wandering maiden, a figurehead for all of us queer women, or she may show up in our lives as a maternal force.

This association that Hekate has with Artemis is very important when examining their history in ancient Rome. Ancient Romans, much like the ancient Greeks did, adopted many of their beliefs from other cultures. The names Hekate and Artemis were changed, but they kept the compilation of powers associated with them. A lot of Artemis's attributes were transferred to Diana. Since Artemis and Hekate are so entwined, certain Hekatean aspects— such as magick—also became associated with Diana. But other aspects of Hekate, or Hecate to the Romans, become more infernal, while her governance of crossroads and roads becomes associated with a figure known as Trivia, which means "of the three ways."

## Working with Artemis

Artemis is typically an energizing figure. When we engage with her, we are likely to find ourselves wandering in the wild—whether that be walking in nature or breaking free of being "too civilized." I've always liked this contradiction—there were countless temples (normative structure of religion) dedicated to a goddess who resisted conformity. But Artemis will always insert the thrum of individual freedom. She is the eternal archer, piercing us with her arrows to wake us up, reconnecting us to the sacredness of the moon and who we truly are.

Symbols of Artemis, beyond those of the moon and arrows, include wild animals, especially deer. When wildlife shows up unexpectedly, it may well be an envoy of Artemis.

## Selene: The Lunar Journey

> *Eternal Mother Moon,*
> *Constantly shifting,*
> *Steadfast transformer,*
> *Quiet and swift.*

Selene's name means "light," and her epithets include Phoebe and Phos. These epithets are often applied to Artemis and Hekate as well, because they have specific associations with lunar rather than solar energies. Selene was ancient, predating the classical Greek period, and was referenced in Hesiod's *Theogony*, which was written almost 3,000 years ago.

Over the centuries, Selene's connection with Artemis and Hekate grew stronger so that the three were often intertwined. In ancient spells, Hekate, Selene, and Artemis were often evoked together as a trinity of lunar goddesses. Selene oversees the moon's mysteries, intuition, magick, and emotions—she embodies all things associated with the moon. Artemis watches over these aspects but also brings the spirit of youthfulness and independence. Hekate is the divine mediator, symbolizing how the moon makes life on earth possible. A modern version positions Artemis as maiden (waxing moon), Selene as mother (full moon), and Hekate as crone (waning/dark moon).

Selene's task was to lead the moon through its nightly journey from an oceanic cave to the celestial heights and back again. She was responsible for the moon's phases. She represents the spirit of the moon, and as Hekate is related to all things lunar, they are deeply interwoven. Like Hekate, Selene was a Titan, part of the family of old gods whose supremacy was usurped by Zeus and his Olympians. Both Selene and Hekate are illuminating night goddesses who are connected to the depths.

## Themes

While Hekate's lunar aspects represent only one facet of her, Selene is purely focused on the intuitive, magickal, depths of the moon. Her nightly voyage from the bottom of the sea to the Starry Road, along with the changing moon's faces, connects us to the cycles of nature and the mysteries of the universe. Turn to Selene when you are feeling lost and seek her guidance.

Selene fell in love with the mortal Endymion, and every night she would pause in her journey to gaze upon his beautiful face. Zeus had placed Endymion in an eternal sleep, so he retained his beauty forever. Selene's dedication to Endymion offers a way for us to explore our own relationships. Selene even bore children by Endymion, and so unlocks our own generative potential and creativity. Thus she is an excellent companion for all manner of gestation and birth, from children to projects associated with the lunar aspects of intuition, emotions, magick, and mysteries.

### History

The ancient worship of Selene was seen as outside mainstream Greek religion. Much like Hekate, but very unlike Artemis, Selene remained on the margins of religious practice. *The Homeric Hymns* contains a beautiful verse dedicated to her, describing her great beauty and her chariot leading the moon across the sky. The ancient Greeks viewed her as both the moon itself and the goddess who oversaw its cycle. This practice of personifying physical objects was common back then; for example, Nyx was seen as the embodiment of night.

### Working with Selene

Selene tends to be a calming spirit, bringing love and healing to those who call upon her. She relieves loneliness, soothes broken hearts, and reminds us that even the darkest moments will yield to brighter days. Above all, she teaches that life, like the moon, goes through phases. Her profound beauty, which we experience whenever we are awestruck by the moon, may lead us to better self-care, acceptance of our own worth, and increased confidence. The stone selenite is named for Selene and is very suited for working with her.

### Persephone: From Innocent Maiden to the Queen of the Underworld

> *Great Goddess, Fierce Queen.*
> *Teach me to craft my own crown,*
> *From the dust, tears, and blood*
> *Of my pain.*

Persephone's journey from Kore (the maiden) to Persephone (the queen of the Underworld) was brokered by Hekate. In the rituals of Eleusis, Hekate mediated the journey to Persephone's secret chamber, and the *Homeric Hymn to Demeter* recounts Persephone's transition from innocent maiden to fierce yet benevolent queen.

Our own relationship with Hekate may place us in the role of Persephone. Hekate often comes to us when we are broken by the nastiness of the world, our innocence having been violated. She emerges from her cave to console and guide us through the healing Underworld journey. Persephone's union with Hades symbolizes our own need to reconcile with our shadow self and perhaps heal our masculine side.

Both Hekate and Persephone are chthonic goddesses who bear illuminating torches and are associated with the riches found only in the depths. In ancient times, the harvest and other treasures were often stored underground or in caves. The chthonic was not viewed as purely hellish but as a complex territory of spirits. Hekate and Persephone were both called Anassa Eneroi (Queen of the Dead); Hekate was the psychopomp who guided spirits to and from the Underworld, and Persephone ruled over them. With Hekate's governance over land, sea, and sky and Persephone's emergence from the depths to awaken the natural world, they shared above-ground powers over fertility and the physical realm of the middle world.

**Themes**

The central tenet of Persephone's story is her transition from maiden to queen, from helpless to empowered, as evidenced in the two names by which she was known. Kore, which refers to her pre-Underworld period, is an epithet meaning "maiden" or possibly "sprout," according to some academical texts—symbolizing the vitality of youth and new growth. Whereas Persephone (Proserpine to the Romans), her actual name, translates as "destroyer," referencing the power of decay and decline.

Like Hekate, Persephone teaches that life is a cycle of creation and destruction; without death, there is no life. Persephone illustrates the transmutation of pain into power and the sometimes brutal adaptions one must make during unpleasant circumstances. Ultimately, she rises to the obligations of her throne, becoming a benevolent sovereign who is both tender and fierce with the spirits in her Underworld realm.

In one story, she grants the grief-stricken Orpheus his wish to bring Eurydice back from the dead but with one condition: that he walk in front and not look back at her until they reach the living world. Orpheus makes the promise, but as soon as he reaches the light, he looks back. Eurydice, not yet having crossed the threshold, is immediately sent back to the Underworld forever. During the trials that Aphrodite set for Psyche, Persephone willingly shared a piece of her own beauty, with the instruction that Psyche not look at it. Poor Psyche couldn't resist peeking, and she fell into a deep sleep as a result. Both these stories provide examples of how we mortals can fall into the temptations of our own shadow selves. When Persephone speaks, it's best to follow her edicts exactly.

**History**
The telling of Persephone's transformation from maiden to Underworld queen dates back almost three thousand years, although some scholars now posit that the story is likely much older. She was a central goddess in ancient Greece and perhaps, like Hekate, was adapted from earlier versions of the Great Mother from cultures visited by the Greeks.

While there were many centers of worship, Eleusis was the main location. The rituals there were incredibly popular and, unlike some other festivals, were available to everyone. People traveled from far and wide to experience them. The ceremonies consisted of two components—the first was a series of minor preparation rituals; these led to the second and greater celebration of the cycle of rebirth.

This second celebration consisted of three main components: purification, descent into the mysteries, and rebirth, echoing Persephone's governance over the natural cycles of life, death, and regeneration. After Christianity replaced the earlier religions, the essence of the Eleusinian Mysteries became syncretized with saints and Christian festivals. Regardless, Persephone has continued to be a very widely appreciated figure in art and pop culture.

**Working with Persephone**
*"Are you the queen of your own life?"* asks Persephone. She can challenge us to let go of the past and offers us great comfort when we are doing personal shadow work, especially when we are trying to resolve trauma. She shows us that spending time in the Underworld is necessary for growth and that our own riches may be lurking down there. If you have buried talents, interests, or

passions, she can shine her torch on them, pointing out that these treasures are our personal throne.

Her cyclical journey connects us to the rhythms of the natural world and of our own lives. Honoring Persephone at the commencement of spring and autumn connects us to her and these cycles, echoing the spirit of the ancient Eleusinian rituals. Reflecting on her union with Hades can help us to find the good in bad situations but also make us aware of the seductive powers of "dark lords."

## Demeter: The Mother

*She who knows the story,*
*She who holds the power,*
*She who is the Mother,*
*Knowing pain and joy,*
*Watching over the cycles of our lives.*

Persephone's mother, Demeter (Ceres in Latin), is very much entwined in her story and rituals. In one myth, Demeter, accompanied by Hekate, confronts Zeus about their daughter's fate. After she goes on a furious rampage, Hekate calms her down, and off they go to sort out the mess. And it was Demeter who gave the Eleusinian Mysteries to Triptolemus, thereby initiating a series of rituals that persisted for hundreds of years.

But worship of Demeter was not limited to Eleusis; she was also an important goddess of agriculture, fertility, and civilization. Like Hekate and Persephone, Demeter was a chthonic torchbearer, although her association was more with the earth itself than with the Underworld. Widely viewed as a Great Mother goddess, Demeter is especially concerned about the sacred feminine in the middle world, although she has her darker aspects. When Persephone was violated by Hades, Demeter swore to destroy humanity by rendering the world barren. Demeter may arrive in our lives when we are veering too far from her priorities; in other words, when it is time to tend to our own crops.

## Themes

Exploring the complex relationship between Demeter and Persephone can help to heal our personal mother wounds. Although their relationship was imperfect, they still came together to guide others into the mysteries. Demeter can remind us not to hold on too tightly to others, as she did with Persephone. She evokes the structured world of intentional growth, but she also challenges us to overthrow systems that confine us. An example of this is the ancient festival of Thesmophoria, when women could temporarily reverse the status quo of the patriarchy and become the leaders.

### History

Demeter was claimed by the Greeks in the same way that they claimed to have invented both agriculture and civilization. The Eleusinian Mysteries represented only a fraction of the widespread cult following and many festivals that honored Demeter, which signaled her importance in a country where only about 20 percent of the land was arable. The Lesser Mysteries—celebrated in the spring—and other first-sowing festivals honored her as Chloe (Verdant Goddess), whose name means "of the green." During the growing season, she was worshipped as Evalosia (Mother of the Harvest). While Persephone reigns with Hades in the Underworld, Demeter was Brimo Cyanopeplos, the raging, dark-veiled mother of the barren world.

### Working with Demeter

As with Persephone, rituals honoring Demeter during spring and autumn are excellent opportunities for seeking her presence. Celebrate your own Thesmophoria during autumn, the time when it was traditionally held, by reversing roles with someone for a day. For personal work, Demeter is unparalleled for helping to heal the mother complex, whether it be with our own mother or how we relate to the archetype. Perhaps surprisingly, connecting with Demeter often signals a period of reconciling with our own rage, and she can guide us toward healthy expressions of anger. She is particularly helpful when we are balancing the need for order, when we are synthesizing our wild and civilized parts, and in all matters relating to the natural cycle.

### Circe: Witch Who Sees Beyond

*Mistress of plants and animals,*
*Knower of secrets and lies.*
*With unique voice and clearest sight,*
*Show me the ways of truth.*

In her mythology, Circe is both biological and spiritual daughter of Hekate. She was born a demigoddess, who fit in with neither the gods nor humans.

After she was banished to an isolated island, she made a home for herself and created the practice of witchcraft. Circe is the original witch in Greek mythology and has a special connection with the natural world. She is one who can see beyond the surface and connect with the spirits of the deeper world—from deities to the departed.

Like Hekate, Circe was an outsider because she was a powerful woman who could wield magick, abiding outside civilizations where females did as they were told. Both evoke personal sovereignty, teaching us to become the keepers of our own cauldrons. Circe often shows up to remind us that we have power as a witch and that reigning supreme over our own "island" is better than trying to fit in where we don't belong. She reminds us to see beyond the surface to reveal lies that have been told to us and to see the spirits of the deeper world.

## Themes

Modern witches often feel like misfits, having experienced rejection and invalidation. We can become mired in feeling like outsiders, continuing to define ourselves through the lens of mainstream society and those who reject us. Circe (Kirke in Greek) teaches us to see our lives through our own eyes and to stop viewing it through others' perception of us. This can be a revolutionary process that can lead to great change. Like Circe, we should shift our gaze toward witchcraft, finding beauty in what speaks truth to us and cutting ties with those who find us peculiar or different.

Circe was criticized because of her voice, but on her island, she learned to harness its power. When confronted by liars, she worked her magick to reveal their true nature—like when she turned a cruel girl into the monster Scylla and men invading her island into pigs. Yet she showed kindness to Odysseus and helped him journey to the world of spirits. Because she was a mother as well as a witch, she is a source of inspiration to all those walking the same path, showing them how to merge the magickal with motherhood.

## History

Circe was a mythical woman, playing supporting roles in several ancient stories, particularly that of Odysseus (Ulysses in Latin). Unlike Hekate, Artemis, Persephone, and Demeter, Circe wasn't worshipped—she was viewed as a minor deity and not a proper goddess. However, Circe has captivated the attention of creatives over the centuries, and there are many great works depicting her. She is usually shown as an evil temptress who caused trouble for civilized men; she embodied the spirit of the dangerous woman in the same vein as biblical Eve.

These days, Circe is being reclaimed as a powerful witch and a symbol of justice for all those who feel marginalized because they have power and a unique voice.

## Working with Circe

It can be lonely as a solitary witch, so Circe can become our companion, alleviating the sense of isolation. If we talk to her, share our emotions about feeling like a misfit, she will render comfort and advice. Be warned, though, she speaks the truth and can be quite stern with her guidance. If we are living a false life, she may point this out.

When concocting spells, Circe is a lovely helpmate. If we listen to her unique voice, she'll make useful suggestions. But most importantly, she teaches us to see beyond the surface—peering into the cauldron, across the veil, and into the mysteries from whence all magick comes.

## Medea: Witch of Shadows

*Teach me how to*
*Stand in my own power,*
*Bring light to the shadows,*
*Where magick is revealed.*

Alongside Circe, Medea can also be considered a "spiritual daughter" of Hekate. As witches of lore, they are entwined with Hekate as queen of witches. Both Circe and Medea were depicted as "evil sorceresses" who worked baneful spells on innocent men. Unlike Circe, Medea received widespread attention thanks partly to Euripides's widely popular (even today) play about her. Beyond that, like Circe, she has been expressed through many works of art, from paintings to operas.

Medea is almost always shown as a horrible yet pitiable creature who slays her own children. Historians have noted that versions of her story prior to Euripides's treatment did not include her killing her offspring. Euripides's play is an excellent example of how views changed from the ancient perceptions of benevolent female magick to the later interpretations of their powers being malevolent.

When I first started writing about Medea in my blog, there was a surprising amount vitriol in the comments, including pointing out that she isn't actually a goddess. Medea activates our own shadows. As for her not technically being a goddess, she is one for me. In reclaiming Medea from the grip of those who use her as a mechanism for vilifying powerful women, I have found great shadow healing. Yes, I am a witch, capable of baneful things, but I choose to not fall into the traps set by others, which could lead to me lashing out. Medea has become an important spirit for those healing from trauma, and she helps to illuminate the witch power that they have pushed deep into the shadows.

## Themes

Medea's story inspires us be diligent in our practice. She reminds us to carefully craft our spells and talismans, giving thought to the true nature of our workings. Her story is difficult but offers great insights. If we are being tempted by a "heroic prince" to do what is not in our own best interests, think of what happened to Medea, who was forced into all manner of deplorable acts. She was used and abused by powerful men, a story all too common, and we can identify with her vengeance as we unlock our own righteous rage in the pursuit of justice and healing.

## History

Medea's story is embedded within that of Jason's adventures, of which numerous versions were known—from ancient times right up until the present. Although there are various tales, generally, Medea is a beautiful daughter of a king in trouble. Jason (or Iason) shows up, seduces Medea, and convinces her to use her magick to capture a powerful talisman, the legendary Golden Fleece. While this ensures Jason's military victory, it also leads to the death of Medea's brother. Regardless, Medea then accompanies Jason on an epic journey.

During their trek back to Jason's home, they encounter Circe—who is Medea's aunt—and she absolves Medea of her nefarious deeds. Eventually, they reach Jason's home and settle into married life, although he continues to ask her for magick "favors." At one point, Jason even has Medea restore his father to life in a sort of cauldron of rebirth. Eventually, Jason casts Medea aside in favor of a younger, better connected woman, leaving Medea completely rejected.

In Euripides's version, she then slays their two sons, while the older versions of the tale have her simply being outcast, which lacks theatrical flair.

Another depiction finds her escaping, driving a chariot led by a dragon. Horrifying and highly entertaining, Medea's narrative has endured in countless forms. In so many of the later stories, she is the dangerous woman, with her evil nature fully revealed, revealing a cautionary tale from those in power to mind our place and do as we are told. According to those versions, we should accept an unwelcome, cruel fate and step aside quietly. More positive retellings of Medea's story exist, and, as witches, we have an opportunity to vindicate her spirit.

### Working with Medea

As a spirit, Medea is a mighty witch—a mythic ancestor who comes to us when we are ready to embrace both our shadow and illuminated aspects. She has no patience with limited views of witchcraft or reinventing it as "light working." Medea reminds us that witchcraft has a complicated history, bound in the portrayal of women and others who use their power to threaten the male-dominated authority. When we are doing shadow work, be it healing our broken pieces or giving light to our hidden talents, she is a most stalwart cheerleader. Rather than being seduced into the trap of conformity, she is a most liberating ally.

### Voces Deae—Corresponding with the Goddesses

*Voces Deae* translates as "voices of the goddesses." The practice involves writing a heartfelt letter to your chosen goddess, then allowing her to write a reply through you. This is a great project to do with a partner so that each of you exchange your written letters, then channel the reply to the other. I try to do this exercise at least once a month, typically with profound results. We do it in the coven at least once a year, and it is beloved by all. When new coven members do it for the first time, many question if the goddess will really reply. She always does.

I recommend creating magickal paper and other supplies to enhance the process. Infusing the paper with sacred smoke, adding images of your chosen goddess, choosing or crafting a special ink, and working in colors that you associate with her are examples. Amethyst, bay leaves, and the color purple are generally good for this project. You can create a special candle for your chosen goddess as a connector, too. Or write her name and symbols on a bay leaf, punch a hole in it, and wear it around your neck as a talisman. Infused bay leaves can also be burned in the cauldron.

Should you want to divine which goddess to exchange letters with, use the Cauldron Council and pull out one. It will be exactly the right goddess for you at that time.

Connect to your chosen goddess through art, create an altar in her honor, play music that resonates with you and your goddess; you will feel what is right.

When you are ready to write to her, with your correspondences and talismans in place, light a candle and place it near your writing area.

Without self-editing, write to her; just let it all flow without censoring. When you are finished, offer the letter to her by ending it with something like, "*These words are my offering to you. I am open to receiving your reply.*"

Seal the letter with wax, bind it with cord, or put in an envelope. Keep it in a sacred space. Try not to reread the letter before sealing. You may want to do an immediate exchange of letters or wait for a special date to get her reply.

If you are exchanging letters with a partner, you can each read the other's letter if you want. Keep in mind, however, that our goddesses don't require that we know what has been written; they do, and they will respond accordingly.

When the time comes to channel the reply, you can have the your letter nearby to better connect to the chosen goddess. Have your chosen correspondences nearby, too. Then ask your goddess to reply through you: "[Goddess's name], *I ask for you to work through me, as scribe for you reply to my* [or partner's name] *letter. May your wisdom and guidance flow through my hands.*"

Don't filter what she has to say, simply be the one recording her words as she wills. Her reply may be straightforward or more symbolic, calling you into her mysteries. It's possible that you may not get a written response at this time. She could respond through other means, such as dreams, inner knowings, or synchronicities.

## The Sovereign Goddesses Ritual

This ritual evokes the presence of Hekate and all six goddesses who are closely aligned with her—Artemis, Selene, Persephone, Demeter, Circe, and Medea—to awaken the goddess within you and connect you to them. Together, they comprise a Sacred Seven Cauldron Council. However, you can also include your own goddesses as you feel led to. We've been doing this ritual for years in the coven, always around the summer solstice. One goddess may come through more strongly than the others, or you may experience them all equally. Enjoy this ritual, trusting in the goddesses to show up as and when they are meant to.

## Preparation

- A khernips ritual (see page 4) with a sprig of dried thyme or rosemary is lovely as cleansing prior to the sovereign goddess ritual.

- Bay leaves with each of the goddesses' names can be created and kept in the cauldron.

- Purple and amethyst are excellent accompaniments for this ceremony.

- Create an altar honoring them all; include images, candles, and symbols associated with them.

- Craft a talisman with charms, symbols, and colors that you associate with each of the goddesses. Select a color of thread that represents each one, braid it, and then add one charm for each of them. The charm can be a disk with her image or name inscribed on it, a stone, or a symbol that you associate with the particular goddess. Finish the talisman by anointing it with Oleum Spirita prior to the ritual. Wear this as sacred adornment for the ritual; afterward, to maintain a connection to them, you can continue to wear it, wrap it around a candle, or place it on the altar.

- Choose suitable offerings, which you will place on the altar during the ritual.

- Wearing a crown is perfect for this ritual, be it a botanical one you craft yourself or something you purchase.

## Procedure

Position yourself comfortably in front of the altar, perform the khernips ritual, light any candles, and then recite:

*Come Goddesses and Witches,*
*Ancient but new,*
*To this place,*
*I beckon you.*
*Artemis,*
*Selene,*
*Persephone,*
*Demeter,*
*Circe,*

*Medea*
*And Great Hekate,*
*I welcome you.*

Raise your arms up high. Then make your offerings, saying:

> *I honor all Goddesses through these offerings, expressing gratitude and connection.*

Continue with this invocation:

> *Hekate, Queen of Wisdom, Anassa Kleidoukhos, grant the keys of magick and mystery. Guide me with your wisdom and open the way.*
>
> *Artemis, Wild Goddess, Anassa Apollousa, reveal your wildness, your unapologetic ways and power of destruction for all that no longer serves.*
>
> *Selene, Mistress of the Moon, Anassa Phoebe, illuminate my journey with your silver light, and loving ways.*
>
> *Persephone, Undisputed Queen, Anassa Eneroi, awaken triumph, tenacity, and ability to rise strong.*
>
> *Demeter, Goddess of Structure and Balance, Anassa Theron, share your compassion, discipline, and force of will.*
>
> *Circe, Original Witch, Anassa Pharmakeia, unlock the knowledge of witchcraft, true voice, and the power to create.*
>
> *Medea, Eternal Witch, Anassa Venificarum, share your passion, cleverness, and the ability to heal.*
>
> *I invite your powers into me now as a proclamation of my own sacred sovereignty.*
>
> *The energy of your fires burns within me.*
>
> *Your mighty winds are my breath,*
>
> *Your blood-water of creation runs through my veins,*
>
> *And my feet walk your road.*
>
> *Like you, I am the darkest night of the Underworld,*
>
> *The starry heights of the Upper World,*
>
> *And all points in between.*
>
> *Eternal,*
>
> *Strong and wise,*
>
> *Powerful beyond measure.*
>
> *Sovereign. Free. True.*

Pause here so that the goddesses can speak to you through words and images. When you feel ready, conclude the ritual by reciting:

*Great Hekate,*
*Artemis,*
*Selene,*
*Persephone,*
*Demeter,*
*Circe,*
*And Medea,*

*I am enlivened with your spirits,*
*May I honor you well.*
*May you forever watch over my crooked path.*
*Hail and Farewell.*

Bring your arms to your sides in a sweeping motion.

As with all rituals, record your experiences and be open to further communications.

## The Great Goddesses Oracle Reading

This reading conveys messages from each of the seven goddesses, drawing upon their wisdom and guidance. It can be done with cards (as in the example below) or other divinatory tools. It is a great accompaniment to the sovereign goddesses ritual, or it can be done separately. Given the complexities of this reading, I recommend doing it only once per season.

If you have inscribed bay leaves dedicated to each of the goddesses, arrange them on your reading space, then place the revealed card beside the corresponding goddess.

The structure of the reading is:

Card #1    Circe: The Seer—what is coming

Card #2    Medea: The Witch—where to focus your magick

Card #3    Persephone: The Queen—where your power is

Card #4    Demeter: The Mother—how the maternal archetype
           will manifest

Card #5  Artemis: The Wild—what to do to reclaim your wild soul

Card #6  Selene: The Journey—what is illuminated

Card #7  Hekate: The Healer—what the medicine is

Begin with the usual opening ceremony: igniting your candle and performing khernips, if required. Hold the deck and say:

*Hail the Great Goddesses,*
*Circe,*
*Medea,*
*Persephone,*
*Demeter,*
*Artemis,*
*Selene,*
*Hekate.*
*Great Goddesses,*
*I welcome you.*
*My intention is pure, my actions true, and will strong.*
*Grant me guidance through these cards.*

*Circe, Seer of the Future, what lies ahead?* [Draw the card]
*Medea, Witch Supreme, where is my magick?* [Draw the card]
*Persephone, where is my power?* [Draw the card]
*Demeter, how do I mother / who is mother?* [Draw the card]
*Artemis, Wild and Free, how do I reclaim my wild?* [Draw the card]
*Selene, Bright Shining Light in Darkness, what is illuminated?* [Draw the card]
*Hekate, Mighty Goddess of the Witches, Wise Guide, Guardian, and Gate-keeper,*
*Where is the medicine?* [Draw the card]
[Finish with] *Hail and Farewell, with gratitude for your wisdom.*

Spend time with the arranged cards after completing the reading, bringing into awareness more details about the messages, then consulting the book that accompanied the cards for standard interpretations. Record the results and impressions from your reading so that you can add notes as more comes to light and so that you can review it all later to see how the reading played out.

# Part III

## *The Craft*

# Chapter 9

## Walking the Crooked Path

*Walking the crooked path,*
*Following Hekate's torches.*
*Guided by the moon.*
*Rooted to the earth.*
*In the company of spirits,*
*Crafting magick,*
*Seeking the mysteries.*
*Entering each crossroads,*
*I claim the keys offered,*
*Entering new gates,*
*On this evolving journey.*

There is a moment of soul-quaking realization when you first awaken to your core identity as a witch. Perhaps it was a film or a book or something you saw on the internet. But something led you here, a calling toward the crooked journey.

Fundamentally, witchcraft is about stepping through the mundane world of everyday life into the deeper world of Hekate. It is entering her cauldron of magick and mystery. I believe we are born to the cauldron, that there is something within our souls that calls us back to what we have always been.

## Spellcrafting: The Heart of Witchcraft

The absolute essence of witchcraft is crafting a spell to achieve a desired outcome, drawing from spirits and energies and calling up our guides for support. Spells can be words alone, but in my system, they typically include magickal objects, such as talismans, along with incantations.

Plants, stones, animal spirits, colors, the moon, the planets, the elements, the realms, and more can be summoned into our workings. Words and numbers themselves have powerful energies, which is why carefully crafting intentions and incantations and using words of power appropriately is so important. Our bodies have immense energy that can also be summoned into spells. We can do this using bodily fluids, breath, and even sex.

All of the above have "daemons," or spirits, that can be evoked and worked with to achieve our intention. They all contain energy that is waiting for us to use to achieve our potential as witches. We can place these energies into spells, potions, energy grids, and more. Once added, our magickly charged creations release the combined energy to manifest the outcome we seek. The energies we work with must not be harmed by our workings. Each object should be honored prior to use. However, the objects exist for our use.

Botanicals, animal spirits, stones, the planets, the moon, words, letters, numbers, and colors are collectively referred to as "correspondences." And while these objects have energetic properties that can be evoked and channeled into magick. there are ancient systems governing their use, such as the Doctrine of Signatures and the Hermetic Principles. We can even add objects with personal meaning, such as jewelry and clothes, just like the ancients did, thereby creating unique correspondences.

The worlds of form and force intermingle when you do magick. The forces you can work with include correspondences, which always have a physical form, and those of pure energy, such as spirits and the elements. With correspondences, we bridge the two worlds by pulling the mystical properties out of the physical object.

## The Essence of Witchcraft

Like correspondences, we have both physical form and a deeper essence. In our souls, we know that we are witches—Hekate's chosen. In our energetic depths is our root, the lower self where emotions and intuition resides. There is the heart center, the intersection between our interior life and the external world. Our lofty crown has a foundation of regular mind yet stretches to the heights of the mysteries. We are the embodied mortal and the etheric being. Witchcraft abides at the crossroads between all these phenomena. Spells that are effective weave everything together, combining ourselves with correspondences and spirits, rendering power and transformation.

# Witch, Know Yourself

When developing or selecting a spell, the fundamental key is exploring what outcome you actually desire. I say, "actually" because we may think we know, but our personal inquiries may yield different results. For example, I may want to do a money spell because I'm short on cash this month. If this is a rare situation, prompted by a huge, unexpected expense, then a one-off money manifestation may be in order. However, if I am constantly overspending on nonessential things, then I may want to craft a spell for changing my overall spending habits. Should those extravagant outflows be driven by deeper mechanisms, such as fear and past trauma, then my spellcrafting can be designed to support healing.

All spells can be self-directed—focused on our own emotions, thoughts, and actions. Although I loved my mother dearly, I usually ended up drained and upset after spending time with her. I wanted to establish firm boundaries regarding our time together; I wanted to see her through love and not resentment; and I wanted to enjoy our interactions during the limited time she had left in this life. So I did spells designed to achieve these outcomes. I also did a cord-cleansing ritual to remove my contributions to our difficult relationships. I favor spells of this nature rather than ones that target other people.

# Emotions Are the Root

I often say that witchcraft is driven by emotions. What this means is that we do a spell that has a specific desired outcome, but this is just a surface goal; in reality, it's all about how we *feel*. In the money spell example, I mentioned fear, and this is often the driving force in spellcrafting. If I don't have enough money to pay my bills, then I am afraid of losing my home, not having food, and so on. If I'm habitually overspending because of deeper issues, they are always rooted in fear. Conversely, our spells may be ignited by love, such as the need to protect our family or send healing to another person.

*Examples of fear-based feelings* include anxiety, aggression, anger, avoidance, codependency, depression, envy, neuroticism, being overcontrolling, and perfectionism. Specific types of fear, such as fear of lack, fear of missing out, or fear of rejection are often involved as well.

*Examples of love-based emotions* include affection, attraction, belonging, connections, contentment, commitment, loyalty, joy, giving and seeking support, responsibility, and trust.

Then there are more complex emotions that are combinations of love and fear. Examples include betrayal, grief, jealousy, loneliness, and sorrow.

## Values: The Points on Our Crown

Some of these feelings are also values, such as perfectionism or commitment. Perfectionism, the unattainable desire that everything be absolutely flawless, links to fear, which often shows up as trying to control everything. Commitment refers to prioritizing, endurance, and reliability.

If you look at the spell at the very front of this book, you will see that it contains emotions and values that are important to you. Our thoughts are often fleeting, but the principles that sustain us endure as guiding values. They are personal spirits that influence all that we do. Here is a selection of such values: accountability, accomplishment, adventure, authenticity, awareness, belonging, commitment, confidence, courage, creativity, curiosity, dignity, discipline, excellence, family, freedom, fulfillment, growth, health, humor, justice, integrity, kindness, learning, nurturing, power, safety, spirituality, stability, strength, and wisdom.

### Divining Values

Write on bay leaves or inscribe tiles with your key values and add them to your oracular set. Put them in your cauldron and ask Hekate and your spirit guide to speak through the set, then pull one out. You can also choose one intentionally to work with, carrying it with you. This is a favorite method in the coven. We often draw them for one another. On one occasion, we even made them into crowns. Here's an example using the Sacred Seven Principles (see *Hekate's Cave* and *Hekate's Garden* for more information).

### Boundaries: Casting Our Personal Magic Circle

Emotions and values, along with intuition and thought, converge at the crossroads of our interior life and the external world, and can affect everything from relationships to our personal appearance. Boundaries keep us safe; they are about acknowledging our limits and capacity to handle specific circumstances. As witches, we are more likely to perceive the energy, needs, and even innermost secrets of others, rendering strong boundaries vital to our lives and ability to practice our craft.

## Sustaining Boundaries

Use the following list to begin your exploration of how much you respect your own and others' boundaries; add any others that may be important for you to work on.

For each statement, indicate from 0 to 3 how frequently you demonstrate the boundary, with 0 being "never" to 3 being "most of the time."

Next, identify how important this boundary is to you: "high," "medium," or "low."

Finally, choose a few to specifically work on. You can prioritize them using stars or another symbol.

- Asking a person if it's okay before touching them

- Being kind to others

- Being wary of others who come on too strong, too fast

- Not tolerating unacceptable actions or words

- Understanding that others may have difficulty communicating

- Being kind to yourself first

- Being clear about your expectations and needs

- Having passion about your needs and interests without harming others

- Demonstrating integrity; living in accordance with your beliefs

- Following through on what you've promised

- Recognizing your own emotions

- Knowing your own capacity and limits

- Making time every day for what nourishes your body and soul

- Saying "yes" to things that feel right

- Knowing what, and who, is inside your personal circle

While exploring your root, heart, and crown centers, record which emotions, values, and boundaries come through to you. Pay special attention to this when doing the daily Unifying the Three Selves meditation (see page 26). Combine this with the Cauldrons Oracle Reading to reveal further insights.

# Developing Personal Ethics and Practice

The power of magick can bring both bane and blessing to ourselves and others and therefore requires us to develop our own code of ethics. Spells can be interpreted different ways, and magick can be beneficial to the recipient or bring unwelcome consequences. The term "white" witchcraft is typically used to describe magick that restricts anything that can be considered baneful. For me, witchcraft has no color; if it did, it would be all hues combined into grey.

"Whitewashing" is hugely problematic, reflecting a toxic "purity culture" and denying history. That being said, a discussion about baneful witchcraft can help us develop our own code of ethics. *Hexe* is the German word for "witch." Separating witchcraft from hexing makes no sense since they are the same thing. In Pennsylvania, the German settlers used the term "hex" to describe all sorts of folk magic, including beautiful "barn hexes." Pennsylvania Dutch folk magick thrived in the less constricted environment of the New World.

Hexing today is commonly used to represent all forms of *baneful* magick, which can be defined as any that interferes with the free will of another—be they human, spirit, or otherwise—with a goal of inflicting harm or gaining control. Healing, as defined by some, seems to refer to all witchery designed to be beneficial—from attraction spells to protection and prosperity charms. Of course, hexing can be healing. Baneful magick wouldn't be done unless the practitioner believed it to be beneficial in some fashion, if only for themselves. Hexing and healing are completely intertwined. It is our personal code of ethics that determines how we see them and the type of witchery we engage in. I would never curse anyone because they've annoyed me, but I would bind—restrict—the behavior of someone who has repeatedly caused harm to me or my beloveds.

Knowing our emotions, following our values, and regulating boundaries form the basis of a personal code of conduct, both in our individual practice and how we focus on others. There has been, and I'm certain will continue to be, much debate about ethics in witchcraft. The old saying, "a witch that cannot hex, cannot heal" implies that how we practice is our choice. Hexing, which is a type of cursing, is sometimes considered baneful magick, since the intention is to inflict consequences that cause harm. But what if the person, known as the "target," was causing great suffering to others?

The issue of interfering with the free will and natural order, whether to prevent someone from causing harm or for healing, is important. There are different ways to approach this. It might be the right decision for you to always seek informed consent from the one to whom you want to send healing before starting any working. Or you could simply add, *"May this be for the highest good of all involved, and should the energy not be needed or welcome, may it go to where it is required,"* while sending energy, crafting a spell, or calling upon spirits for assistance. When we are doing work for those who cannot consent, such as animals, children, the land, people we cannot contact, or organizations, the affirmation example above may be the appropriate solution.

Sharing our witchery is another consideration when developing our personal code of ethics. Whether it is displaying altars and talismans prominently in our home or posting photos on social media, considering the possible consequences before doing so is important. We have a right to keep secret what we keep secret. Additionally, the energy evoked by our witchery could impact others. If I do a cord-cutting spell, I keep the talisman used far from my home. My home, however, is filled with magickal treasures that are designed to benefit all of us.

Developing a personal code of conduct, or creed, gives us a framework for how we engage in witchcraft involving others. It also speaks to our capacity to help others. Are we truly able to devote the energy necessary to support others in their healing, whether through protection or binding someone who is causing harm? Having firm boundaries around what we will and won't do, what we can and cannot do, gives us a clearer decision-making framework.

# Chapter 10

## The Apothecary, Magickal Supplies, and Tools

*I cast this circle round*
*Such delights and treasures,*
*True helpmates.*
*Full of possibility and promise.*
*Awaiting my witch's touch,*
*Through which I render*
*Life into my craft.*
*Like me, they are much more than they appear.*
*Hail to objects claimed,*
*Each one special and true.*
*Great Hekate and my Spirits,*
*Watch over this apothecary,*
*Banishing what blocks and binds,*
*Protecting from harm,*
*Guiding my work,*
*Ever blessing all that is rendered.*
*As it is spoken,*
*So it becomes.*

This invocation can be used as your personal ritual for all the contents in your apothecary. Group them all together, if possible, or perhaps choose your most prized helpmates to stand in for everything; you could even do it over your entire witching space. The apothecary is our collection of supplies, correspondences, objects, and magickal tools—all awaiting our witch's touch. From intuitively repurposed kitchen gadgets to intentionally acquired specialized treasures, each witch's apothecary is unique, yet there are some common items that you may want to have in yours.

An apothecary can be in an antique cupboard, on a shelf, or even take up an entire room. Above all, apothecaries are workspaces and storage areas. When I was renovating my home, the smallest bedroom became my witching room. I redesigned the closet to be my apothecary by taking off the door and building a workbench at the right height for me. It extended across the entire closet, stretching from one side to the other. I added shelves above the bench and cupboards below, and there is also a family heirloom armoire. To be honest, the entire bedroom is the apothecary. I even added shelves on the back of the door to the room for storing candles, cords, and such.

## Commencing Your Apothecary

You probably already have the most important item for the apothecary: a cauldron. Maybe you have more than one by now. If you have a candle, a deck of cards, bay leaves, a piece of amethyst, and any other items I've mentioned previously, then you are well on your way to having an established apothecary. But just to cover the bases, here are all the fundamental items you should have:

- First and foremost, cauldrons that are exclusively for spell work. A large one is good for concocting potions—a modern kitchen pot will work and is ideal for workings with contents that require heating. Use smaller cauldrons for sacred smoke or Cauldron Councils.

- A selection of candles. White or natural beeswax can be adapted for any purpose. Small glass votive holders are great for shorter workings; two-inch pillars last about a month, and larger ones are good for long-term devotional candles.

- A mortar and pestle for crushing and combining botanicals.

- A diffuser for distributing sacred oils.

- Cording: black cotton and hemp are all-purpose choices.

- An oracle or tarot deck.

- Scissors, spoon, and a sharp knife dedicated only to witchcraft.

- Bags and boxes specifically for spellcrafting.

- Large storage jars, bottles, or other containers for moon waters and infusions; smaller ones for things like oils and tinctures.

- Salt, the non-iodized variety.

- Kitchen staples that are ideal to have just for witchery include strainer, heat-proof measuring cups and bowls, tea pot with strainer, baking sheet, parchment paper, gauze, and cheesecloth. I even have a dedicated electric coffee grinder that is very useful.

- For sacred smoke, charcoal disks designed for burning botanicals are excellent. A censer for burning the botanicals can be just about any heat-proof vessel, especially a cauldron.

- Fabric for making bags and poppets and other doing workings. I love to give new life to worn-out clothing, such as my beloved black leggings or old bedsheets.

- Special paper and pen(s), inks, paints, and other tools for writing and drawing. My black acrylic paint marker might just be the one item that I would choose as most important after my cauldron.

Having these additional staples in your apothecary will provide you with foundations for crafting potions, oils, and more:

- Water that has not been chemically treated—such as natural well water, spring water, sea water, fresh water from a river or stream, or rainwater.

- A good-quality base oil, such as organic extra virgin olive oil. Olives are associated with Hekate.

- High-proof alcohol, such as a top-of-the-line gin that is actually made using the traditional juniper (sacred to Hekate). An alternative would be one of the glycol alcohols.

- Fixatives—quality glues that can be enchanted with correspondences so that they become truly magickal.

- Pebbles and sand—these are especially good as the base in cauldrons that are used for sacred smoke.

- Blank charms, which can be wooden disks or, my favorite, hand-crafted clay ones. The head chef in Hekate's Kitchen in the coven came up with the idea of using small, black-cardboard cupcake boards as foundations for charms. They have become one of my go-tos. I'm always reaching for one to create a charm.

As for correspondences, they include botanicals, colors, numbers, and stones. Select them intuitively, working with what you have on hand and feels right or intentionally choosing based on their standard properties, also known as signatures. You can develop personalized meanings for correspondences, and your individual ability to connect with any specific one varies.

- For botanicals, there are diverse forms to explore: fresh and dried herbs, flowers, various foodstuffs, and oils. The list of botanicals associated with Hekate is very lengthy, from those found in the ancient Hekate's Garden to modern associations based on her characteristics. Bay leaves, however, are especially sacred to Hekate and can evoke banishing, protection, connection, and well-being.

- Colors are ideal for layering into any working, The traditional colors linked with Hekate include black, dark blue, green, gold, purple, red, silver, and white. The properties of colors can be summoned through mediums such as candles, cords, fabric, inks, paints, and papers.

- Hekate is also associated with numbers, from the "hek(a)" in her name (which refers to one hundred) to her typical three-formed self. Nuanced inclusion of numerical meanings into a spell add depth. Hekate is also attuned to the number seven, and some ancient statues—such as the one at the Chiaramonte Museum in the Vatican—depict her with the seven-rayed crown.

- *Chthonia* means "of the earth" in ancient Greek, so stones are literally chthonic and are absolutely wonderful to work with. I get a bit fed up with the "love and light" crystals crowd, yet my coterie of stones is part of my Cauldron Council. The precious pretties, like highly polished amethyst, are fabulous. Equally so are the rocks that call out to us as we wander in nature. Stones that can evoke banishing, protection, connection, and well-being are black obsidian, clear quartz, and amethyst.

Shapes and symbols—which are themselves correspondences—along with specialized items, such as keys and wheels and anything of personal significance to you, are lovely to include in workings. When using them, focus on the intersection of the standard meaning and your personal experience of the object.

- The triangle is especially linked to Hekate. Ancient triangular altar trays, such as those found in the excavations at Pergamon and Sardis, are evocative of her triple nature and reinforce the triangle as being a most magickal shape.

● The circle is a sacred space. Circles and representations of the lunar cycle are ideal to have on hand. As was stated earlier, each phase of the moon has its own energy: the dark moon, as a symbol, is the most sacred; the first appearance of the waxing moon signals new beginnings; the growing waxing phase is for "drawing in" and protection spells; the full moon is usually suitable for any working; and the waning moon is good for banishing, removal, and cleansing spells.

● Keys symbolize both openings and closings and are always suitable for Hekatean witchcraft.

● Hekate's Wheel, aka the strophalos, is the great spinner of the natural cycle, perfect for workings that include peering into the future or rectifying past wrongs; it is generally associated with our journey through life.

● Shapes or symbols of the three realms are welcome representations, such as waves for the sea, crossroads for land, clouds for sky.

● Representations of the elements—earth, air, fire, and water—can be simple or elaborate. It is especially important to include fire (a match, a candle—any flame) in incantations to ignite their power.

● Stars also evoke fire energy, and the five-pointed star can be used to combine the four traditional elements with the deeper fifth one—spirit. The star (which can also be viewed as a flower) within the usual illustrations of Hekate's Wheel has six points—five rays for the traditional elements plus spirit and one left over to represent the deeper mystery.

● Sacred geometry can be incorporated as well. As Hekate traditionally wears the seven-rayed crown, symbolic of the original seven celestial bodies in astrology, the septagram (sometimes called the heptagram) is highly suitable.

## Working with Magickal Tools

There is a distinction between the tools used repeatedly in witchcraft and those reserved for one specific purpose. Cauldrons and scissors, for example, are used multiple times for many different workings; other objects perform one task only. One of the highlights in the coven is an annual ritual featuring the personal magickal tools we work with purely on their own. I love seeing the diversity—from handcrafted versions made with found and repurposed components to expensive purchased items. Unlike the multipurpose tools that are usually kept in the apothecary, the reserved ones are often included on altars. Here are some examples of magickal tools you can reserve for use on their own:

- A special feather talisman to summon sky/air energy. Found feathers are perfect, as they were messages sent to you.

- A sacred blade to cast a protected sacred space and to reopen it after a ritual

- A wand for directing energy and for igniting the spirit of fire

- To represent sea/water, dedicate a cup to this purpose.

- Bells are excellent for clearing energy and for creating a connection to the deeper world. Place them at thresholds to ward off unwelcome spirits.

- Among your keys, reserve one for unlocking the mysteries during rituals.

- Use a physical Hekate's Wheel to align with and connect to Hekate, the deeper world, and transcending the ordinary.

- Brooms, also known as besoms, when dedicated to witchcraft have a dual nature wherein their energetic vitality for cleansing accompanies their practical purpose. You can have several, each devoted to a specific task. Small versions are useful for clearing the workspace and altars. Full-sized models are potent symbols of reclaiming the witch as sacred, given their sometimes very derogatory historical depictions. Adorning the broom with talismans, either ones chosen solely for it or those that hold special remembrances of workings, enhances its power.

- A special staff can also be adorned with charms and keepsakes. Whether inspired by the ancient caduceus (a symbol of Hermes) or modern takes on "talking sticks," a staff can become a tool that is both record of your witchery and useful for casting circles, banishing, and more. Again, you may need several so as to dedicate each to a specific purpose. Most witches seem to already have special sticks even before they begin their practice; perhaps you already have one or more awaiting enchantment.

## Preparing Supplies for Use

Our supplies, correspondences, and other objects may require cleansing before engaging in witchcraft with them.

- Khernips works well for this purpose. Arrange the supplies needing cleansing, then sprinkle them in a counterclockwise direction with charged khernips water and recite:

*I banish the unwelcome from* [name the objects].

- A similar process using a sacred smoke of purifying botanicals—such as bay, basil, or juniper—can also be used, especially for supplies that shouldn't get wet. Add the names of the botanical spirits to your incantation.

- Another alternative is to set the objects under the waning moon and recite a similar incantation.

- Purificatory stones, including black obsidian, can be placed alongside supplies. Adapt the incantation to name the specific stone(s) doing the cleansing.

- For supplies that need a deep "scrub," a bed of salt in a cauldron, with any desired botanicals and stones mixed in, works very well. If an object seems sullied or unsettled, place it in this cauldron for purification. This done during a waning moon amplifies the process. Usually, a couple of days will remove all miasma. Objects will feel lighter when cleansed. You can recite an incantation, such as the one above, when you place the item in the cauldron. This type of cauldron is useful to keep around so that you always have a cleansing station on standby.

- To enchant an object for magickal use, proclaim it as such, reciting an incantation that clearly links your intended purpose with its nature, such as:

*I call upon* [botanical/moon] *as helpmate for* [correspondence]. *May all the work we do together be to our benefit. As it is spoken, so it becomes.*

- You may sometimes get "willful" objects, those that resist our incantations and ideas. If you feel that any supply, correspondence, or tool doesn't want to work with you, or should you not feel a kinship to it, then it may be best to not use that object.

### Enchanting a Cista Mystica

Drawing from archeological discoveries, the *Cista Mystica* is a sacred container used to house all that you wish to keep safe, especially that which you are safeguarding from others. It can be an antique wooden box or something simple that you adorn yourself. Whatever you use, you'll want to make sure that it closes tightly and perhaps has a lock and key. The Cista Mystica is meant to be your secret treasure trove of whatever you feel called to include. Here are some ideas of things to keep in it:

- Personal keepsakes, such as photos and trinkets

- Cards, notes, and other papers

- Components of retired spells and other workings

- Drawings of symbols or other images received during meditations and rituals

- Mementos from rituals, including those from "Honoring Hekate on the Dark Moon"

- Anything else that you feel belongs in there

Once you have your container ready, you can vivify it through a ritual. Vivification refers to rendering life into an object; in other words, enchanting it. Since this focuses on rendering life into your Cista Mystica, it is not recommended that you do it during a waning moon. Aside from the Cista Mystica itself, you will need a few things:

- A candle of your choosing

- Sacred smoke of bay or frankincense oil simmering in a diffuser (which can represent the cauldron)

- A marker for writing the date, including any astrological signatures, on the Cista Mystica.

A few items to immediately place in the Cista Mystica.

When everything is ready, light the candle and say:

*Sacred Flame, bring to life this sacred vessel before you.*

Hold the candle above the Cista Mystica and recite:

*In the name of Hekate and her allies, Sacred Flame*
*Render life to this sacred vessel,*
*Spirit made flesh,*
*My Cista Mystica.*

Rotate the candle counterclockwise around the Cista Mystica three times, reciting:

*Cleanse this sacred vessel, Sacred Flame.*
*Spirit made flesh,*
*My Cista Mystica.*

Bring candle back above the Cista Mystica and pause for a moment. Then encircle the box three times in a clockwise direction and recite:

*Protect this sacred vessel, Sacred Flame.*
*Spirit made flesh,*
*My Cista Mystica.*

Set the candle down. Now pass your Cista Mystica through the sacred smoke or over the diffuser, reciting:

*Container of magick, and mystery,*
*Spirit made flesh,*
*My Cista Mystica.*
*Awaken as sacred vessel,*
*Container of keepsakes,*
*And secrets.*

Put down the container and finish with:

*Great Hekate and my allies,*
*This is my Cista Mystica,*
*Keeper of Secrets and Memories.*

Write the date on your container and place your chosen items inside.

Given that this is your secret keepsake vessel, you may want to disguise it under a cloth or otherwise keep it hidden and not tell anyone about it. Pull it out whenever you have an item to add and also include it on your altar during rituals. Over time, the secrets you put inside it will begin to merge, and the container will take on its own personality.

## Magickal Mixtures: Oils, Waters, and More

Magickal mixtures can be used on their own or as foundations for other formulations. The difference between mixtures and spells is that the former can be adaptable to further witchery, while the latter is a finished working. Mixtures are added to anything we're working with that needs a bit of magick. The ingredients may begin as mundane items, but then we render magick into the mix and can apply it to our witchcraft.

The basic technique is to add plant essences, stones, and colors to a "regular" item—such as oil, water, glue, paint, ink, or clay—thereby infusing the properties of the correspondences into the mundane item so that it becomes enchanted. This can be accomplished directly, such as by adding botanicals to an oil, or indirectly by, for example, placing a stone beside a jar of moon water. If you wish for the mixture to be attuned to specific aspects of Hekate, include your chosen epithets in any incantation.

While preparing any mixture, the action of stirring can amplify the potency; stir clockwise if you want the mixture to draw something toward you, counterclockwise for a potion designed for cleansing. You can elevate this technique by aligning the stirring motion to the magickal properties of each botanical as it is added. Juniper, as a mighty banisher, matches well with counterclockwise, for example.

Certain "hard" stones can be added directly to the mixture, while others are best enjoined into the mixture by placing them beside it. I have a rhodochrosite heart that I've been including in spells for years, and no harm has come to the stone. However, putting a stone adjacent to the liquid is safer and protects more fragile stones, like selenite, from possible damage.

### Basic Mixtures
**Oils**: Begin with a base such as high-quality olive oil, then add your chosen botanicals and stones. Olive oil is quite adaptable, yet it also lends its own properties of cleansing, protection, and well-being. It's also safe for the skin, so

there's no concern when using a mixture designed for topical use. Completed oils can be used to vivify countless items, from the Cista Mystica to ourselves.

**Waters**: Moon waters are endlessly useful. They can be enhanced by attuning them to the moon's phases and astrological placements. Botanicals and stones can also be included. If the botanicals added are safe to consume, the water can be used as a libation during rituals. (Be sure to remove any stones before drinking!) Moon water can also be used as the basis for potions, cleansing your altar and workspace, and as offerings.

**Glues**: Some botanicals, be it finely ground dried herbs or a few drops of oil, add magick to any fixative. Magickal glues are wonderful for creating collages, from devotionals depicting Hekate to spell boards. One of my favorite projects is the Roses of Rebirth, which are crafted from paper petals held together by rose-infused glue. Magickal fixatives can be used to seal witchcrafting, too. If you seal—or set—your spellcrafts, you create a sort of enchanted membrane that amplifies the power while unifying all the components. Much like a binding agent used in cooking, a magickal glue can harmonize the pieces within a spellcraft. Uses for this technique include finishing a vision board like the Artifex Vita, sealing an image to render it into a sacred icon, coating a written incantation in magickal glue, completing charms, activating a scrying mirror, and so many others. In the coven, our magickal glues find their way into just about all of our spellcrafts.

**Paints**: As with all the above, a few botanicals render life into paints. Mixing a bit of paint into fixatives is a way to include some color magick in them.

**Inks**: Depending on the type of ink, a bit of magickal oil or water can be added. To craft your own ink, make an infusion by pouring boiling water over colorful botanicals, such as saffron or pomegranate. Let the brew steep and evaporate until it reaches a consistency thick enough for writing, then strain and bottle it. Another method is to add a charm to your creative tools, such as pens, markers, and paintbrushes.

**Clays**: For charms and more, gently knead some ground botanicals or oil into the clay. To make this easier, create a slurry by mixing a little of the clay with water and the botanicals, then reincorporate it into the larger piece of clay.

## Creating Circe's Wash

This is an all-purpose wash for cleansing and enchanting objects, supplies, altars, and even yourself. It can also be added to magickal mixtures. Amplify it by crafting it during the waning moon. You can adorn your completed mixture with the sigil of Circe, which combines "regina" (Latin for queen) with a "K" from her Greek name ("Kirke"). The implicit "P" in the sigil design represents *pharmakeia*, the practice of Hekatean plant spirit witchcraft. The three dots represent the three realms and selves.

### Supplies

- ¼ cup cleansing and enchanting botanical, such as mugwort or worm-wood
- strainer
- 2 cups boiling water
- 2 heat-safe lidded vessels: a large one and a small, watertight one that will fit inside the larger
- piece of fluorite that will fit in the smaller vessel
- Oleum Spirita or other suitable oil

### Process

Place the botanicals in the strainer. Hold the strainer over the large vessel and pour the boiling water through it.

Let cool to room temperature.

Insert the fluorite into the small vessel and seal it tightly. Place the small vessel inside the large one. Add a few drops of oleum. To activate the mixture, stir in a counterclockwise direction. Seal the large vessel. (As an alternative, if you don't have two vessels, the stone can be placed on top of the closed single container.)

Let the mixture blend for a few days, repeating the activation each evening after moonrise.

Keep stored in a cool, dark place, such as the refrigerator. The whole thing can even be frozen, as long as you have used appropriate vessels.

*Use this method to combine the essences of any botanical and stone.*

## Applications

● Cleanse any water-safe sacred objects.

● Use as a hand rinse before any sacred practice.

● Place in cauldron to cleanse the space.

● Mix with glue, paints, etc., to add power to your witchcraft.

# Chapter 11

## *Magikeia—Spellcrafting*

*One by one,*
*The spell's begun.*
*Plants, colors, and stones,*
*Coming together,*
*Spiraling out.*
*Two by two,*
*This spell is true,*
*Weaving magick throughout.*
*Three by three,*
*Great Hekate,*
*Guide me.*
*As I speak it,*
*So it becomes.*

All spells begin with an awareness. Something unlocks within us, bringing into our consciousness the knowledge that there is a problem, challenge, or calling. Coupled with this is the intuitive wisdom that witchcraft can help our efforts to overcome or transform, be it for manifesting money for an unexpected expenditure or healing from deep trauma. While we may reach for an existing spell that fits our need, crafting our own will always yield better results. It all begins with a word.

## Word Witchery

Our voice, internal or external, is the most important part of any working—be it the careful thought process of developing a spell, our dialogues with Hekate and our allies, or the spell itself, spoken aloud or written. Conversing with our plants, stones, and spirits as we work with them generates power and personalizes them for us. Yet words are only one expression of our power; there is also our will, which is displayed through the actions and emotions involved in our spells. "Will" is like the power source for our witchery—a mixture of confidence, connection, knowledge, and power.

If you've ever experienced what's known as a flow state, those moments when you lose all self-consciousness and you know you are doing exactly what you are meant to be doing, you've connected to will. Yet when crafting spells, we go beyond a regular state of flow by truly attuning to Hekate and her deeper world. Witchcraft gives us a true and powerful voice. In the ancient world, spells calling upon Hekate's intervention thrummed with empowerment, as shown on curse tablets seeking punishment for transgressors and in the mythic spells of Medea.

Creativity is the key to connecting to the deeper world, whether it's following an established working or doing intuitive witchery, and it often begins with words and the complementary objects that we associate with them. The ancients utilized ingredients that held meaning to them in very creative ways that manifested their incantations. While some of their techniques and components may be contrary to our modern practice, the spirit of their spoken spells and creative witchery is still inspiring today.

Correspondences are our contemporary magickal palette, offering up their properties as we render our intentions for life. Hekate shares her aspects with us, so that we may call upon them as spirits for our spells. Epithets are archetypes, energetic underpinnings for the very essence of the universe. When we evoke them in spells, it is to these archetypes that we appeal, as well as to Hekate herself.

Often our dialogues with Hekate and our guides are spontaneous; we simply share what is in our heart, and they often give guidance. When we purposefully work with words to evoke specific energies, that is very different. In magick, just the words can become spells, whether one word on its own or a combination of several. This is known in Latin as *Voces Magicae*, "magic voices." A single word can be a potent talisman, evoking transformation and power. You can create keywords by infusing magickal meaning into an existing word, or you can invent your own unique words. Hekate's name, which always causes a stirring deep within when spoken or written, and her epithets are incredibly powerful. Simply stating her name can evoke her presence and cause archetypes to emanate.

## Word Weaving with Acrostics

An acrostic is a method of weaving together the different aspects of a spell into one primary word for the working. A *taglock* is a small item that connects to a much larger whole; it's a "tag" that "locks onto" the whole. The base word in an acrostic becomes a taglock, giving fuller meaning to each of the connected words. Epithets—along with descriptive words, emotions, and verbs—are excellent for use in acrostics, thereby evoking their power. Acrostics solidify written verses into a talisman.

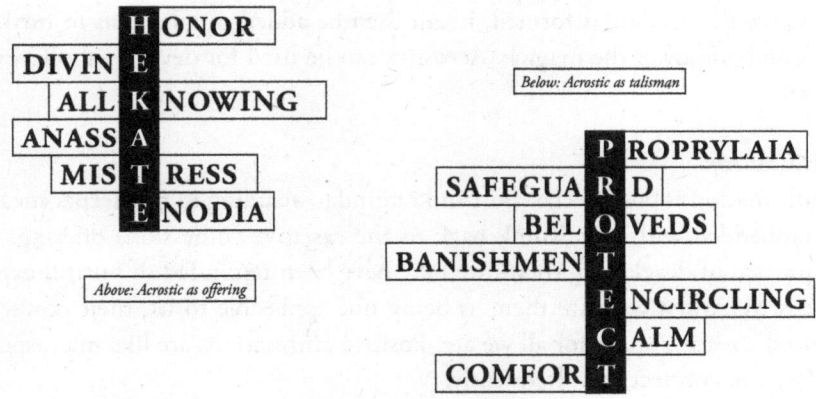

*Above: Acrostic as offering*

*Below: Acrostic as talisman*

For example, in the offering acrostic, the keywords draw from a longer expression of devotion:

> *Hail Hekate,*
> *on this Dark Moon, I honor you as the Divine*
> *Queen of Witches,*
> *Three-Formed, All-Knowing Goddess.*
> *Anassa Chthonia, Guardian of the Depths.*
> *Mistress of Magick,*
> *All my witchery is both offering,*
> *And keys you have given me.*
> *Enodia, my Guide, may I always*
> *Follow your torches.*

Anassa translates as "queen" or "empress," and Chthonia reflects Hekate's Underworld aspects. Enodia connects our journeys and crossroads, the liminal space where witchcraft abides.

In the acrostic spell of protection, the incantation goes as follows:

*Great Propylaia, Guardian of Thresholds and Gatekeeper,*
*Safeguard my home and beloveds from all harm.*
*Bringing swift banishment to those who would do us wrong.*
*Encircling us in harmony,*
*With calm and comfort for all.*

Propylaia means "She of the Gate," so it is most suitable to call upon this epithet for protection, keeping the wrong ones out and blessing those within.

Once the acrostic is formed, it can then be added to talismans to further unify and empower the magick. Acrostics can be used for devotional offerings as well.

## Affirmations

An affirmation is both declaration and reminder, attuning to the deeper meaning embedded within it. Think back to the negative confessions offering. In the process of developing them, we may have been reminded of hurtful experiences; yet when we state them as being not applicable to us, their power is reversed, creating space for all we are. Positive affirmations are like microspells that we can connect with frequently.

**I Remember**: Write "*I remember who I am*," which connects us to being a devotee of Hekate. This can be further distilled as "*Remember.*" Write it on a piece of paper and keep it within view.

**E"no"dia**: Creating affirmations incorporating epithets enhances their strength. For example, Enodia is especially suitable for boundaries and crossroads. It also contains the word "no," so what are you saying no to? What are your personal no-fly zones? We've been doing the E"no"dia exercise in the coven for years, writing it on our left hands and then sharing what we are saying no to.

## Affirmations by Color

Amplify an affirmation's potency by writing it in a specific color. Light a candle in the matching hue, and also try to wear something in a similar shade. Here are some examples:

**Black**: *Paionios, the Healer, I am protected from all harm.*
  Properties: banishing; mediumship; protection; reversals; shadow
    healing; witchcraft

**Blue**: *Skotia, the Darkness, I am connected to my intuition, and I shine the light of truth.*
Properties: boundaries; communication; curiosity; education; transformation; thoughts; speaking; truth; writing

**Brown**: *Triformis, the Transformer, I am rooted, and I am honest with myself as I change.*
Properties: earthiness; gestation; grounding; growth; land and property; roots

**Gold**: *Propylaia, the Threshold, I am sacred, valuable, and enter into the mysteries.*
Properties: creativity; illumination, initiation; outward appearance; sacred rituals; the solar; transcendence; worth

**Green**: *Enodia, the Crossroads, I am abundant, I value the in between, and I am growing into what I'm meant to be.*
Properties: attracting objects and possessions; abundance; the environment; finances; harmony; manifestation; natural cycles; interpersonal dynamics; prosperity

**Grey**: *Rixipyle, Breaker of Barriers, I am wise, and free, and I see the possibilities.*
Properties: allowing; convergence; complexities; identity; protection; temperance; understanding; wisdom

**Orange**: *Chthonia, Of the Depths, I am deeply supported and cared for, and my relationships sustain me.*
Properties: calming; career; children; healing; personality; self in relation to others; sustenance

**Pink**: *Kore, the Reborn Maiden, I am gentle with myself, and I accept tenderness.*
Properties: compassion; happiness; kindness; love; rebirth; self-care

**Purple**: *Drakaina, the Dragon, I am powerful, sovereign, and fierce.*
Properties: alignment; divine; expansiveness; expressivity; growth; integrity; renewal; sovereignty

**Red**: *Borborophorba, the Catharsis, I am cleansed of all that harms, and within me truth and power flows.*
Properties: creativity; generativity; passion; romance; sexuality; union

**Silver**: *Psychopomp, the Soul Guide, I am attuned to my own soul, and I lead from within.*
  Properties: attunement; emotions; initiation; intuition; the lunar; magick; manifestation; the soul; value

**Yellow**: *Lampadios, the Torchbearer, I am illuminating my abilities, powers, and capabilities. I accept them all.*
  Properties: acceptance; assertiveness; confidence; forgiveness; justice; self-esteem; vitality

**White**: *Anassa Eneroi, the Death Queen, I release all that no longer serves. I am reborn.*
  Properties: ascendence; evolution; harmony; initiation; psychic development; protection (attracting); purification

## Intentions

Affirmations can be intentions, phrases that we work with to summon what we are developing. Another form of microspell, they can form the foundation for an incantation or be worked with on their own. Intentions can be set for specific events, such as a meeting to discuss finances or dealing with boundaries-violating relatives. Setting intentions for the day, week, month, season, and year help keep us on track. Using the same technique as with the affirmations, we can start with a more detailed intention and distill it down into one keyword. For example, my intention for the month may be to spend more time with my spiritual practices, from witchcrafting to doing a daily tarot reading. This can encompass quite a bit.

Distilling it into one keyword that evokes how doing this will make me *feel* provides an energetic tether to my detailed intention. "Connected" is a keyword that works for me when my intention is to deepen my practice, because that is the *feeling* I am evoking. Keywords can be like a taglock, the piece of the focus of the magick within a poppet, that attunes us to the greater objective. Attune your intentions to the moon's phase, especially the major moons (full and new), to enhance the potential. (Refer to "Hekate in the Signs" on page 55 for more moon information.)

Intentions are like personal policies for how we conduct ourselves, what our boundaries are. They can also be used to draw toward us what we are manifesting and to rid us from what blocks and binds. Intentions are usually self-directed, focusing on changing ourselves from within so that we can heal, better deal with issues, and generally navigate the complexities of life with greater skill.

Generally, an intention is written in active voice, much like the colorful affirmations. Featuring strong verbs and short sentences, intentions are brief enough to easily remember.

## The Cauldrons Three and Creating Intentions

Working with the energy of the three cauldrons to craft intentions gives you a magickal framework. You can do the Cauldrons Oracle Reading (see page 18) in advance to help you discover the keywords or afterward to give you further guidance. You can also add aspects of Hekate to strengthen your intention.

*Cauldron of Sky*: This aligns with our crown, higher self, and mind. Regarding intentions, this references the driving thought. What are your primary thoughts regarding the intention? See if you can come up with just one word to encompass them.

*Cauldron of Land*: Symbolizing the middle world and self, it speaks to our heart and links with our actions. What are the actions associated with your intention? Determine the main action.

*Cauldron of Sea*: This is evocative of the Underworld and the intuitive/emotional root that is the lower self. What feelings are underpinning your intention? Distill it down to one primary feeling.

Once you've found the three keywords, form them into a sentence or two to create your intention. Work this into a talisman for reinforcing your personal commitment to the intention, writing it in appropriate colors based on the "Affirmations by Color" list on page 112 and calling upon aspects of Hekate to help. Here's an example of three keywords, the aspects of Hekate that can help, and the resulting intention.

- **Thought**—wise, without the inner critic interfering; Phaenno—Brilliant Light (for illumination and burning up that negative chatter)

- **Action**—create; Pammetor—Mother (for generativity)

- **Feeling**—joy; Makairapos—Blessed (for allowing all good things to come)

- **Intention**—I am illuminating my wise mind, creating a joyful life that nourishes and sustains.

# Crafting Your Own Spells

While affirmations and intentions certainly can be types of spells, more involved spells feature specific components—especially correspondences—and usually involve the crafting of a physical object. We may start from scratch or adapt an existing spell.

## Stages of Spell Development and Casting

Developing a spell includes stages, sometimes done sequentially, sometimes in tandem. There may be occasions when we are doing an emergency working and don't have the luxury of time to plan; then there are spells that we carefully map out for weeks in advance. This is a summary of the "elements" needed to craft and perform a spell:

- Keywords: keywords and intentions form the basis of an effective spell.

- Focus: self, others, situations, events, and so on

- Type: attraction, removal, combination

- Hekate and other allies: selecting the aspects of Hekate and other helping spirits

- Components: selecting correspondences and supplies

- Method: crafting a charm or talisman, bottling a potion, etc.

- Timing: your personal optimal time, along with astrological considerations

- Location: where the spell will be cast and kept or, if doing removals, disposed of

- Incantation: once the above are clarified, synthesize it all into a powerful verse.

- Connection: casting a spell requires us to connect to the deeper world—Hekate herself, our guides, the properties of correspondences, and more.

- Casting: finalizing the enchantment process—the incantation is recited and any magickal object completed. The spell will feel alive.

- Relationship: once the spell is cast, it becomes a living spirit, a helpmate that supports you as you engage in supplemental activities that reinforce the spell. Tend to the spell, perhaps lighting a candle to renew it or talking to it.

- Completion: spells have a natural life cycle. When renewing the spell no longer enlivens it, it may have finished its work.

## Incantations

Our incantations speak a spell into life. A word, affirmation, or intention can be an incantation. However, I'm distinguishing between Voces Magicae that are purely words and the verses that call forth correspondences, spirits, and more into a living spell. Incantations, thus, are evocations and invocations, summoning a magickal creation to life while infusing us with the power.

Incantations usually begin with the crafting of a solid intention, which is then fleshed out with correspondences, epithets, and so on. When crafting a spell, there is a process of going from intention to incantation that includes selecting the components of a spell, distilling it down to one theme, determining what type of spell it will be, and other considerations, such as astrological timing.

## Themes and Focus in Spells

Establishing a theme for a spell, such as abundance or healing, helps to contain it's potential, reducing the likelihood of unintended results. Themes can be linked to the root (emotions), heart (actions), and crown (thoughts), thereby aligning ourselves with the theme. Themes can also be connected to epithets. Often, certain epithets will jump right out at us, compelling us to work with them as we explore a theme.

The focus of a spell refers to the intended recipient, be it people or circumstances:

- Ourselves: spells to empower, heal, and transform us

- Other people: sending healing or designing a spell to help someone out of a difficult time. My usual advice is to keep a spell focused on ourselves or situations, rather than other people. It's almost always easier to work with a spell focused on our own issues than anything external.

- Problems: hassles like a broken washing machine or major obstacles, like needing to acquire safe housing or a new job

- Situations: ongoing challenges such as problematic social interactions or inhospitable environments. You could do a calming spell to smooth out a difficult conversation or a banishing spell for a toxic work climate.

- Events: one-time or infrequent situations, such as Thanksgiving dinner with the family or a job interview

- Attachments: the bond between us and other people, objects, and situations. Oftentimes, it is the bond rather than the person or object that needs work. Cord cleansing and cutting are effective types of workings for these problems.

## Types of Spells

It is helpful to categorize a spell into a type once we have an intention, theme, and focus. That being said, some spells resist this, and others are a combination of categories. Several of Hekate's epithets evoke certain types of spells, such as Erototokos (Bringer of Desire) for spells awakening our own passion and connecting with another or Phileremos (Lover of Solitude) when we are banishing someone from our lives. The two broad categories of spells are attraction (what we are drawing to us) and removal (what we are sending away).

## Spells of Attraction

When performing spells of attraction, any movement—be it stirring a potion, setting protective boundaries, and so on—should be done in a clockwise direction. Generally, the right hand should be used.

**Attraction**: These are spells that draw something toward us—from financial freedom to finding a romantic partner.

**Abundance**: This is a highly personal construct, and defining what "abundance" means to us helps to narrow the focus. I recommend Enodia as an aspect for abundance witchery, layered with other aspects that are more specific to your definition.

**Growth**: From biological fertility to birthing creative projects, growth spells focus on planting a seed and helping it grow to fullness. Kore, which is also associated with Persephone's above-ground aspects, is excellent, since Kore means "sprout" as well as "maiden."

**Protection**: We do this spell encircle ourselves and what we hold precious so that any potential harm is minimized.

## Spells of Removal

When performing spells of removal, movements—be it stirring a potion, setting protective boundaries, etc.—should be done in a counterclockwise direction with the left hand.

**Avoidance**: These are spells that prevent something from happening.

**Banishing**: This is the complete removal of energies, memories, people, spirits, and ways of being.

**Binding**: Any spell has a binding component; for example, the words we use are connected (bound) to their meanings. Binding as a technique refers to a containment of the recipient; we may want to do a spell to bind us to someone or to bind someone onto themselves so that they can no longer cause harm.

**Reversal**: Use this to flip a situation or energy around to something more positive; this would include "return to sender" spells.

## Combination Spells

Spells that combine attracting and removing include a multitude of possibilities. Amplify the potency by incorporating the appropriate motion clockwise/ attracting or counterclockwise/removing and hand use.

**Clarity**: When murkiness exists, be in in figuring out our own motivations or the nagging perception that someone is not being truthful, clarity spells can reveal what is really going on. It is a combination of removing obstacles while manifesting our ability to get to the truth. The three-fold epithets, such as Triformis, are suited for clarity workings, allowing us to see in all directions.

**Cleansing**: Cleansing is evoked to get rid of unwanted energies, thereby creating space for what is welcome. Its twofold in nature removes what no longer serves and also protects from any harm. Hekate as Borborophorba (Filth Eater) gladly accepts our offerings.

**Hastening**: There may be times when processes are moving too slowly or feel stuck. A hastening spell speeds things up, removing barriers and clearing the way. Calling upon Hekate as Podarke (Fleet-Footed One) can help.

**Healing**: The duality here is to remove dis-ease while protecting against further damage. Call on Hekate Paionios (Healer) plus other aspects suited to the specific type of healing.

**Transmutation**: There are times when we have an abundance of something that needs to be transformed into something else; this begins with removing any toxicities, then transforming into what is desired. The three-formed epithets work well for such spells, as well as Hekate Rixipyle's forceful energy.

## The Daily Threefold Incantation Cauldron Spell

*I banish all that blocks and binds.*
*I am protected from all harm.*
*I have all I need to be healthy and whole.*

Said as part of the daily practice, this incantation cleanses, protects, and invokes well-being. I do this every day with my cauldron when releasing sacred smoke. Here's how:

- Focus on the coming day, whatever is on your agenda, setting intentions for how it will all proceed. Record these in your journal. This connects you with the spirit of the day.

- Select well-dried botanicals, such as a bay laurel leaf, thyme sprigs, finely cut mugwort, or wormwood, for the sacred smoke; use a heat-proof cauldron that you can safely hold. I usually make my selections intuitively, based on what is appropriate for the day. There are many formulations that work excellently for this ritual in my book *Entering Hekate's Garden*.

- Ignite the botanicals with your "torch" of choice.

- Once the smoke starts to rise, hold the cauldron with both hands at your heart center.

- Then, with the cauldron in your left hand, circle it counterclockwise while reciting,

  *I banish all that blocks and binds.*

- Return the cauldron to heart center.

- Transfer it to your right hand and rotate it clockwise, while proclaiming,

  *I am protected from all harm.*

- Now raise the cauldron high up with both hands, announcing,

  *I have all I need to be healthy and whole.*

I typically do this spell while I am in water (the "giant cauldron") after I've unified my three selves and connected to the Sacred Flame through a candle. I don't take my cards with me, so I do that part of the daily practice once I'm back on dry land.

# Chapter 12

## Connecting to the Essence of
## the Deeper World

*Moon, moon,*
*As you grow,*
*Take my intention,*
*And make it so.*

The moon's phases offer us a portal to the deeper world. The waxing moon called forth in this simple incantation renders a powerful spell for drawing toward us what we desire. While all correspondences have essences (spirits), it is perhaps the essence of the moon that is most important to the practice of Hekatean witchcraft.

Generally, the waxing moon is for casting attracting spells, and the waning is for removals. The full moon is suitable for most workings, especially combination spells. While we may reserve the night of the dark moon for honoring Hekate, the following evening is the ideal time for spells that launch new beginnings. The astrological meaning of the sign that the moon is in can further amplify the potency of a spell. Refer to "Hekate in the Signs" in chapter 7, especially for the dark moon.

The moon is as much a part of who I am as the air I breathe. I am never not aware of the moon. I can't imagine casting a spell without calling upon dearest luna. I tend to the moon—talking to her, watching her movements—and I've built the entire schedule for the coven on the moon's phases rather than the chronological calendar. This is an act of devotion, honoring Hekate and her moon. The moon is testament that invisible forces exist, reminding us that our spells, like her, work their magick in mysterious ways—but they are certainly very real. The power of a spell is created by calling forth these unseen energies and combining them into a cohesive force that manifests a specific outcome.

Once added to our magickly charged creations, we release the combined energy to achieve the desired result.

## The Phases of the Moon

There is no greater force that we can attune to as Hekatean witches than the moon. Beyond honoring Hekate on the dark moon, the other phases offer specific energies that we can work with in all areas of our practice, from healing moon bathing to incorporating a phase into our spells.

- Generally, the dark moon, which occurs during the astronomical new moon, is a time for rituals and offerings. The dark/new moon is both the end and the beginning of the lunar month, representing a crossroads portal for connecting deeply with Hekate.

- In the following days, when the crescent appears igniting a new lunar month, intentions for this cycle can be cast. The ancients referred to the time as "Noumenia," or "new moon," which is different from our modern definition of the new moon that occurs when it is not visible. Noumenia is the beginning of the waxing moon period. In keeping with the growing light of the moon during this time, workings dedicated to drawing toward, from spells of attraction to manifestation, are indicated.

- The full moon is ideal for most practices, especially those that combine both attraction and removal components. The full moon lights up the night, so spells for revelation, from healing our personal shadows to getting to the bottom of a confusing situation, are suitable.

- The moon wanes after its fullness, and the decreasing light provides energy for removing, releasing, cleansing, and banishing.

Strengthen your lunar workings by corresponding them to the sign the moon is in, referencing again "Hekate in the Signs." Combine the phase with the notes I provided as a template for your own workings. Set your intentions for the new month on the night the moon first appears. For example, a Capricorn crescent waxing moon is good for work focused on discipline and organization. A waxing moon in Scorpio is particularly suited for practices focused on awakening the mysteries. If working, instead, with a waning moon, one in Gemini is ideal for removing barriers in communication. A Libra full moon is an opportunity for illuminating the truth about relationships.

Eclipses are especially potent, but I caution against doing witchcraft during these times unless you are confident enough to manage the power. Generally, the week before or after an eclipse is not recommended for performing spells. During the eclipses, rituals that align with the energies can be incredibly beneficial but only if you are comfortable. I've led rituals during eclipses for almost two decades, but I've yet to do any spellcasting. Refer to "Goddess of the Eclipse and the Rise of Christianity" on page 45 for a Hekate invocation suitable for your personal eclipse practice.

## Lunar Cycle Themes and Practices

- Dark moon is both end and beginning of the lunar month. This phase represents harmony, as the sun and the moon are in tandem in the heavens. It should be reserved for practices honoring Hekate. Journaling about dreams, writing a letter to Hekate, working on your altar, and other personal practices are recommended, in addition to more formal ceremonies.

- Crescent waxing moon is for setting intentions for the new lunar month, organizing, and planning. For me, this includes a "forecast" reading for the coming weeks, such as "The Cauldrons Oracle Reading" on page 18. This is a time to look toward the upcoming full and dark moons and to start to connect with what you'll be doing during them. Mapping out the month in your journal or planner can become a type of spell for manifesting the coming weeks.

- During the waxing moon, focus on the keyword of "approach"; it is the time for drawing toward you what you are seeking. You grow with the moon, so it is also good for making your presence known, speaking truth, and pursuing goals. Setting objectives, crafting vision boards, and starting projects are all indicated during this phase.

- The full moon holds the balance of opposites, since the illumination is created by the moon being on the opposite side of the Earth from the sun. Often my preferred timing for casting spells, this phase is equally potent for illuminating insights—including vivid dreams and spontaneous transcendent experiences of deep attunement to Hekate and the moon. Balance is different from harmony (new moon), since it also holds the possibility of friction between opposites. For personal contemplation during the full moon, reflect on what you are manifesting and releasing, or approaching and avoiding.

● Continuing with the "avoid" aspect of the moon, the waning phase offers the energy of release, the opposite of "approach." To truly manifest our desires, there is always the need to create space for the new. The question posed by the waning moon is, "What do you need to move away from?"

## Correspondences: The Crossroads of Form and Flow

Apart from the moon, many other things can be woven into our workings—the elements, the realms, botanicals, stones, colors, and more. All these things have "daemons" or spirits that can be evoked and worked with to achieve our purpose. They contain energy waiting for us to use to achieve our potential as witches.

If I had to pick one place to begin exploring the essences of correspondences, it would be learning to connect to the spirit of a botanical. Botanicals have much to share if we only open up to them. I believe this so much so that I wrote an entire book dedicated to botanical witchcraft, *Entering Hekate's Garden: The Magick, Medicine, and Mystery of Plant Spirit Witchcraft.*

To begin, hold your cauldron, with sacred smoke spiraling skyward, and speak your spell to life. Words and correspondences can unlock the deeper world, as long as we look beyond their mundane properties to their essence and spirits. Hekate's epithets attune us to their underpinning archetypes. Calling upon Hekate and our allies connects us to their energy. A spell without a connection is just arts and crafts; with a connection it is witchcraft. We establish this connection by transcending beyond the confines of our physical existence, becoming etheric beings that can move outside the regular rules.

The worlds of form and force intersect in spellcrafting. With correspondences, we bridge the two worlds by calling upon the magickal properties of a physical object. This applies to botanicals, stones, and even animals. And though we may not be able to hold the moon or even stand under it for one reason or another, we can attune to it via symbols. All correspondences have a physical manifestation.

Whenever we work with a correspondence, we are seeking a piece of the whole that exists purely in the deeper world. Even a small portion of a correspondence—be it a plant, stone, color, or even one of Hekate's epithets—

contains the whole. The physical representation connects us to the spirit that is released through the material world.

## Connection, Attunement, Synchrony, and Vibrational Essence

Opening up to the spirit of a correspondence is the first step to working with one. The next is to attune ourselves or our intention to the spirit. This works by aligning the energetic signature of a specific correspondence with your purpose or your personal vibration. All spirits have a vibrational essence that is a mix of the archetypal energy plus unique characteristics and experiences. This is where the standard definition of a correspondence can vary. For example, you may start to work with a correspondence based on its standard properties, but then find that your specific example (especially with animal spirits) is nothing like the established qualities.

There are some correspondences that we naturally avoid or are even repulsed by. This can be caused by a variety of factors, including previous experience with that spirit (in this life and previous ones), a physiological aversion (such as an allergy), or resistance by the spirit to us. Sometimes this can be shadow energy, so it's best to try to connect with your chosen correspondence a few times before giving up. It may be that your energy signature and that of the correspondence simply don't connect, just as we don't get along with all people.

Once we are attuned to a correspondence, we can merge its spirit with the task at hand to create a synchrony within our working. This is accomplished by using our will to direct the correspondence as we intend it to be used. Incantations are most helpful in focusing our instructions, as is envisioning the process of everything coming together to achieve the desired outcome.

Here are some tips for connecting with correspondences:

- If the item is new, it may require a "rest and recovery" period and/ or cleansing. You'll know if this is required because you'll feel it in the energy emitted by the correspondence.

- Once the object is ready, hold it in your hands at heart center and dialogue with it, letting it know how you wish to work with it.

- Listen to the emanations from the correspondence. Depending on your natural talents, you can receive the transmission as images, hear words, or experience sensations in your body.

- When you feel connected, let the item know that you will only borrow what it has to give and that you honor its spirit.

- Allow any new correspondences or other objects to sit with the established ones for a while so that they can get comfortable with one another before you introduce them into a working.

- When writing an incantation, turn to your correspondences for inspiration.

## Classifying Correspondences

Understanding the typologies of correspondences expands our understanding of them, rendering them available for our workings.

### Forces

The moon, sun, planets, stars, and other celestial bodies are forces that exist as energetic currents that we can tap into for witchery. The elements and natural phenomena are forces that exist as pure spirits but have material representations. The three realms are layered forces, and their pure energies are reflected in land, sea, and sky—each also having material representations. Time, whether in the chronological sense of moving backward or forward, as well as kairos, the cyclical rhythm of the deeper world, such as the Wheel of the Year, is another force.

### Naturals

These are the plants, stones, and animals that are embodied creatures with strong energetic signatures. All stones, minerals, crystals, metals, and chemical elements are chthonic.

### Energetics

Lesser-order spirits that have properties but usually not distinct personalities are filtered through human understanding. For example, colors exist in nature without human interference, but their properties are interpreted through human knowledge. One color has a refractive structure that makes it appear to our human vision as "purple"; we now associate the color with powers like sovereignty. The color purple can be evoked as a pure energetic wave, so it stays in the ether, but we usually use material representations, such as candles.

Numbers and letters have properties but require something else to enliven them, like writing them down or using candles to activate their properties.

## Creations

Creations are exactly that, things that we have created and given spirit to. They are usually comprised of naturals and energetics that can be connected to the ether. Sigils, symbols, and tools (e.g., wand, stang, blade, sword, scourge) are all examples. Others include words (phrases, prayers, etc.), systems (divination systems such as tarot and the runes, societal structures like a matriarchy or patriarchy), formulas (from alchemy), and alloys (manufactured metals such as brass).

## Self and Others

Our three selves and the unified wholeness of spirit can be summoned as correspondences, calling forth the power in ourselves and then adding it to spells. Use the lower self to summon emotions. The active middle self can be summoned to add haste and agency. The higher self can be used to summon any intellectual, reflective, and mystical aspects.

Characteristics, abilities, energies, images, physical features, possessions, and corporeals (bits of the physical body) from humans and animals make excellent correspondences. Including a piece of the spell target acts like a taglock and boosts the probability of a spell reaching its goal. We can use all these aspects of ourselves in witchery. Always remember that we are the most powerful correspondence in any working; including pieces of yourself, such as hair or a photo, augments the process.

## The Elements and the Zodiac

Elements are foundational forces, scaffolding the universe, and utilizing them provides a secure base in our workings. Within the Cauldrons Oracle Reading, the spirits of the elements abide: air for the mind, earth for the heart, and water for the root, with fire running through all. The signs of the zodiac are associated with the elements. Aries, Leo, and Sagittarius are associated with fire. Aries is illuminated as courage, but in shadow it can be aggressive. Leo is all about taking up space, which can be beneficial or troublesome. Sagittarius uses fire to fuel the quest for adventure. Taurus, Virgo, and Capricorn are earthy, focused on daily life. Gemini, Libra, and Aquarius are governed by air. Their concerns are of the mind—communication, truth, and humanity are applicable keywords. The watery signs of Cancer, Scorpio, and Pisces signal emotions and intuition—with Cancer evoking caregiving, Scorpio the mysteries, and Pisces the imagination.

When you are working with the elements, it is good to have a symbol on hand. For example, sacred smoke or a feather representing air, the burning botanicals and candles for fire, a cauldron with sand or pebbles for earth, and one with water for water. This will help you to connect with these forces on the macro level. Including tools on your altar that contain the energy of each of the elements and realms is another way to evoke and honor them. We can connect to these objects as conduits to the larger forces. They can also serve as mediators to make the forces more manageable.

## Characteristics of the Elements

- **Earth**: associated with the north and "earthy" colors like green and brown. Connect to this element in muddy places, the forest, caves, and basements. A downward-facing triangle with a line bisecting it is the symbol for earth.

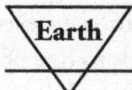

- **Air**: associated with the east and the colors white, yellow, and gray.. You'll be able to feel the power of this element the strongest when standing on top of a windy cliff, along a sea-blown shore, or at the top of a tall building. To represent air in your sigils and spells, use an upward triangle with a line through it.

- **Fire**: associated with the south and the colors red and orange. The sun and the stars are the ultimate fiery sources of energy, but when it comes to the elements, we're sticking to earth-bound fires. Lighting a candle or sitting by a campfire are accessible ways to explore this element. An upward-pointing triangle is the symbol for fire.

● **Water**: associated with the west—although some traditions reverse east/ air and west/water (I use water for the west in this book)—and the color blue. You can connect to this element by being in a lake, river, ocean, or even on a glacier. A downward pointing triangle is the symbol for water.

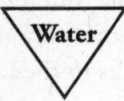

### Elemental Awakening and the Tarot

Practice awakening one element at a time within you. Notice when you are feeling each element. Water represents emotions, earth is for action, air is for intellect, and fire is for intuition. Consider journaling using the elements as a tool for interpreting your experiences. Then try using the elements for balancing.

If you are being too "air," contemplate ways of balancing it with "fire," "water," or "earth." Using the tarot is an excellent way to study the energy of the elements; each suit corresponds to one of them. Wands can either be fire or air, depending on your perspective and the individual deck, and the same goes for Swords. Cups is water, and Pentacles/Disks/Coins is earth.

### Working with Correspondences

The right correspondences seem to call out to us, lighting up on the page or thrumming in the apothecary. Our incantations call them forth into our workings, and I recommend speaking to them during the preparation process. When it comes to choosing them, oracle decks of botanicals, stones, and animals can be very helpful. You will intuitively draw the right cards for your working.

Layering correspondences in any working strengthens the power of our rituals, spells, and altars. This is the process of synergy: creating a unified whole much greater than the sum of the individual parts. Usually, layering is done in a number that corresponds to the intention of the working.

# Chapter 13

## Sigil Crafting—Rendering a Spell into a Form

*Into this sigil, I now rend:*
*The crossroads, sacred ground.*
*Meeting place of land, sea, and sky.*
*All the phases of the moon,*
*Waxing bringing growth,*
*Waning removing what no longer serves.*
*Fullness illuminating and protecting the crooked path.*
*And the hidden Dark Moon for the sacred mysteries.*
*I draw within the elements;*
*Earth for grounding,*
*Air for flying,*
*Water for feeling,*
*And fire for spirit.*
*Three becomes one,*
*Becomes thirteen,*
*For Hekate, harmony, and witchcraft.*
*As it is created, so it becomes.*

This is a sigil of Hekatean witchcraft, evoking the power of our craft through the components of the invocation, associated symbols, and numerical properties. Examine the sigil to see if you can discover how these individual components are represented. You can add this sigil to your cauldron, candles, and more, or be inspired to create your own versions. A sigil is a spell that is made of symbols, letters, words, and images. A sigil can be a simple line drawing or as complex the one above. Sigils often include glyphs, which are symbols representing a force or correspondence—astrological signs are an example.

Sigils, as with many forms of magickal creations, work because they are attuned to the essences contained therein. Known as sympathetic magick, it is the process of infusing properties and spirits into either something we entirely create, such as sigils, or by enchanting objects, like talismans.

Aside from using ink, sigils can be drawn using chalk; by shaping earth, ash, or salt into patterns; by pouring water or oil to create shapes—be inventive. Sigils have been used in magick since Neolithic humans scratched them out on cave walls. The most common way to construct a sigil is to reduce a keyword or intention down to its basic components. You can leave the letters in their original form in the language you wrote them or use a different language or use symbols to represent each letter. To connect more deeply to your primary epithets and sacred name, render them into sigils.

## Basic Sigil-Making Technique

- Choose a keyword, then craft an intention or incantation from it.

- Reduce this down to as few words as possible.

- Cross out repeated letters.

- Group the letters that have common features, like circles or straight lines.

- Reduce each of your groups to one form.

- Combine the forms into a unified sigil.

- Activate the sigil using the intention or incantation you crafted.

- Strengthen the sigil by invigorating it with Oleum Spirita and passing it through sacred smoke.

## Sigil Components

Beyond letters, symbols of energetics like the moon and realms, numbers, and shapes can be woven into sigils, infusing the sigil with their properties.

## The Moon

- Dark (astronomical new) for the mysteries and the sacred

- First returning moon, the emerging crescent (Noumenia) for beginnings and initiations

- Waxing for attracting and manifesting, including protection

- Full for the entirety of the moon, illumination, revealing, and attunement

- Waning for removals, including cleansing, banishing, and release

## The Three Realms

- Land (quartered circle; three-way crossroads; bisecting arrows): matters associated with the middle world and the heart, such as actions and the intersection between the interior self and the external environment. Examples: relationships, work, home.

- Sea (waves; downward arrow; drop of water): Underworld and the root concerns, emotions, intuition, and the deeper world.

- Sky (clouds, stars, crown): themes related to the upper world, including the higher self, astral realm, psychic abilities, mysticism, intellect, education, and thoughts.

## The Elements

While the elements are connected with the realms, they also have their own unique essences. The glyphs are described in the "Characteristics of the Elements" section of chapter 12 (see page 129).

- Earth: release, healing, cord cutting, burying, ancestor work, material success, prosperity, finances

- Water: emotions, cleansing, purification, transformation

- Air: beginnings, communication, travel, thought, the mind

- Fire: creation, destruction, passion, heat, intensity, prophecy

## Shapes

- Triangles, evocative of Hekate's transforming triple nature and crossroads. Also contained in the elemental glyphs.

- Circles represent wholeness. They can be included for protection, such as keeping the unwelcome outside, and for nourishing all that is contained within.

- Squares can be included to infuse a sigil with structure and containment.

- Diamonds can be two triangles fused into one. Evocative of abundance.

- Stars: the five-pointed version is symbolic of the elements and spirits; the six-armed version is at the heart of Hekate's Wheel and is evocative of the Sacred Flame.

- The septagram, which symbolizes Hekate's seven-rayed crown and the Sacred Seven forces of realms and elements. It is seven triangles formed into a star.

- Many other shapes from sacred geometry.

## Other Symbols

- Punctuation marks: ampersand (&), question mark (?), and period (.), for example

- Astrological symbols: the glyphs for the zodiac signs and planets

- Lines and arrows: use directional arrows to indicate the type of magic

- Tarot: pentacles, wands, swords, and cups

- Musical notes: each note corresponds to a letter

- Others: infinity loop, spiral, heart, dollar sign

## Design Features
Work with the properties of numbers and colors to further enhance your sigil's potential.

## Enchanting

As you develop the sigil, focus on your intention, repeating it in your mind or out loud. This will infuse your energy into the sigil as you create it. Once the sigil is complete, trace it with your finger, then in the air above it. If it is a sigil of attraction, do this clockwise. If it is removal magick, counterclockwise. Recite the intention or incantation. Envision the power of the sigil becoming a spirit in its own right.

## Using Sigils for Witchery

Once the sigil is activated, you can use it in various ways, especially for adding vitality to candles and talismans.

A sigil can be a personal talisman that you can connect with to activate characteristics within you, so it is a good idea to carry it with you. This personal sigil is called a touchstone. Sigils can also be created for others. Sometimes you'll want the recipient to know about it and use it; at other times you may want to place the sigil in a hidden spot in their personal space.

Sigils can be placed on objects, such as computers or appliances, or in vehicles—anyplace that needs a little magickal help. They are excellent as threshold guardians.

Continue to monitor the energy of the sigil. Like all spells, they can become depleted for a variety of reasons. Reactivate as necessary. Generally, continue to use the same sigil until the goal is achieved.

As with all spells, sometimes the sigil will fail to work as intended. If that happens, revisit your intention. If necessary, "mortify" your sigil by disconnecting it from the associated powers, then cleanse and destroy it.

## Crafting Your Own Power Sigil

Craft a personal sigil that conveys your unique energetic signatures, abilities, and talents. Use it to adorn candles and talismans and when contacting your primary epithets. This will render a connective tether between you, Hekate and her deeper world, and whatever you have enchanted it with. Craft a poppet with the sigil on it, creating a unique helpmate spirit.

## A Modern Mystery: The Hekate Sigil

Consisting of a key that opens three ways, evoking the spirit of the crossroads, this contemporary sigil of Hekate has no clear origins, although an internet search revealed it's connected with the Hekate asteroid. The version I've been working with for years includes three lines for numerical synchrony with the three key "blades," the part that goes into the lock. The key "head" evokes the moon, with the "hole" representing the full moon, and the outer ring the dark; the head also represents her wheel. The waxing and waning moons are found in the opposing blades, with the top one being the base of her torch.

Add this sigil to candles, talismans, poppets—anything you want attuned to Hekate. In the coven, we often adorn ourselves with it for High Rituals. It's particularly powerful when applied using henna or ash, as inspired by ancient practices. Trace it with your finger or wand to call upon Hekate.

> *By the power of three,*
> *And the mysteries of the keys,*
> *Within the heart of the crossroads,*
> *There Hekate abides.*

# Chapter 14

## Witchcrafting—Making Magickal Creations

*Through words and will,*
*I enchant,*
*Weaving together,*
*as I craft.*
*Blending force and form,*
*Rendering so much more.*
*What once slumbered,*
*Now awakens.*
*Helpmates and companions.*
*As it is spoken,*
*So it becomes.*

Putting the "craft" in witchcraft is done by creating enchanted objects brimming with the essences of correspondences and calling them into life. Charms, talismans, candles, and much more become vivified spirits with the witch's will and touch. There's no limit to spellcrafting, from the more traditional candles, tools, and poppets to collages, masks, and statues.

Charms, which are single objects featuring symbols and correspondences, are the most basic type of magickal item. In the ancient Mediterranean, magickal gems were a popular type of charm, often depicting Hekate with her companions. Create charms from flat stones, clay or wooden disks, or even paper. A talisman incorporates a charm and correspondences into one unified form, such as a witch bag, knot spell, or a magickal collage. A regular candle, be it wax or LED, becomes a talisman when infused with botanicals, adorned with charms, and so on.

# Knots and Cord Work: Weaving Magick to Life

From simple square knots to elaborate macrame creations, cord work weaves talismans to life through the act of tying, especially when energetic motions and numerical properties are included. Knots tied to the left and counterclockwise are for banishing and cleansing. Those tied to the right and clockwise attract. Here are two examples of spells featuring intentional knot work; you can craft them as presented or be inspired to make your own unique version.

## Enodia's Abundance Talisman

This spell is built upon knot work and cording. For manifesting abundance, however you define it, call upon Hekate Enodia and the botanicals of bay laurel, pine, and cinnamon. You'll also need a steadying piece of smoky quartz for this cording spell. If you are new to macrame, there are instructional videos on the internet for the knots in the spell. You can adjust the following instructions to accommodate more or fewer of the correspondences—do whatever calls to you.

## Correspondences

There are seven correspondences in this working. The number seven itself (repeated throughout the spell) aligns with the theme of abundance. So, in addition to abundance, here are the properties of the correspondences in this spell:

- Bay laurel: awakening, divination, protection, purification

- Cinnamon: motivation, passion, sustainability, rebirth

- Pine: growth, happy home, second sight, vitality, wealth

- Smoky quartz: alignment, clarity, choosing the right path, connecting to higher purpose/consciousness, grounding

- The properties of the color of green (for the beads) and white (for the cording)

## Supplies

- 12 (or more) dried bay leaves for writing personal abundance declarations

- Acrylic marker for inscribing the leaves; black works well, as does gold

- 12 yards white 2 mm, 3-ply macrame cord

- 6 cinnamon sticks that have a clear inner channel so that a cord can run through

- 8–14 10 mm beads with 2.5 mm opening (these can be plain wood ones that you paint green, or use pre-colored ones or stones with a hole bored through)

- Smoky quartz stone

- 30 gauge jewelry wire for wrapping beads and stones, if working with them

- 7 pine or other conifer (spruce, fir, hemlock) cones

- Scissors and wire cutters

- Anchor to secure the cording (tack, nail, etc.)

- Something to make small openings, like a hole punch

**Procedure**

Craft an intention regarding the abundance you are calling toward you.

Inscribe the bay leaves with any combinations of your chosen symbols, words, and/or sigils, leaving room in the center to punch a hole. You can even craft a sigil just for this spell and add it to the talisman. Inscribe another bay leaf with the same sigil to carry with you to connect you to the spell.

Cut a piece of the cord about 45 cm (18 inches) long and push it through a cinnamon stick. Then cut a cinnamon stick in half. Slide one bead, then a cinnamon half, then another bead on one side of the whole cinnamon stick. Repeat on the other side. Make sure they are centered on the cord and tie the two ends together. Anchor this assembly to a flat surface so that you can create tension when doing the knots.

Cut five more strands of cord about 2 meters (2 yards) each in length. Secure the five strands to the middle of the whole cinnamon stick by folding over about 10 cm (4 inches), then binding with a wrapping knot to hide the ends.

Pull the middle of the five cords up out of the way for now. Do seven basic four-stranded square knots. In my design, I then added a bead to each of the two middle strands, and then tied just a regular knot underneath each bead to keep them from sliding. You can add more beads here or no beads at all. Just do what feel right to you.

Punch or poke holes into the middle of six of the bay leaves. Bring the fifth cord down behind the work you've already done. Slide two of the bay leaves onto this cord and tie a knot to keep them in place. Then slide on two more and tie a knot; finish with the final two and one more knot.

This next bit may be a bit tricky. You'll need to tie knots while leaving space to add the smoky quartz stone. First establish the size hole you'll need by measuring the stone against the cords. You'll want the opening to be slightly smaller.

Using half-hitch knots, tie the first two lefthand cords together, leaving the space for the stone. Then tie the second and third cords together, and so on until all five cords are connected, making a little nest for the stone.

Insert the stone into the space you've left. It should be a snug fit. Once the stone is in place, make seven two-stranded square knots using all five cords. You'll need to alternate between the five strands, using two at a time. The pattern doesn't specifically matter, but you'll want to end up with three square knots approximately in a row at the bottom. At this point, you'll sort of have three groups, one under each of the bottom row of square knots.

Add a bead to any strand in each section, then tie three regular knots to secure the beads. Finish with a final bead at the end of each grouping and tie a knot. Attach a bay leaf to one of the strands in each group.

Do one "four-stranded" square knot using all five strands. For this one, pick any two strands and hold them together as if they were one. Add the final bay leaf to the center strand and tie a knot to keep it in place.

Slide a cinnamon stick onto each of the four outer cords, then tie a knot under each one so they stay in place. Tie a loop at the end of each cinnamon cord.

Split the middle cord into three strands. You now have a total of seven cords.

Cut seven pieces of wire, each approximately 10 cm (4 inches) long.

Attach one piece to each of the seven cones: Fold the wire in half; slide it under the second or third row on the cone; twist the wire against the cone to secure it. For three of the cones, twist the ends of the wires together and form a small loop at the end.

In each of the three strands of the split cord tie seven knots all in a row. Attach one cone to each strand by sliding the loop onto the strand below the final knot and twisting the wire around the cord. Then braid the strands together (just a couple of braids) so that the wires are anchored. Tie seven more knots in each strand, then tightly knot all three strands together. Trim off any extra cord.

Attach the four remaining cones to the four outer cords, using the loops at the bottom.

Add your personal declarations.

Spray with Circe's Wash, then anoint with Oleum Spirita while doing the incantation below.

> *By the spirits of bay laurel, cinnamon, and smoky quartz, the power of the Sacred Seven, and the blessing of Enodia, I call this talisman to life.*
> *I call abundance to me now* [repeat seven times, stating the declaration for each of the seven personal abundance aspects and touching the seven components each round].
> *May this talisman align me with true abundance. As it is spoken, so it becomes. Hail Enodia.*

## Working with the Talisman

Hang the talisman in a suitable location within your home. When there are specific aspects of abundance that you are manifesting, add them as charms to the talisman, repeating the incantation and adding a few words evocative of the specific aspect.

## Creating and Working with Taglocks

While certain components in a working can be considered taglocks, as discussed in earlier sections, they can also apply to physical beings and spirits. They are often used in spells that focus on people, whether for ourselves in our spells or for workings that focus on others. Personal taglocks include bits of the physical body (blood, hair, nail clippings), prized personal possessions (e.g., jewelry), and images. These kinds of taglocks are traditionally most associated with poppets and other forms of "baneful" magick, such as putting a curse on someone. You can out find more about poppets in *Entering Hekate's Garden*.

## Arkyia Binding Cord Torch Spell

Hekate's epithet of Arkyia (Entrapper) is ideal to call upon for binding someone who is harming others; you bind them onto themselves, thereby preventing them from causing further damage. This is best reserved for when other methods, such as protection, have failed. To ensure that there is no blowback from the spell, cast it somewhere away from your home. The completed talisman also needs to be disposed of far from your home; if at all possible, place it close to the targeted troublemaker. This is a tried-and-true spell, so be certain that you genuinely want to bind the target because this will not only prevent them from causing further harm but will also cause them to feel the consequences of their prior actions.

You'll be using three ten-inch cords to bind the taglock: a black one, a red one, and a white one. The black cord is for emotions, the red for actions, and the white for thoughts. While you are braiding the cord, light a black candle for protection.

A torch spell is one wherein a created talisman is burned to release its power. A binding spell traps the energy onto the target using a symbolic representation of them to create a tether; this is the taglock. A cord spell is activated by braiding and/or knotting it while reciting an incantation.

## Supplies

- Approximately 1 cup of salt for sprinkling around the area of casting (I prefer sea salt, but just about any type of salt does the trick)
- Piece of black cloth large enough to contain your completed talisman
- Taglock (image) of the target printed on regular paper (if you are unable to obtain an image, use a blank piece of paper)
- Binding botanicals, such as skullcap and birch (optional)
- 10-inch cords (such as embroidery floss) in black, red, and white
- Black candle
- Lighter
- Water for extinguishing the torch (waning-moon water works well)

    **Correspondences**: the three colors, plus any botanicals used

    **Timing**: do this is spell during waning moon

    **Preparations**: The three cords can be soaked in birch/skullcap potion in advance; make sure they are completely dry before using in the spell.

The same botanicals can be burned as sacred smoke while casting. Add a protective botanical, such as oak, to the incense to eliminate the risk of spell blowback (*do not* add oak to the potion).

**Method**

Begin with connecting to Hekate Arkyia, saying something like:

*Great Hekate Arkyia, guide my spell, binding* [person's name] *from causing further harm and sending the consequences back to them.*

Spread the salt over your work area or place it in a dish in the space. Lay out the black cloth and place the paper on the cloth. Place the botanicals (if using) and anything else you wish to involve (e.g., hair or a snippet of their clothing) on the paper.

Roll the paper containing whatever else you've placed on it into a tube and fold over each end to seal it. Light the sacred smoke if you are using it.

Wrap the black cord around the tube three times, reciting:

*By cord of black,*
*Pain, suffering, and despair I do send back.*

Knot the cord three times.
Wrap the red cord around the tube three times:

*By cord of red,*
*All acts of harm done are bound to them.*

Knot the cord three times.
Wrap the white cord around the tube three times:

*By cord of white,*
*I bind them this night.*

Knot the cord three times.
Light the black candle. Braid all three cords together and knot it at the bottom, while reciting:

*As I weave, so I proclaim*
*No more can* [name of person] *cause pain.*
*As for the consequences their actions rendered,*
*They are now returned to sender.*

Light both ends of the "torch" on fire. Place it in a fireproof container. The kitchen sink with an open window and water at the ready works well if the spell cannot be conducted outside at a fire pit.

Recite the whole incantation until the flames extinguish themselves.

Envision the smoke surrounding the target, wrapping the smoke around them until they are completely bound. Finish by thanking Hekate for her guidance.

Douse the torch in water to make sure the fire is out, then wrap the remnants in the black cloth and get rid of the whole thing—bury it, put it in the compost if safe to do so, or wrap it up and take it to a garbage bin away from your property.

## Spell Bags: Magick Inside and Out

Spell bags are talismans with correspondences, symbols, and keywords that can be enhanced by adding sigils and charms. They are a go-to method that's quick to assemble. First choose, or create, a bag in a color that aligns with your purpose. Bags can be fabric or paper, even an envelope. Then select correspondences that map onto the theme and let your sacred creativity flow.

### Rixipyle Transmuting Spell Bag

In the spirit of Rixipyle, the barrier-breaking aspect of Hekate, this spell is truly liberating. This talisman takes what brings us pain and transmutes it into power by writing the incantation using magickal methods, creating a spell bag to contain it, and using botanicals to boost the working. You can also add a unique sigil, such as one made from the components of "Rixipyle," to the bag and add it to the candle you will use during the spell.

This spell can focus on anything that you want to transmute, from false to true. Transmutation combines the power of a reversal with clarity and healing.

### Supplies

- Markers and paper for writing the transmuting declarations; the paper should be of a size that when rolled into a scroll will fit in the bag

- A short-burning candle, such as a votive

- Sigil, if using

- Bag (premade or crafted) in a color that reflects the theme of your spell. Grey is a good choice for this spell, since it combines black (a traditional hue for banishing) with the rebirthing energy of white

- Botanical correspondences, divided (see below); you will add some to the bag and burn the rest in your cauldron

- Incantation (see instructions below)

- 2 10-inch pieces of cord (such as embroidery floss) in the same color as the bag

- A key, for locking up the false and unlocking the truth

**Botanical Correspondences**

Botanical allies of fennel, lavender, and rose work well in this spell.

Grinding these three together yields a blend that burns well, smells lovely, and is so evocative of rebirth and transformation. In addition to all three having cleansing and protective powers, some of their attributes are supportive of transmutation include:

**Fennel**: breaking curses and bad luck, clarity, communication, courage, self-discipline, visions

**Lavender**: calm, clarity, connecting to the deeper world, love, self-confidence

**Rose**: beginnings, calmness, emotional healing, psychic abilities, rebuilding trust

**Mirrored Writing and Forward Spirals: The Incantations of Transmutation**

You create your incantation by combining backward, or mirrored, writing for what you are rejecting as false and spiraling forward script for what you declare as true.

Reversed writing releases the hold of the "false" over us, but even writing backward in a straight line can be a bit tricky. You may want to practice, particularly before trying the reversed spiral technique. Once you've completed your practice writing, make sure to destroy these trial incantations.

Determine what you deem to be false or negative, then come up with an opposing truth or positive. Write the false statement in reverse on one side of your scroll paper. Then flip the paper over and write the true statement forward on the other side.

**Casting the Spell**

Activate the candle by adorning it with sigils and symbols, then light it. If you created a sigil, add it to the bag.

Add the botanicals to your cauldron, reserving one tablespoon for the bag. Ignite the botanicals in your cauldron and perform the threefold process of banishing, protecting, and assuring health; then proclaim:

> *This spell's begun. In the name of Hekate Rixipyle, I transmute what blocks and binds into healing and power.*

Now recite your incantation, beginning with the false and then proclaiming the true.

Once spoken, roll the incantation into a scroll and tie it with one piece of the cord (trim any excess). Place it in the bag.

Add the remaining botanicals to the bag, and recite:

> *Fennel, break what is false, and grant courage and voice to what is true.*

*Lavender, calm and steady this spell, bringing clarity and compassion. Rose, banish the false, and open the way to truth.*

Place inside the bag anything else you wish, then close it.

Slide the key onto the other piece of cord, tie it around the top of the closed bag using three knots, then recite:

*This key locks the false and opens the truth. Knot of one, the spell's begun; knot of two, this spell is true; knot of three, the spell is free.*

Keep the spell in a suitable place.

You can continue to burn the candle to enhance the spell, replacing it as required.

## Witch Bottles and Jars: Wet or Dry Magick

Like spell bags, witch bottles and jars are talismanic creations that contain botanicals, charms, words, and sigils. They can be dry or wet; a potion activates the spell for the latter, and a base activates the former. There are numerous examples in *Entering Hekate's Garden*. A wet spell jar features a liquid as the harmonizing base, while a dry spell jar doesn't.

**Meisoponeros Worry Jar**

This is a dry spell. Paint a jar black and fill with a mixture of salt and activated charcoal (or dirt). Write your concerns on slips of black paper and cast your worries into the jar, calling upon Hekate as Meisoponeros (Vice Hater) to free you of troubles. Keep the jar sealed and out of the way. You can add any new concerns to the jar as necessary.

## Creating a Spell of the Year

This has been one of my traditions for many, many moons. It is a highly personal spell, so the way you craft yours will be unique. It can be wet or dry, although I always do a wet jar. The Spell of the Year (SOTY, as we call it in the coven) is a guiding talisman that will truly be a companion as you journey throughout the year. Follow any of the previous instructions for spellcrafting to create a SOTY that feels right for you. Journey from keyword to companion in this magickal project.

# Candle Magick: Spells with the Sacred Flame

Hail Hekate, Torchbearer and Sacred Fire. In candle magick, we connect to the power of the flame for banishing, clarifying, creating, illuminating, and so much more.

Simply lighting a candle and stating an intention can be powerful.

## Selecting Candles

There are countless options for magickal candles, from creating your own to purchasing ones that are already activated for witchery. In general, the more of your own energy you put into the candle, the more effective it will be for your specific purposes.

Ethically sourced candles, such as handcrafted beeswax ones, are usually more amenable to witchcraft. However, basic white tea lights can be the most useful tool in your witch's cupboard. Candles with scents that correspond to your intention can also be used.

Beeswax and white candles are suitable for most types of spells. Black candles are excellent for all forms of removal magick, from banishings to curses. Refer to the "Affirmations by Color" section on page 112 for help with choosing which color might work best for your intention.

Candles in the colors of the elementals are excellent choices, for you can summon the corresponding elemental spirit in addition to fire.

Choose a candle that matches the method you are employing. If you are doing a one-off spell, candles that have a short burn time should be used, such as a tea light or a small taper. You can also cut larger tapers into smaller pieces.

## Technique

The basic technique is to speak your words of power (intention/incantation) into the candle, then release it using the spirits contained within the candle. This can be a one-and-done spell or be carried out for days or weeks. The Seven Day candle spell (available online) and the Spell of the Seven Fires, from my book *True Magic*, are two techniques that I personally find very effective, especially when more powerful witchery is required.

A seven-day candle spell works best with a candle that will last for the entire time. It can stay lit for the entire week if it is safe to do so, or ignite it for periods during each day. The Spell of the Seven Fires is one that consists of seven seven-day spells, using a new candle for each week. The former is best for quick resolutions and the latter for enduring workings. For spells cast during one working, it's best to use candles that will be completely consumed during the session. Once the candle is exhausted, the spell is set. Incorporating the lunar phase into candle spells amplifies their power.

### Cleansing the Candle

Candles can require preparation before use in witchery. Cleansing it with sacred smoke or resting it on a bed of salt usually does the trick. The candle will be noticeably lighter and feel cleaner once it has been purified.

### Enchanting Candles

Techniques for activating the candle are sacred smoke, anointing, inscription, and adornment. Recite an incantation while activating any candle, such as:

> *Candle, I call you forth, weaving magick into your essence, attuning you to the Sacred Flame of Hekate.*

**Sacred Smoke**: "Smoking" a candle refers to passing it through burning herbs, incense, or another source of flame to either purify it or to charge it with the spirits of the botanicals.

**Anointing**: To dress a candle, rub it with a sacred oil, such as Oleum Spirita; or a high-quality olive oil will work for almost any purpose. In general, you can rub the oil either clockwise for attraction magick or counterclockwise for removal magick. Roll the candle in scattered herbs as well.

**Inscription**: Carving, drawing, or transferring words, sigils, and/or symbols onto candles infuses them with power.

**Adornment**: Candles can be enchanted by attaching charms, botanicals, and stones to them, or by setting them on a foundation of correspondences.

### Casting a Candle Magick Spell

Clear your mind for a few minutes, then light the candle. As you watch the flame, concentrate on your intention for the candle.

For calling Hekate's torchbearer, light, or sacred fire aspects—such as Lampadios, Phos, and Hieros Pyr—to connect to both her and the flame, light the candle and recite:

> *Hekate, she who is the Sacred Flame, may this spell burn true.*
> *Candle, candle burning bright, grant this spell I speak tonight.*

Rotate the candle counterclockwise in your left hand:

*All that blocks this spell is banished.*

Rotate the candle clockwise in your right hand:

*I cast this circle around me and this spell, protecting all from harm.*

Then proceed into your incantation with the candle held at heart center. When extinguishing the candle, thank Hekate and the Sacred Flame.

## Creating Transfer Candles

A fabulous method for infusing candles with sigils, symbols, images, and words is using a transfer; you first print the image, then attach it to the candle. There are many ways to do this, from using clear sticker sheets to the following technique using tissue paper. Most printers can accommodate tissue paper if it is carefully taped onto a piece of regular paper. Ink-jet printers will work, but laser printers are better since the transferred images are less likely to smudge.

The Hekate sigil (see page 136) is ideal for a transfer candle.

## Supplies

- Candle: plain, high-quality pillar candles work well for this; LED lights set in wax work, too

- Printing supplies: tissue paper, printer paper, tape, scissors, image to print

- Transfer tools: parchment paper, blow-dryer or heat gun, gloves

## Steps

Cut a piece of tissue paper about 6 x 9 inches and completely tape it to the center of a piece of regular printer paper, making sure that the edges are secure the whole way around like a frame.

Edit the image to a size that will fit onto the candle. Copying a screenshot into Word is a simple way to edit. Once the image is printed, cut it out of the tissue paper.

Position the image, printed side up, on the candle. Wrap the candle tightly in parchment paper and put on the gloves.

With the blow-dryer or heat gun on a medium setting, gently heat the image. It's fine to unwrap the parchment paper to check your progress, then rewrap and continue until the image is fully transferred. At this point, the tissue paper will no longer be visible, and the image will look sealed.

Anoint the candle with Oleum Spirita to further enchant it.

**Paionios Healing Candle Spell**

When sending healing to ourselves or others, appealing to Hekate as Paionios (Healer) is certain to amplify the working. When doing spells for people you specifically know, including yourself, add relevant sigils and symbols to the candle. Yarrow, an all-purpose healer, can serve as the foundation for the candle, or you can anoint the candle with a yarrow-infused oil.

Write a healing intention and distill it into a keyword. Either write this on a charm or choose a physical symbol to represent the keyword. Keys are always appropriate symbols; they lock up pain, disease, and suffering and unlock recovery and wellness.

For long-term healing, a jar candle works well. Work with small votives for shorter-duration healings, such as when someone is undergoing surgery or has a virus.

Once the candle is ready, light it, then hold it with both hands at your heart center and recite:

*Hekate Paionios, I seek healing for* [person's name].

While holding the candle in your left hand and circling it counterclockwise, say:

*Removing all that would block healing through your sacred flame.*

While holding the candle in your right hand and circling it clockwise, recite:

*Encircling* [person's name] *with healing.*

Once again hold the candle in both hands at your heart and recite your specific incantation.

Conclude with:

*Hail Hekate Paionios, As it is spoken, so it becomes. May healing abound, for*
    *the highest good of all. May any extra energy go to where it*
    *is welcome.*

# Part IV

## *The Mystery*

# Chapter 15

## *Crossing the Threshold—Spirits of the Deeper World*

*The night comes alive.*
*Black hounds howl.*
*The Queen beckons her chosen now.*
*Your feet twitch,*
*And your soul awakes.*
*Crossing the threshold,*
*Entering the mysteries.*
*Found in the depths*
*Of Hekate's Cauldron,*
*Where spirits abound.*

Spirits come in all shapes and sizes and have diverse personalities and abilities. Our spells, synchronicities, intuition, and dreams remind us that there is no separation between the spirit world and the waking one. Our altars are the focal point for the spirits we work with. We enliven them through our work, and they have much to teach us.

Often on our altars we place statues, stones, and animal talismans. These are all spirits as well. Typically, we have already deeply engaged with spirits without being consciously aware of what's going on. From connecting with an amethyst or owl to feeling the frisson of a wandering ghost, spirits are always with us. If we shift our gaze beyond the illusory veil of separation between the physical and the etheric, we can see how much we are already walking in their world. The witch abides in both the worlds of form and force. We are liminal creatures who occupy both landscapes as we follow Hekate's torches into the mysteries of the world of spirits.

Hekate is ever companioned by spirits, and she is their mistress. She is the epicenter of the deeper world, and we have used many methods to call to her, from ancient suppers to modern mediumship. In ancient times, Hekate led a mighty horde of spirits, including the restless dead, etheric beings, and companion animals. Witchcraft, like Hekate, is about spirits. We dialogue with the departed, have etheric allies, and are comprised of many aspects that are spirits unto themselves.

While physical spaces can hold spirits, and we can intentionally journey into the deeper world through transcendent experiences to encounter them, all of us travel in Hekate's country every night. The dreamworld, the juncture of our personal lives with the realm of spirits, offers rich treasures for understanding ourselves and the universe. I wrote extensively about dreams in *Entering Hekate's Cave*.

## A Taxonomy of Spirits

Animism is the idea that all beings, objects, and locations, even mundane ones, have a spirit. These spirits are a convergence of how we experience the things/places and their innate characteristics. Going beyond spirits that have a corporeal (physical) form, there are those that are based in the deeper world and are purely etheric, although we can certainly sense their presence (their emanations) in the material world.

Spirits, by their nature, resist structure. They speak to us symbolically through inner knowings, visions, and dreams. The world is enchanted by those of form and force; our task is to connect with them. The underlying forces that emanate from specific deities, spirits, and correspondences are archetypes. Myths are archetypal stories, and their characters can be higher-order, middle-order, or lower-order spirits. Fictional characters, celebrities, and even our own lives reflect archetypes. Hekate's epithets are archetypal.

### Etheric Entities: Spirits of the Deeper World
Etheric beings are those who never knew flesh or are no longer contained by it. They range from the divine to energetically dense bothersome spirits.

**Deities**: The divine Hekate is the ultimate spirit, whether we connect to her through her totality or in a more focused manner through the use of epithets.

**Forces**: The realms and elements, along with the earth, moon, and other celestials, are foundational archetypal forces. Time, both the standardized chronological type—based on the natural cycles of the earth, moon, and stars—and the deeper time of the universe, known as kairos and symbolized by Hekate's Wheel. These cycles create the seasons and weather, both of which are very spirited. Then there is the unified essence of the universe, such as Hekate being referenced as Physis, the wholistic spirit of nature.

**Ancestors**: Blood ancestors are departed family members, which certainly can include adopted relatives; while spirit ancestors are the long departed whom we honor as part of our spiritual lineage, such as witch ancestors.

**Higher-order spirits**: Angels, as messengers of the divine, are linked with Hekate in ancient sources, particularly in *The Chaldean Oracles*. They are fierce communicators and protectors. Some ascended beings, who were once human, have evolved beyond mortal limitations, but they often come as teachers, descending from the celestial into our visions and dreams. These spirits are sometimes called the "Mighty Dead."

**Middle-order spirits**: These are the dead who are still tethered to the earth plane and their former humanity; however, they possess insight into their condition. This category also includes some land and sea spirits that are brimming with intelligence and personality. They can be quite willful but are generally mature. Depending on how you experience them, nature spirits—such as the fae, dryads, and wights—can be like this.

**Lower-order spirits**: These are denser entities that lead with emotion and instinct rather than will or wisdom. The restless dead, disruptive ghosts that interfere with human life, and some land spirits that are prone to interfere with humans are examples. Entities like "shades" are often encountered late at night, especially in places where there are portals to the deeper world; they can also appear in dreams. Lower-order spirits can be very beneficial, though, sometimes acting as protectors.

## Corporeal Beings: Spirts of Flesh

Spirits with a physical form, generally mortal living beings, are those who have a physical embodiment (or corporeality) along with etheric essences. Corporeal beings can fall into the categories of higher, middle, or lower as well.

**Humans**: There are two Greek words that are helpful for understanding how we are spirited. *Daimon* (or daemon) refers to the spirit in all living and etheric beings, whereas *psyche* signifies the essential soul that transcends mortality. Within us as individuals, we may have multiple daimons, or selves, from former lives to past versions of this incarnation. There is also our personal shadow self, the side of us that contains our fears and anything we keep hidden from others. Now add all these personal spirits to those of others, from individuals we have relationships with to groups, organizations, and societies.

**Relationships, groups, and organizations**: Within a relationship, a spirit develops between those involved and also within each individual based on their perceptions of the relationship. For example, someone can believe they are in a satisfying, committed, and monogamous romantic partnership only to discover the other person doesn't share this view at all. Each perception we have about anything in our lives can create a spirited thoughtform that can be both beneficial and detrimental. All these personal and interpersonal spirits can take on lives of their own.

**Thoughtforms and egregores**: Psychological complexes, such as the "mother" or "savior," can overtake our own agency. Egregores are spirits that go beyond thoughtforms, developing their own consciousness and will—for example, an egregore of a group such as a coven. Keeping in mind that archetypes work on us and through us, thoughtforms and egregores are connected to their mysterious deeper nature.

**Emotions**: Feelings can be archetypal, having spirits far greater than our personal experiences of them. Physiologically, there's a growing stack of evidence supporting that though emotions are based in the body, they are much more than mere physical phenomena.

**Naturals**: Animals, plants, stones, and physical aspects of forces—such as water and the earth—have their own spirits. Familiars may take the form of naturals, from beloved pets that are so much more than everyday companions to botanical spirit guides.

**Locations and physical spaces**: Places can also be very spirited—"imprinted" locations, such as haunted places, or those that are portals to the deeper world, like certain crossroads and monuments. The expression "reading the room," referencing being aware of the vibe in a space, demonstrates this. If you've ever felt awkward for no obvious reason in a specific space, it could be caused an intuitive reaction to the energy of the place.

**Creations**: Magickal objects, ranging from candles that reveal messages in their wax patterns to altars that connect us to Hekate, are certainly spirited—at times developing their own personality and will. Regular physical objects can also be spirited, as well as buildings and other features in the manmade environment. Possessions may take on the spirit of their owner, or how their owner perceives them, and become infused with an essence. Photos, works of art, music, and literature, as well as digital content can be spirited.

**Symbols**: From tarot cards to keys, symbols evoke the deeper archetypes they represent and can develop relationships with their beholder.

**Forms**: Colors, letters, and numbers have spiritual qualities, although they typically lack the will and consciousness of higher-order corporeal spirits.

## Navigating the Spirited World: Balancing Connection with Protection

Deities are complex spirits with whom we can have enduring or fleeting associations; although they often respond when we seek them, they certainly come and go as they will. We may wish to call forth specific deities for specific workings, even if we don't have a close bond with them. In this case, we are more likely to connect with their energetic currents than to truly evoke their presence, but the latter is certainly possible—especially when evoking epithets, which align to aspects shared by other expressions of the divine.

Hekate's known associates, from Persephone to Pan, can become our allies, and we can appeal to them during workings. Given their connection to Hekate, they are often easier to call forth than disparate deities. However, some deities far removed in historical connection to Hekate could also appear. Those that have similar energies, such as Freya or The Morrigan, ride connected energetic currents that can bring them closer to us.

As with deities, we can develop enduring relationships with spirits, or we can call upon them for specific workings based on certain characteristics and abilities. Etheric spirits, like the Mighty Dead and ancestors, can be quite willful and should be treated with the same respect as the divine. The elementals—those spirits of the four forces—as well as the embodied spirits of land, sea, and sky are usually amenable to connection without issuing demands, although they can be unpredictable. The lower-order spirits can be complex creatures but are typically more emotional than intellectual—in contrast to the higher-order entities, such as angels and the Mighty Dead. While these lower-order spirits reside in the etheric world, they can take on form here in the middle world. We often perceive them as shades or shadows, existing just outside our perception.

**Tips for Working with Spirits and Processing Deeper-World Experiences**
Keep yourself cleansed of toxic waste and stay protected. In addition to the methods previously discussed, a salt scrub for your body and an open dish of

salt by the entrance to your home, amplified with an herb such as lavender or better yet juniper, will ward off unfriendly spirits.

Some spirits are fierce but are on our side. Shadow allies are our protectors and are super intimidating but not harmful. You'll know the difference based on your reaction to them—are you frightened *of* them or are they just frightening in general? Think of them as your spiritual bodyguards. Here are some tips for working with them:

● Let the mystery be the mystery. Spirits communicate through symbols; they have their own will and resist our expectations. It can be tempting to try to reduce these experiences into tidy interpretations that are immediately crystal clear. It doesn't usually work like that. Not everything will make sense to the limitations of the conscious mind, yet to your deeper Self, it does.

● Be respectful of the mystery, Hekate, and all the spirits. They are not convenient push-button entities that perform on command. They will do what they want.

● Keep unwanted visitors at bay by protecting yourself and your environment. Spread salt while walking counterclockwise around your home and place it at entrances along with a bay leaf and black obsidian; this will do wonders for keeping out unwelcome visitors—both the physical and etheric varieties. A bowl of salt at the threshold or in your ritual space also works well.

● Spirits communicate in diverse ways, usually symbolically in dreams and meditations. Pay attention to how they looked, anything they shared with you, what they did, the setting, and even the time of day.

● We can receive communications in other ways, too. Sometimes called the "clairs," these are "psychic" methods of perception—clairaudience for hearing messages, clairsentience for physical sensations, and claircognizance for knowings.

● A *sumbolon* is a material representation of an object that was found or given to you during a deeper-world experience. You may create a sigil based on a sumbolon. Sumbola are links between the practitioner and the deeper world. Sigils can be used to connect with these forces. Both are highly symbolic energy but acquired differently. Sigils are usually manifested first in the material world by the practitioner, while sumbola are found or given to us.

## Ancestors of Spirit

Allowing yourself to feel the presence of the ancestors can be healing, empowering, and incredibly spiritual; the experience will transform you. Sometimes, our ancestors are "famous" figures from myths, folktales, and history, such as beloved Circe and Baba Yaga. More often, though, they come to us without renown in visions and dreams, unique beings traveling through time to connect with us. Discover more about Circe and Medea in *Entering Hekate's Garden: The Magick, Medicine, and Mystery of Plant Spirit Witchcraft.*

Ancestors of spirit can be anyone who has passed from this life and who holds a special place in our hearts—a caring teacher who helped us through a difficult time, a kindly neighbor, a former boss. There are ancestors of spirit who are symbolic of who we are today. We stand on their shoulders and remember their sacrifices. Often our ancestors suffered greatly for being who they were. They reach across time to guide us as their kindred. We can reciprocate through showing them our appreciation, offering them any healing, or perhaps even forgiveness, that they need.

Many of us have ancestors of spirit who were public figures that inspire us and perhaps guide us along our journey. Our witch ancestors who persisted in their pursuit of their truth deserve our veneration. We can also express our gratitude to our former incarnations. Across lifetimes, I've always been some form of healer-witch. These ancestors of my soul are part of who I am today. I honor them. I am part of a great lineage.

## Witch Ancestors as Our Guides

Witch ancestors are always keen to be our spirit guides. They see how their suffering and efforts are finally leading to a cultural shift in the perception of the witch. We honor them well by listening to their whispers and heeding their signs.

Identifying as a witch comes with the mantle of our complicated, and often troubled, history. Working with witch ancestors offers a way to heal the witch wound—the grief and pain associated with centuries of mistreatment, abuse, and torture that those labeled as witches often suffered. Go gently into this work if it is your calling.

**Ritual with Ancestors of Spirit**

To connect with your witch guides, set a place for them at your table after your home has been cleansed and protected. You don't want any troublesome spirits showing up. Generally, set the intention for only one guide to come forward.

Offer a meal suitable for the type of guide you seek. Cakes and tea are universally welcome by all the witch ancestors I call upon. Sit at your table, light a candle, and call out to the witches who are already silently watching over you. I know you can feel them even while reading this. They're a curious bunch, those ancestors of ours, always looking over our shoulder to see what we're up to.

To connect with your witch allies, and to give them a most welcome offering, brew a pot of "Crossing the Veil" tea. It's made from mugwort, mint, yarrow, and juniper berries. Mugwort is for opening your third eye to the ancestors, mint is for connecting to the departed, yarrow is for healing all involved, and juniper berries are for banishing any unwelcome visitors. Juniper also helps us overcome self-doubt. As with all botanical medicine, the specific amounts used will vary based on your unique constitution. However, 1 teaspoon each of mugwort and yarrow, with about a ½ teaspoon of mint and 13 juniper berries steeped in two cups of boiled water is a good formulary for most of us. As always with botanical witchcraft, do your research to see if there are any health reasons why you should not consume this tea.

After sipping your tea, connect with your visitors. Express your gratitude for their lives and for coming to spend time with you. Ask one who is aligned with your intention to come forward. Listen to what they have to say. Ask them to give you guidance through your tarot cards.

## Cauldron Companion: Connecting with a Spirit Guide

*Great Hekate, Queen of the Cauldron.*
*I seek one of your spirits as*
*Helpmate, ally, companion, guide.*

As mentioned, there are many different types of spirit guides in the deeper world. Spirit guides give us advice and assistance, acting as teachers and helpmates. Hekate sends them our way. They are usually our protectors as well, ensuring our safety in both the physical and spirit realms. You have a special guide, perhaps a witch ancestor, who will become your cauldron companion.

To connect with your spirit guide, create a safe space, set intentions, and visualize a meeting with your guide. Connect with them in Hekate's Cauldron and be open to their messages and guidance. Reflect on your experience and stay aware of any signs or messages from your guide in the future.

## Ways of Discovering Your Spirit Guide

Since spirit guides usually attempt to communicate with us through signs and symbols, our witch's power of observation comes in very handy. Sometimes, it can just be a feeling we have that a certain type of spirit is watching over us. Although there are countless ways that a spirit guide can communicate with us, here are some of the more common ones.

## Signs

Be aware of unexpected symbols. Stay on the lookout for random things showing up in your life. Other signs often include spontaneous encounters that are totally out of keeping with what you're doing. There will also be signs that are meaningful only to you.

## Journeys

Another way spirit guides speak to us is during our journeys—dreams in particular. This is because our busy minds are quieted by sleep, allowing our established connection with a possible guide to flow more freely. While the guide may come to you as themselves in a journey, they may also use signs. They could even appear in a human form that's quite unexpected. A spirit guide will appear in whatever form is most appropriate for getting your attention. When you later write about your journey, you may remember signs that you might otherwise have missed.

## Meditations

Meditation leads to an opening between us and the energetic realms. In this altered consciousness, we are more open to receiving direct messages from a spirit guide. These messages can be audible—like a whisper—or they can appear as written text in your mind's eye. Guides may even appear and talk to you directly. As in dream journeys, symbols may also appear during your meditations. However, you need to pace yourself. Meditating too often in the hope of receiving direct communication from a spirit guide is likely to be exhausting and ineffective.

## Direct Messages

A spirit guide may directly communicate with you during magickal or spiritual activities. You could use automatic writing to receive a direct message. Then there is a special type of direct communication—what I call the "instant download." This happens when you are going about your regular life and suddenly a guide speaks to you. It can take the form of a vision, you may hear them speak, or a message may suddenly flash across your mind's eye. When this happens, it can be quite startling. Do your best to journal your experience as soon as you can.

## Events

There are times when a spirit guide speaks to us through events in our lives—when a scenario plays out that is so unusual that the entire situation seems to be a message from a spirit guide. For example, I know someone who unexpectedly altered her morning route because she was late. On this different way to work, she found a heart-shaped key with "you are loved" engraved on it. At the time, she was going through a very difficult period in her personal life and was feeling quite unloved. No one came forward to claim the key. This is an example of an entire event being a message. Hekate became her guide and goddess.

## Inner Knowing

There are times when we just *know* something. There's no other explanation. For me, this often happens when I wake up in the morning. One way of looking at this is that it is our intuition talking, while another is that this is a message that flowed through an established energy channel with our spirit guide. It's like when you look at someone and instantly know what they are thinking. Typically, the inner knowing accompanies one of the other types of messages, but there are times when we just know without any other evidence.

## Spirit Guide Meditative Journey

I draw a distinction between evoking a spirit or Hekate and an invocation. The former refers to calling upon their presence, the latter concerns drawing their essence into ourselves. For example, journeying to meet your spirit guide is a type of evocation, whereas invoking their attributes would allow you to take on certain characteristics they have.

This journey works whether you are hoping to make initial contact with your guide or you have already received signs and are looking to meet your spirit guide formally for the first time. Set aside at least one hour for the journey.

A ritual bath infused with the Crossing the Veil tea (see page 162), homemade rose water, and salt is one of my favorite ways to prepare for this type of experience.

I like to do this sort of work in the evening, but the choice of time is up to you. Wear loose clothes. Get comfortable, preferably lying down on a bed or the floor. You may want to cover up with a warm blanket. This will help avoid any physical coldness that may set in during your journey.

Activate your imagination. Set the intention to go where the imagery takes you. Do not resist any images or experiences. You'll be protected and completely safe. When the journey is over, you'll return from the meditative state to normal waking, feeling calm and refreshed. You'll feel strong and confident and fully supported by your new guide.

Close your eyes. Begin to feel the weight of your body sink into the bed or floor beneath you. Feel the weight of your feet and ankles as they press into the surface below you; now feel the weight in your calves, then your knees, your thighs. Take a moment to feel how heavy they are. This is a pleasant sensation of heaviness, like being under blankets—warm and soothing.

Now shift your attention to your torso. Feel your bottom grow heavy, your lower back. Go up your spine as all the weight of your organs is released into your back. Your body is deeply relaxed.

Let the backs of your arms accept the weight from the front—heavy, warm, relaxed, comfortable. Pull the feeling of heaviness into the back of your neck, the back of your head.

Pause here to feel how light the front of your body has become. Notice that all tension has been released. Your mind is now clear of thoughts and stress. Your head is relaxed, your face is relaxed—smile a bit. Your throat is soft, your breath relaxed and easy.

Your heart rate is slowing. Your belly is calm, your legs are at rest, as are your ankles and feet—warm, relaxed, comfortable.

Now let the weight in your feet melt into the bed or floor beneath you; do the same for your ankles, calves, knees, thighs.

Pause here to enjoy their lightness—no pain or tension, just relaxed.

Do the same for your back. Release all the heaviness into the bed or floor.

Feel the lightness as it moves up your body.

Now move on to your arms. Release the weight into the bed or floor. Your neck follows, then your head.

Your feel light, calm, relaxed, comfortable.

Envision all this weight traveling down through the bed or floor—down into the earth. All tension, worries, and cares go along. Thank the earth for accepting the heaviness.

In this state of lightness, allow the strength within you to open up. Imagine your spine as the center of this strength—a great silver sword along your back. Silver strength energy fills every part of your being; the silver energy wraps you in a protective cloak that nothing can penetrate, but it is as soft and light as your body. Your hands wear silver gloves. Your feet are covered in boots that match. You are entirely strong, protected, and light.

You are now in a state of perfect balance: lightness and strength are the true components of love. All heaviness, all fear is long gone.

See yourself standing before Hekate's Cauldron. See the cauldron as the source, the womb from which all creation flows. The mystical nexus where the energetic realms come together. It is the entrance to the deeper world. Connect with the cauldron, be it by diving in or just taking a sip.

As you peer into the cauldron, a door takes form.

When you are ready, walk through the door. A new world is before you. Take time to notice the details.

Call upon your guide to come forward:

*I ask you, great guide, as a powerful teacher, and helpmate, to come to me now.*
*I know that you, great guide, are coming forward*
*To bring me guidance that is deep within me*
*So that I may live as my true self*
*That I may be true in my words to myself and others*
*That my magick will be in my highest good and for that of others*
*That I will do so with honor and respect for myself, others, and the land.*

*Out of great respect, I call upon you, Great Guide, to guide me on my journey.*

Your guide is coming toward you. Greet the guide; take in their physical being. At this point, your guide will deliver a message to you and give you the name you are to call them. Listen patiently. File away their name and appearance for reflection after the journey.

Call them using this name. Say that you are ready to follow them back to your true self.

The guide beckons you to follow.

Walk with the guide; let the images flow.

Now your time with your guide is coming to an end. Thank them for their guidance. Ask for any final insight.

Carefully store in your mind the wisdom of your journey.

Turn around. You discover that you are no longer in the cauldron.

Take off the silver coat, boots, and gloves. See yourself in your everyday clothes.

Breathe deeply, feeling the strength and wisdom but retaining the lightness.

When you are ready, walk back to your regular consciousness.

Now that you are back in your body, in everyday life, take time to notice any physical sensations that are occurring. Note these as well. Activation of certain body parts or systems after a journey shows us further information for healing.

Take time to reflect upon your journey. When you are ready, open your eyes.

As soon as possible after the journey, journal about it. Spirit guides often speak to us in riddles and symbols. Writing about them can help us unravel their meanings. Remember that this is very intense work that can take time to process.

## Journey Processing

1. Immediately record all the details of the journey that you remember. Using the voice memo function on your phone is a great tool for doing this; it's quicker than writing and you can allow your thoughts to flow freely. Later you can summarize the journey in your journal.

2. Processing the journey should occur soon after, but can wait until later, especially if you make a recording. Here are the things you should be thinking about:

- What is my current emotional state? (You'll carry the dominant feelings of the journey over into the mundane world.)

- How did the realm of my guide appear?

- What did my spirit guide look like?

- What were the activities that they were doing?

- What did they say to me?

- What did I say?

- What were the symbols? (This can include many things. Journeys are notoriously cryptic. Look for colors, things associated with the deities you wanted to connect with, animal messengers, etc.)

- What happened? (Did you do something with your guide?)

- What time period was it? (Past, present, future?)

- What do I need to do for follow-up?

3. Now that you've processed the spirit-guide journey, you should move on to your interpretation of it. First evaluate your own understanding and write it down. Then seek other sources, such as a standard journey-interpretation guide or references on the type of spirit you encountered (e.g., animal medicine, angelic types, deity), for further interpretation guidance.

4. Follow up on your experience.

- Be gentle with yourself for the day after the journey experience. The emotions of the journey may carry forward into your waking life. Take time to notice these feelings and release them if they don't serve you well.

- If there was something you were asked to do during the journey, explore how you can make it happen.

- Pay attention for further messages from your guide in your dreams; you may see symbols or get other messages that reinforce your connection with them during the days afterward.

- Arrange a tribute to your guide, with symbols and images associated with them, on your altar or in a separate space.

- Return to the cauldron when you wish to communicate with your guide again.

## The Mirari: Crafting and Working with a Spirited Mirror

Scrying with black mirrors can connect us with a host of spirits, from what lies within our own shadows to the departed and spirit guides. *Mirari* is a Latin word that means "to wonder at," but it later developed into the English word "mirror." For our purposes, spirited mirrors can be used to illuminate Hekate, communicate with spirits and guides, or reveal truths about others.

There are many ways to create a spirited mirror for scrying. Generally, the surface of the mirror is darkened so that reflections are dimmed. This can be accomplished by painting over a mirror or using regular glass and placing a dark surface underneath it, such as painted cardboard. Using metallic paints adds dimension. Here's one way to create one.

## Supplies

- A 5" x 7" photo frame that feels like it wants to become enchanted. Generally, this smallish size works well because it's big enough to convey the spirits that you are seeking a connection with but not so big as to attract invaders.

- A heavy piece of cardstock. Sometimes, frames come with this, but you may need to find an appropriate piece. Make sure it is strong enough to take the paint well.

- Dark-hued metallic paint, such as black, deep blue, or dark red. Alternatively, you can mix gold or silver with flat black paint. Mix some Oleum Spirita in with the paint to add energy. Magickal glue, especially with glitter in it, can further enhance the paint.

- You can add sigils and symbols to augment the mirror. Place these around the perimeter so as to keep the surface bare.

## Process

Remove the glass from the frame and set it aside. Cleanse the frame with Circe's Wash or another magickal cleanser.

Paint the cardstock with the prepared paint. A pour-over technique is a favorite method of mine for creating a mystical surface. Let it dry, then add a second coat.

While the second coat is drying, you can paint the frame (if desired) and adorn it with sigils and symbols.

When the cardstock is completely dry, rub a little Oleum Spirita over the surface in a clockwise direction and say an incantation, such as:

> *Mirari, I enchant you with this oil, banishing the unwelcome and revealing wisdom.*

Once the oil has dried, insert the cardstock under the glass and reassemble the frame.

## Vivification Protocol

The full moon offers an excellent opportunity for vivifying a scrying mirror. Once you are satisfied with your creation, it's time to enchant it with the illuminating energy of this lunar phase.

Hold the mirari under the light of the full moon so it reflects in the mirror.

While washing the mirari with a suitable formulation, such as Circe's Wash, and anointing it with sacred smoke from the cauldron (mugwort is ideal for this), recite the incantation. (Mugwort's Latin name, *Artemesia*, is used in the incantation.)

> *Hekate's Moon shining bright,*
> *Empower this mirror with true sight.*
> *Bringing clarity and banishing doubt,*
> *So I may see within and without.*
> *Blessing me with guiding sight.*
> *Artemesia grants the boon of visions,*
> *While protecting me from invasions.*
> *To Artemesia, Hekate, and the Moon above,*
> *I offer trust and purest love.*
> *As I speak it, so it becomes.*

*Hail Hekate.*
*Hail Luna.*
*Hail Artemesia.*

Feel free to add your own verses to the incantation, especially if they reflect any symbols or correspondences you've evoked to enchant the mirror.

I recommend leaving the mirari under the moonlight until dawn to ensure full vivification.

The name your mirari wishes to be called may come forward right after the vivification or at a later time. Consider adding a monogram of this to the mirror.

Take your time with your mirari, getting to know it's ways. You can ask it questions. Hekate, the moon, mugwort (*Artemesia*), and other spirits will send images, sensations, and wisdom as you soften your gaze into the mirror.

Your mirari will acquire a unique voice and personality. Like any relationship, the more time you spend talking to it, the deeper the connection will become.

Keep the mirror on your altar, covering it with a cloth when not in use.

It is an excellent idea to keep your tarot and oracle cards on or near the mirror; and you can use the mirror as the foundation for readings, setting the deck on it to begin, then placing the cards you draw around it or on it.

### Scrying with the Mirari

Generally, scrying works best when mundane distractions are minimized and a general atmosphere of magick abounds in the space. Be sure to protect your space from unwanted visitors before you begin.

Ignite sacred smoke in your cauldron; use a botanical that will amplify your connection to the deeper world, such as the aforementioned mugwort or a bay leaf.

Light an enchanted candle, such as one infused with botanicals and a sigil. Situate the candle and cauldron near the mirror so that both are reflected in the mirror's surface.

Attune yourself to the deeper world, such as with the Unifying the Three Selves meditation. Perform the Cauldrons Three Ritual, with a counterclockwise motion for banishing any unwelcome energy, then circling clockwise for protection and connection.

If you have a specific query for the mirari, ask it without expectations; that way the mirror can transmit the wisdom of the spirits without your interference. For example:

*Mirari, may your surface reflect the wisdom I seek for* [question].

Soften your gaze into the reflective surface, shifting your vision from the physical to the deeper third eye. Images may be reflected on the mirror, or you may have visions in your mind or perceive things some other way.

When the session is over, express your appreciation and make notes of your experiences.

# Chapter 16

## Connecting with Animal Spirits

*Hekate's hounds, ever watchful*
*Attending to their mistress.*
*Horses, companions along her road.*
*Deer, under her watchful care.*
*Serpents, bringing the mysteries.*
*Creatures of flight, soaring the realms.*
*And those of the sea, plunging into the depths.*
*Allies, familiars, and spirits.*
*Connecting to the natural rhythm.*
*Reminding us of who we truly are.*
*Hail to all the animals,*
*Tame and wild.*

Where there is Hekate, there are animals. From her favored black dogs to sea creatures, Hekate is companioned by creatures that walk on the earth. If we have an uncanny animal encounter, it may be a conveyance from their mistress. Over the years, I've had countless such encounters, often featuring unexpected black dogs—like one that showed up at my front door during the dead of winter. I've heard many tales of black dogs, winged creatures, and other animals appearing without any discernable reason—other than they were sent by Hekate. Think back to any unexpected animal visitors that you may have had. Perhaps they were Hekate's messengers.

Animals, like all spirits, are complex beings with their own will. When we have a visitation from an animal, it is really the deeper archetypal spirit of the creature that is visiting. However, the physical embodiments of the archetype can become loyal companions, with their own unique personalities.

# Hekate Physis: Goddess of the Natural World

In *The Chaldean Oracles*, Hekate is referred to by multiple titles containing the word "zoo" and is given the role of φύσις (Physis, meaning "nature"). "Zoo" comes from the Greek words ζωη (zoe), meaning "life" and referencing living beings, and φύω (fyo), which means to "bring forth or grow," especially in the natural world. In the *Oracles*, Hekate is a mediating force between the mortal world and the deeper realms. The modern definition of "zoo" as a place for viewing contained animals or describing a chaotic scene dates back to the 1800s. What an apt metaphor for how society views the natural world.

Reclaiming "zoe" as sacred liberates us and animals from our respective cages. While animals can be incorporated as correspondences into our workings, we should not act as "zookeepers" but rather as conservationists.

The *Oracles* are believed to have been created and used from the 3rd to 6th centuries CE, so this giving-life view of Hekate coexisted with the more folkloric one that was portrayed in popular plays at the time, such as versions of the Medea story. Also at this time, Christianity was becoming more influential, so the cultural acceptance of animal sacrifice was diminishing. This period was a convergence of the old ways with the new, and the mindset toward animals was changing along with the times. The sacrificial dogs offered to Hekate were becoming a thing of the past. Yet alongside this came an increasing separation between humans and "zoo," which is now sometimes used in Greek as a derogatory term, like how English speakers might say someone is "acting like an animal."

Before and during the time of the ancient Greeks, Hekate's connection with the natural world and animals spoke to her earthiness. Hekate was a goddess among humans, neither residing on high in Olympus nor dwelling entirely in the Hades's domain. The earliest records describe her as a Great Mother, thereby associating her, as in her role of Physis, with all of the natural world.

There is a great deal of healing to do regarding our relationship with the natural world. Part of our witches' work is to connect with Hekate's animal menagerie in ways that nourish everyone involved.

## Hekate's Ancient Animal Horde

Hekate's association with animals—bulls, deer, dogs, horses, and snakes—is found in several of her epithets. The members of Hekate's animal horde—wild and tame—are diverse, from those associated with her throughout the centuries to the personal emissaries she sends to you.

There is power in the different attributes of Hekate's animals—her hounds are fierce, her serpents more symbolic. In many ancient written sources, Hekate's zoological connections are reflected in her epithets, descriptions, and in images and iconography. Hekate's epithets show when she is being called an animal, said to have animal characteristics, or is otherwise associated with an animal. In the *Greek Magical Papyri*, she is referred to as Phroune (She-Toad) and Lyco (She Wolf). Leaina (Lioness) comes to us from her cult in Caria (modern western Türkiye), where she was seen quite differently compared to her mainstream Grecian image that often associated her with a horde of fierce hounds wandering the night.

In some documents, she is described as having a specific role, such as leading her hounds, holding snakes, or blessing horses. Indeed, Hesiod's version of Hekate in his *Theogony* illustrates that she "sits by" kings and "stands by" horsemen. Porphyry in *On Abstinence from Eating Animals* describes a four-headed Hekate with the heads of a horse, bull, lioness, and dog. This theme of Hekate having multiple animal heads is a rather common one throughout the ages, harkening back to her Physis and "zoo" titles.

## Dogs: Balancing the Wild and Tame

In ancient times, dogs were viewed as spiritual go-betweens from the Underworld to the land of the living. Cerberus was Hades's three-headed hound, connecting dogs with Hekate and her three-formed nature. In depictions of Hekate with animal heads, a dog is typically one of them. Dogs now, as then, have the potential to revert to their ancient wildness. They can be dangerous to humans and domestic animals, yet also serve and protect. Dogs, like Hekate and her witches, have sharp teeth and are prone to nonconformity. Unlike any other deity, only Hekate had dogs sacrificed in her honor, speaking to her uniqueness in the Greek and Roman pantheon.

## Other Animal Associations from Antiquity

Yet there were many other creatures associated with her, particularly bulls, deer, and horses. The bull connection links to multiple meanings, from their majesty as king of domestic animals to how their horns symbolized the crescent moon in the ancient world. The bull, like the moon, was more powerful than man but also served his needs, much like how some viewed Hekate then and even today. The deer association is dualistic; Hekate is both their hunter and protector, and this animal connects her with Artemis. The deer motif runs throughout ancient hymns and epithets, although there is scant visual evidence linking her with them. Regarding horses, there are relics, such as coins and religious icons, showing Hekate with them, signifying her aspect as Enodia.

Hekate was also associated with other animals, giving her quite a menagerie—boars, cows, donkeys, fish, black goats and lambs, lions, lizards, owls, polecats (a type of weasel), snakes, toads, and wolves. There are also indirect associations through her deity companions, especially Artemis: bee (from the Ephesian version of Artemis that is quite different from the mainstream Greek one), bear (also associated with Bendis), and rabbit. Artemis was also linked with gold finches, while Circe was linked to hawks, large cats, and pigs; Hekate's mythological mother, Asteria, was linked to quail. Then there is the wryneck (called an iynx in ancient Greece), a bird that can turn its head almost 180 degrees; it is connected to Hekate's Wheel and was used in ancient spells. A vulture is in the *Greek Magical Papyri* but not directly connected to Hekate in a spell or hymn. If we include mythical beasts, she is connected to dragons (Drakaina) and hydra in multiple sources.

## Hekate's Cauldron of Animals

Physis is the essence in Hekate's eternal cauldron. All creatures can be found within it, and you may be surprised by the envoys she sends forth to you. Some animals—like the bat, cat, crow, and owl—accompany Hekate as the queen of witches. Owl has an ancient association with her, as seen in ancient manuscripts and on old coins; the owl is an envoy she commonly sends to teach us wisdom. Bats, cats, and crows have been strongly linked to witchcraft since ancient times. Hekate is still portrayed today with the animals she has been associated with throughout history.

More fascinating to me are practitioner's reports of the animals they associate with Hekate. Over the years, I've compiled a lengthy inventory of the unique creatures that Hekate sends as allies. The list is incredibly varied, ranging from beetles to dolphins. Insects were a common theme, and there were several reports of butterflies, moths, and fireflies. The most popular creature, though, was the spider. Her ancient epithet of Klothaie (Spinner of Fate) is definitely arachnid.

There are no incorrect animal guides. Given that Hekate is Einalia (Goddess of the Sea), it's not surprising that practitioners associated many aquatic creatures with her, including dolphins, seals, otters, sharks, and several types of fish. Birds included the immensely popular raptors (eagles and hawks), crows, doves (which apparently travel in groups of three—very Hekatean), ravens, vultures, chickens, finches, owls, and even cardinals. The mythical phoenix was also reported. Mammals have included bears, cats (domestic and wild), deer and antelopes, elephants (one of mine), mustelids (ferret, mink), muskrats, rabbits, raccoons, possums, and skunks. I'm sharing this inventory to highlight that there are no "correct" animals that Hekate may send or through which we can connect to her.

## Connecting with Animal Allies: The Crossroads of Wild and Tame

Whenever we connect with an animal ally, we enter the intersection between the civilized world and the natural one. Witchcraft is essentially resisting to the world of man; it is of the wild by nature. Even the most domestic animal still bears the ancestral memory of being wild. Hekate is Physis, the essence of the natural world, all that is natural is natural to my witchery. Like botanicals, animals exist in physical form, have their own spirit, and are emanations of a much deeper archetype. For as much as etheric entities accompany Hekate, so do those that are made of flesh and form. Animals are our allies, guides, and teachers. We may have them as pets and familiars or be their caregivers in other ways. I certainly am connected to the wild creatures who inhabit my property, including the countless birds, bears, deer, porcupines, rabbits, coyotes, wildcats, and so on.

Animals have complex spirits; they can be our closest companions, or we can seek their participation for a specific working. We can develop long-term relationships with them as spiritual helpmates. You may have primary animal allies that abide with you. For me, these are ospreys and elephants. We can learn from animals by intentionally studying the physical creature or through transcendent encounters during a journey. Every lunar month, I teach about a different animal, and our work with them includes many different ways to connect with them. A favorite activity is "color and contemplate," which focuses upon attuning with the animal's essence as part of our spiritual development. I've included an example in "Creating an Animal Ally Art Talisman" on page 180.

We also work with animals as correspondences, but they can be very challenging, since, unlike colors, numbers, and such, animals have their own will, personality, and experiences. They have their own ideas about their inclusion in our workings. We connect to their archetype, but we can also evoke specific animals. In addition, the animal spirits we connect with through a corporeal representation, like a deer skull or a used horseshoe, will still be attached to the essence of the former animal.

## Including Hekate's Animals in Witchcraft

Beyond the symbolic significance ascribed to animals by the ancients, animals were also included in ancient spells. There are numerous examples found in the *Greek Magical Papyri* and on curse tablets. Animals were placed next to Hekate on ancient amulets and magical coins. Naturally shed hair, fur, nails, skin, and teeth can be used in spells, which both honors the animal and helps us achieve our desired outcome.

**Animal spirit attunement**: Select from the ancient epithets, or simply use Hekate Physis, then state your intention. Envision a cord linking you to whatever creature you have chosen, which will connect you in a manner that is nourishing to both. Practice opening up this way often and with different animals to strengthen the ability. The more you do, the better you'll be able to include animals in your witchery.

**Living animal connection**: If you connect with the same live animals over a period of time, you may be able to influence their actions. Animals can also mirror simple actions that you perform. My deer nod back at me, for example. You may have already noticed this with your pets.

**Altars**: Include objects on your altar that connect you with your animal allies to honor them and Hekate.

**Offerings**: When making food offerings, take a moment to thank the animal from whence it came.

**Animal messengers**: Hekate often comes to us using her menagerie, either in the spirit world—as in dreams and journeys—or by actually sending an out-of-the-ordinary physical creature into our day. Pay attention to these messengers.

**Animals as Hekatean go-betweens**: Call on Hekate's animals to get her attention.

*Mighty Hound, I seek your Mistress's attention now.*

**Divination**: Casting bones and other animal parts (nails, feathers, etc.) that have been given assigned meanings is an excellent way to strengthen your animal spirit abilities and enable you to peek into the future.

**Spells**: Include their bits and pieces in your potions, talismans, and charms. While adding them, focus on the nature of the animal spirit you're including. If you are new to this, eggshell magic is a great place to start. Grind up eggshells to use in protective spells and more.

**Shapeshifting**: Expand your connection with the animal so you actually take on its characteristics. This permits you to access or strengthen abilities and characteristics within yourself. I've provided a meditative shapeshifting journey on page 184.

## Types of Animal Allies

Whether temporary or long-term companions, we can have different types of connections with our animal allies.

**Familiars**: A familiar is usually an embodied (physical) companion animal that is a magickal partner and is more or less in service to the witch. In folklore and mythology, witches have almost always had familiars, anything from rabbits to goblins. I have witnessed fierce debates about the nature of familiars. My thought is that if an animal feels like a familiar to you, then it is.

**Primary animal ally**: Typically, this is an independent spirit that we have a deep relationship with. We intensely identify with or as the animal. Explore the animals that mean the most to you. Use trance and journeying to connect with them, or, if you don't know what your animal ally is, you can use your journey to find one.

**Spirit Companion**: This can be your power animal, a companion, or even a guide to the mystical realms. Look for signs in everyday life for animals that are applying for this position.

**Fetch**: Sometimes referred to as a servitor, a fetch is an animal spirit we have trained to do our energetic bidding. This is a bit complex. If you have a strong connection to an animal spirit, petition Hekate to direct it to follow your magical instructions.

## Working with Animal Allies

Here are some tips for connecting with an animal ally finding what you can learn from it:

- Put meaningful symbols of the animal in your sacred space and craft talismans in their honor.

- Ask what the animal means to you. What emotions are evoked? What images? Are their memories associated with the animal? How is the animal portrayed in popular culture? Is there a historical thread to research?

- What are the underlying archetypes associated with the animal? Rabbit is swift and productive, while Deer is gentle and timid yet very adaptable. Having a set of animal cards (oracle deck) can be helpful.

- If an animal has a strong presence, set up a little sacred space just for it or incorporate it into your altar. I have a little temenos (sacred space) for Elephant that is completely private.

- Trust in what the animal brings forward. At times, this can be difficult. Serpent brings skin shedding and venom. Both images are very helpful but perhaps not as easy as what a friendly dog might bring.

**Exploring the Soul and Shadow of Animal Allies**

In traditional tarot, the Moon card features a dog and a wolf, representing their connection to the lunar world of intuition and emotions while evoking the duality of wild and tame. From our mortal perspective, all creatures can be seen as having a shadow and a soul.

Vultures, for example, are often treated with disrespect, even though they perform the sacred service of tending to the dead. Pets can be destructive, sneaky, and downright maddening in their shadowy behaviors. With vultures, the shadow energy is projected at them by some humans, and how we interpret our pet's behaviors is us projecting shadow energy onto them. Connecting with an animal ally to reveal not only their own dualities but also our own, while they simultaneously provide guidance for us, can be a deeply meaningful experience.

**Creating an Animal Ally Art Talisman**

Select an animal to work with for this exercise, then develop a template for creating the talisman. You can do this by drawing or digitally creating one or even gluing pictures onto a piece of paper. There are oodles of coloring books and sheets available. Choose images that represent how you perceive the soulful, or "illuminated," aspects of the animal and ones that are more "shadowy," so that you have two specific sections. These can be side by side, a back-and-front arrangement, or two separate sheets.

Here are a few example animals with themes for exploring shadow and soul:

- Dogs for their wild and tame aspects. Personal inquiry: *How are my wild and tame aspects shadowy or soulful?*

- Vultures for the way humans view them and what purpose they actually serve. *How do I let others define me? How am I connecting to my own sacredness?*

- Owls for exploring their self-awareness, who they truly are and what they are not. Individuation is the process of becoming our true authentic selves. Owl is an excellent guide for this. *What are my attributes, and how are they owls? What I am not, like what Owl is not? Or what am I giving up?*

- Horses for the way they support others. *Am I overly dependent on my relationships or am I, like Horse, independent and connected?*

Once you have the template designed, you are ready to "color and contemplate." Start with an incantation:

*Great Hekate, Queen of the Natural World,*
*Reveal in me what lies in shadow and what truly nourishes*
*As I connect with your animal guide.*
*Creature, may we both find value through the crafting of this talisman.*

Add specific epithets to the incantation as suitable.

Write in the shadow and illuminated sections any aspects of the animal that come through. When you are done writing, add color to the talisman as you contemplate your lists, especially how the aspects connect with you. Ask your animal helpmate for messages about how they can guide you.

When you have finished, release the shadowy aspects that surfaced; you can simply flip over a back-to-front design, rip off and tear up the shadow side, or destroy the separate sheet.

## Shapeshifting into an Animal Spirit

Hekate is the Shapeshifter, transforming from life to death and back again. Ancient images and spells also describe her morphing into animal forms. Her triformis incarnation takes on animal heads, or she may be adorned with horns and robed in serpents. Several modern depictions echo these historical ones. The witch, following the heed of our mistress, can transform into an animal, too. In folklore, witches often changed into their animal familiars. Most folk tales have an element of truth in them. Such is the case with the stories of witches' transformations into animals to work their magick or escape capture. The grain of reality in these stories is the witch's inherent ability to adapt and survive.

The process of intentional shapeshifting requires opening ourselves up to the creature into which we will transform. This is accomplished by modifying our own appearance, conjuring imagery of the spirit in our imagination, opening ourselves to the spirit through consciousness-altering techniques, and ultimately merging with the spirit so that we take on its energies.

Shapeshifting can be spontaneous when we are in trance, whether it be through deep meditation or other methods. We can shapeshift during our journeys in the dreamtime as well. Temporarily acquiring the characteristics of an animal ally through intentionally merging ourselves with them can be a profound experience. Shapeshifting connects to the spirit of the animal, the underlying archetypal being that flows throughout the physical embodiments of the creature.

For example, we may call upon the spirit of Wolf so that we can run as they do, freeing ourselves from the shackles that bind us. This spirit wolf will come to us as we are meant to receive it, taking a unique form that flows from the larger archetype. Wolf also teaches independence and connection, as well as commiserating with us on the plight of the natural world. Wolf knows what it's like to be an outsider, judged as problematic by the powers that be.

As a shamanic technique, shapeshifting has been practiced across centuries and cultures. We take on the attributes of an animal so that we can not only become more like them but also receive their wisdom. Although I'm focusing on shapeshifting into animal forms, this method can also be applied to other many types of beings, from plants to becoming a channeling vessel for spirit guides. Shapeshifting changes our perspective of the world, liberating us from our regular selves, becoming more and entering into the mysteries in a deeper way.

I've been teaching shapeshifting for over fifteen years, and I have been fortunate to witness immense healing in those who have shapeshifted. If you begin your explorations of shapeshifting with an animal that you already have as an ally, one that you are deeply connected with, it will help the process. As your skill as a shapeshifter strengthens, you can change the animals you call for shapeshifting. Animals also walk the wheel of time, so you can work with the same animal but at differing parts of its life cycle.

Shapeshifting honors the spirit of the animal called in, nourishing both the creature and the practitioner. As a continuum of experience, shapeshifting ranges from receiving energy offered by the animal to fully immersive shamanic experiences. In the former, an awareness of our own self is maintained; in the latter, we suspend our self-awareness, fully taking on the energy shared by the creature. The animal's shared qualities linger after the transformation, allowing us to draw from them. Shapeshifting can be done as a lone experience but also as part of a working, where we attune with the animal as part of a spell. It is vital that we be clear in our intentions with the animal spirits we call upon and specifically ask for their involvement, much in the same way we would petition Hekate or our spirit guide for assistance.

## Preparation

**Connecting with the animal ally**: Make a connective talisman evocative of your animal; perhaps use one you crafted earlier, or create a new one. Start with a powerful symbol of the animal you are calling toward you. Images, statues, and figurines can work, but the best option will always having a direct encounter with the living creature whenever possible. Animal oracle decks are an excellent place to find animal ally symbols. Deciding whether you want to work with physical pieces of animals—such as bones, feathers, and teeth—is a personal matter. There are legal considerations, too. For example, it's illegal in the United States to own an eagle feather. What I've always done is to accept any bones and such that naturally come to me. These are real treasures.

Wood blanks in the shapes of different animals are available; one can be crafted into a talisman, merging the invitation with the symbol. You can make your own with clay or trace the shape of the animal on paper.

You can create an entire altar dedicated to the animal you will be calling upon, including the aspects of Hekate you connect with the creature.

**Crafting an invitation to the animal ally**: Ask the animal to join you for the experience, specifically explaining in a respectful manner what you are seeking. Here's an example:

*Wolf, Wild and Free.*
*I invite you to join with me.*

*May I run as you do,*
*Without fear or inhibition.*
*May I know the safety of your den.*
*May you teach me of your ways.*
*I honor you, Wolf.*
*Come to me.*

Write this in advance and place it beside your symbol or incorporate it into your talisman.

## Shapeshifting Journey

Place your animal talisman beside a candle, light the candle, and speak your invitation while focusing on the talisman. Begin your journey:

Welcome your animal. Close your eyes so that you can see the animal as it wishes to be known.

Bring your three selves into attunement, starting with breathing into your sitting bones, then reciting:

*I am rooted in myself, tethered to the nourishment of Chthonia, and from*
*here I freely enter into the spirit of shapeshifting with* [animal].

Breathe into your heart center:

*I am open to this experience and seek only to receive what is freely given and*
*honor* [animal].

Draw your the breath into your mind, clearing away mundane thoughts, so that you can open to the energy offered by the animal:

[Animal], *I see you through the vision of my soul. I am ready to receive what*
*you offer for our highest good.*

Envision your deeper self, your soul, standing with the animal. It invites you to touch it or it comes to rest on you.

With this physical connection, gently open up to the energy offered.

As the creature shares its physical appearance, you allow it to merge with your own. Your feet become like its; your legs, torso, arms, head, and so on. Your skin becomes like its, too.

The animal continues sharing, lending you its characteristics. You remain aware of your own self but are equally conscious of these characteristics.

Now the creature invites you to move as it does, and you follow its lead.

As the two of you move in tandem, the animal shares its wisdom and experiences, bringing to you what you are meant to see. Let this last as long as it needs to.

By mutual agreement, the time to separate arrives. The connection between the two of you gently dissipates. You no longer have the creature's physical form or characteristics within you, yet its wisdom remains.

Thank the animal for sharing.

The animal places a gift for you on the ground, then slowly disappears.

Open your eyes, returning to your physical self and environment.

Gently relax the root, heart, and crown, coming back into your conscious self.

Notice any sensations, emotions, visions, and thoughts that linger from the journey.

When you are ready, make notes and sketches about the experience, the appearance and characteristics of the creature, and the gift you received.

In the days following your shapeshifting journey, pay attention to how the experience continues to work on you—in dreams, synchronicities—and try to apply the characteristics of your animal to daily life.

# Chapter 17

## *Transcending the Ordinary—Mystical and Shamanic Experiences*

"What I am here to say to you is this: you are not disconnected from Hekate. In fact, you are of her. Do not continue with this belief that you are not sacred. There is a great change to come, you are required for this. In all things, consider that you are necessary. That you are here to do Hekate's work. Should you be lonely, know you are not alone. Should you be afraid, know that you are protected. Should you wander from the path, follow her torches back home to the crossroads. Do not persist in foolishness, or trivialities. There is a truth that you already know. Abide in it, and all shall be as it is meant."

—APPHIA

I didn't intend to become a channel for the spirit of an ancient priestess of Hekate. It all began several years ago when I woke up with a word looping in my brain, "Apphia." Having learned enough to pay attention to such occurrences, I sat down with my morning brew to let my hands try to make some sense out of this. I drew a sketch of a woman. "*I am Apphia; I am here to help,*" was what the drawing said. Then one day, while reading an obscure scholarly article on the worship of Hekate at Lagina, there she was listed as a temple key bearer. Imagine how I felt. She was not merely an etheric guide but also a spiritual ancestor.

Over the years, Apphia has stayed beside me. During High Rituals in the coven, she speaks through me. I don't have a full awareness of what she says and does during these channeled sessions, but I know that she always brings great truth and healing to the participants.

Contrast that with waking up, drenched in sweat, heart pounding, struggling to pull myself back into the waking world from a nightmare—a horrible creature was ripped out of me by a mysterious woman. The curtains in the hotel room were rustling, even though the window was closed and the AC wasn't on. When I finally oriented myself to the physical world, I realized it was time for my early morning appointment with a First Nations healer. I went to our rendezvous location still shaky from the dream. She never showed up. When I tried to track her down, I found that the number I had didn't work, and nobody had ever heard of her, even though she had been present the day before at the retreat I was speaking at. Realizing she had worked her medicine on me in the dreamworld, I stopped trying to find her in the everyday world. I knew her as "Millie," and she stuck with me during the worst period of my life. She quietly exited when things got better. For me, Apphia represents the mystical, and Millie reflects the shamanic.

Going beyond the limits of our physical beings, crossing into Hekate's deeper world where we can glimpse the essence of the universe, can be richly rewarding. We may receive messages for ourselves or become channels for sharing them with others, or dream spirits may perform spiritual surgery on us. These are some of the characteristics of transcendent experiences. Difficult to describe, yet profound. If everyday life concerns the rational and structured, the deeper world is transcendent and limitless.

Our ventures beyond the threshold into the deeper world can have a great impact on us. In the ancient sacred text known as *The Chaldean Oracles,* Hekate is described as the mediating guide between regular mortal existence and the mysteries. She is Anima Mundi (World Soul), the essence that runs through all, referred to in the *Oracles* (a channeled text) as the Fiery Flower of Creation (sometimes translated as "fiery rose"). Reflecting her roles as gatekeeper and crossroads goddess, the *Oracles* convey how she governs the liminal and can grant entrance to the mysteries.

She offers us the keys of transcendence in different ways. She may lead us into our own personal Underworld for healing our shadow, encountering former versions of ourselves and our own "hungry ghosts" of these selves, along with those we have hurt or those who have deeply wounded us. Or Hekate may unlock a path of enlightenment, where we evolve beyond our prior limitations, perhaps even channeling transmissions from her or other spirits.

## Having Mystical and Shamanic Experiences

I'm using two distinct terms to categorize these experiences to help you better understand:

- Mystical experiences are the times when we see beyond the limits of regular vision, gaining insight into our own journey and unlocking knowledge relating to universal truths and our encounters with guiding spirits. Receiving messages from spirits and prescient dreams about external events are examples.

- Shamanic experiences, using the contemporary definition of the word, are those that are similar to the mystical ones yet fundamentally transform us—body and spirit—through a complex web of forces and spirits. Profound shapeshifting experiences, spiritual dismemberment and death, and soul retrieval are examples.

The mystical typically is the domain of the higher self and the upper world, reflected in Hekate Kleidoukhos (Keeper of Keys), Ourania (Celestial), and Astrodia (Star Walker). Hekate as Chthonia (Of the Underworld), Psychopomp (Soul Guide), and Borborophorba (Filth Eater) often evoke shamanic experiences, such as deathwalking and soul retrieval. If the middle world is the crossroads of the realms and the home of Hekate's Garden, the mystical is located in her temple and the shamanic in her cave. The mystical is refined, the shamanic dense. The difference between the full moon and the dark moon, for example. While the mystical may, at times, unsettle us, it is the shamanic that shakes us to the core. A beautiful ritual in which you deeply connect with Hekate, finding meaning and healing, can be mystical. A wild nightmare that we wake up from utterly in shambles may be a shamanic dismemberment and death initiation. Both unlock the potential for profound transformation, yet the experiences are very different.

## Understanding and Navigating Spiritual Upgrades

Mystical and shamanic experiences are initiations that beckon us into times of intense transformation. Having swum in the depths of Hekate's Cauldron, we simply aren't who we were before. Soul progression, also known as enlightenment, is designed to be challenging. These spiritual upgrades awaken, empower, and heal us, yet they can be difficult.

Many of the characteristics of an upgrade are wonderful. We form stronger connections with Hekate and our guides, and new allies may come to us. Increased curiosity, motivation, inspiration, creativity, embodiment, deep emotional work, and the falling away of harmful thought patterns often ensues. We might feel energized or require long periods of rest. We may feel compelled to find a community of supportive others.

As our transformation amplifies, there can be accompanying root, heart, and crown changes. The root of the lower self unlocks intuition, so that we become connected to our own truth and can see through falsities. The heart of the middle self shifts us toward opening up to those who nourish and connecting to the natural world, while also strengthening our boundaries. The higher self's crown stretches into the mystical, ascending beyond the ordinary.

There may also be physiological indications of a spiritual upgrade, such as a very strong feeling of the heart center being "on fire," headaches (crown), and digestive or reproductive disturbances (root). We may become very sensitive to smells and colors, bodily sensations, and temperatures. We may perceive the physical world more vividly, being able to see beyond the manmade environment to the essence of the natural world, including encountering land spirits or the dead.

Spiritually, we may channel messages, have visions, receive dream oracles, and experience a strong desire to detach from the mundane. The third eye, our connection to the unseen worlds, will open up as well. This is the awakening of the soul. So much will be going on.

Before diagnosing yourself as being in the midst of a spiritual upgrade, ensure that there are no other reasons for the way you are feeling. If you're otherwise healthy, then you may be undergoing a spiritual upgrade. Spiritual upgrades provide us with an opportunity to not only become more enlightened but also to make peace with being uncomfortable. Distress tolerance, abiding outside our comfort zone, is an important skill to develop as you advance along your witch's journey. There is no transformation without friction.

Here are some general tips for navigating a spiritual upgrade:

- Stay with your daily ritual, adjusting it as your feel called. It is natural for our practice to evolve as we "level up."

- Wear a calming stone, such as selenite. Sleep with red jasper. Use black obsidian as a touchstone and release vessel.

- Dialogue with Hekate and your spirit guides about this transformation, seeking advice and support.

- Seek to understand the process. Record your experiences, whether in your journal or making audios or videos, so you can reflect on them.

- Embodied activities—such as dance, yoga, or simply going for walks—can balance the spiritual energy with the corporeal, while also providing time to connect with and contemplate the messages being received.

- Nourish your body well. Making extreme changes during the upgrade can lead to increasing problems, but small changes can be helpful.

- Manage the changes in your energetic field and neural networks with the help of natural supplements, but only when it is safe for you to do so based on your own health needs. The dandelion spiritual upgrade soother in *Entering Hekate's Garden* may be helpful.

- Ritual bathing with purifying salt and equanimity-invoking botanicals—such as yarrow, lavender, and rose—can be very helpful.

- Foot soaks using cornmeal and grounding botanicals—such as dandelion and the ones above—are very grounding for when we feel as if we can't keep our feet on the ground.

- Release stressors. Get rid of anything that isn't serving your highest good, whether it be people or possessions, but consider the consequences and be graceful as you do so.

- Every time you go to the bathroom, envision the feelings that don't serve you getting flushed down the toilet.

- In all areas of your life, be as gentle with yourself as possible.

What works for you will be very personal. Try things. Record the results. Cast off what doesn't work. Try new things. Repeat as necessary.

## Bringing Past Lives into the Present

Hekate is Psychopomp (Soul Guide). As we connect to this aspect, she may illuminate our prior lives, leading us on shamanic treks into our own mysteries. Our eternal souls have known multitudinous incarnations. We may have glimpses into these prior embodiments in dreams, inner knowings, and intuitive feelings, such as with déjà vu.

As witches, our past lives reach out to us, crossing through time and ether, offering us the opportunity for reunification. We are "reuniting" because the unborn self, the soul, which is like the pinnacle of the crown, already knows all of its incarnations—past, present, and future. In our everyday consciousness, there are barriers between us and this higher self, yet we often have inexplicable sensations and encounters that evoke strong feelings of familiarity. If you have ever "met" someone, but felt like you've always known them, it may be a past-life connection.

Memories of long-ago lifetimes surface when we connect with images and places evocative of them. Strong emotions can be involved; we may have intense fears unrelated to our present life, especially if the demise of our past self was difficult.

Children, freshly into an incarnation, often have vivid recollections of their past one. Psychiatrist Jim Tucker has spent his career documenting children's spontaneous past-life memories. I've had several past-life reunions; perhaps the most profound is the one with Apphia, who is both guide and a previous life.

As witches, our former incarnations were often practitioners of the Craft. Given the historical treatment of our kind, they may bear deep wounds. Reconnecting with these past lives can be immensely healing to them and ourselves, bringing strong emotions and a sense of wholeness. However, there can be feelings of loss and grief as well.

I've been deeply touched when any of my students has shared one of their past-life reunions; often, the memories have been tinged with bittersweetness but have been profoundly healing. The science of genetics shows us how we truly *are* comprised of limitless former lives, encoded within our DNA. Add to that the mystical aspect of souls, traveling from one life to another. We can reunite with prior incarnations of biology or these more mystical ones. They all live on through us. It is our task to honor them by reconnecting.

If you're new to recollecting and reuniting with past lives, go gently into this work. At times you may question what's coming through; my response is to look within yourself. If this *feels* like a former self reuniting with your current embodiment, it is.

**Gifts of Past Lives**

The perceptions we have about past lives—like a trail of breadcrumbs leading back to them—are real treasures. You may be very attached to a certain type of antique, a style of clothing, old music, or even a particular historical era. Follow these hints as you journey back in time. Should you have these things in your life at present, contemplate how they may unlock a past life.

When we spontaneously retrieve these memories, make these things manifest in the physical world. Sketch it, craft it, or, if it's something you already have, see it as a belonging of your former self. These things are touchstones that connect us with our previous incarnations.

## Past-Life Reunion Journey

Different from spontaneous recollections, journeying to connect with prior lives—also known as past-life regression—can provide answers and healing to both versions of yourself. Should you have objects that evoke a past life already, arrange them into an altar, along with items that attune you to Hekate Psychopomp. A special candle adorned with the Psychopomp sigil can be crafted; you'll find it in the eponymous chapter in *Entering Hekate's Cave,* along with more on soul retrieval.

As with any meditative journey, it is beneficial to write an intention or declaration in advance; this helps you to prepare energetically and gives you a focus for establishing the process once you begin the working.

The process can be augmented with botanicals and stones. Damiana, dittany, mugwort, and thyme, burned as sacred smoke or rendered into an Oleum Spirita with which you anoint your body, can deepen the experience. Sodalite and several of the quartzes facilitate past-life recall, while stones such as shungite encourage harmonious reunions. Balance the experience by wearing them on opposite sides of the body, whether as bracelets or by placing them in your bra or pockets.

When you are ready, get comfortable next to the altar and light the candle. Begin with your intention, declaring the focus for the journey, such as:

*Great Hekate, Psychopomp,*
*Guardian, Guide, and Gatekeeper.*
*Mistress of Souls.*
*I am here to reunite with a former self.*
*I do this in sincerity,*
*May it benefit both of us,*
*With healing and fulfillment.*
*Illuminate this reunion journey.*

Close your eyes. Now attune your three selves to the journey. Begin by breathing your root awake, drawing the breath deep into your sitting bones, then reciting:

> *I am rooted, grounded into the safety of Chthonia as I seek reunion with a former self.*

Move onto the heart center; take a breath that expands the rib cage fully, then exhale forcefully and state:

> *My heart is open to reunion, and my strength supports this process. Enodia, guide this journey.*

Envision the heart stretching down to meet the upward moving root energy, unifying the two.

With short breaths stopping at the throat, each exhale removes clutter from the mind, shifting your gaze from regular vision to the deeper one, guiding the energy with:

> *My crown opens the way to the deeper world. Kleidoukhos, grant me the key of reunion.*

See with the sight of the soul an entrance to the deeper world; cross over into this realm. As you enter, declare your intention:

> *I am here to be reunited with a past self.*
> *I am a soul living one life,*
> *and I'm a soul who's had countless lives.*
> *I'm here to reunite with one of them.*

The historical era in which your former self lived takes shape around you. Make note of your surroundings.

In the distance, you see yourself as you were in that life. As you approach, they greet you warmly, and you reply in kind. Let them know who you are in your present incarnation and encourage them to share some details of who they were when they were embodied and living on the earth as a mortal. They share with you a gift that will become your touchstone for connecting with them.

It is time to bid them farewell for now. But this is temporary. Do not despair as you say goodbye; you're not really leaving them behind. You can return, especially using that touchstone, and dialogue with them whenever you wish. You may use your cards to help you. They may speak to you through automatic writing. Be aware of other ways they may communicate.

Now you must journey back to your waking self; walk down the path back into regular consciousness. As you cross back, work with your breath to relax the three selves and make a big smile; this pulls you back into your physical being.

Make a few initial notes so that you don't forget anything. May you have a wonderful relationship with this retrieved past life.

**Integrating Past Lives into the Here and Now**

There may be a busy period of reconnection with a lot of dialogue; this will simmer down as you integrate this past life with your current one. Tend to this relationship and something great will develop. There may be strong emotions linked to the recovered memories and the conversations you have with this reunited self. The stones recommended above will steady this period of integration. This is an opportunity to heal past trauma and patterns, which we may unconsciously repeat until we intentionally engage with our prior selves.

While there is deep work to be accomplished, there is also a lot of fun to be had. Your former self may not be familiar with modern life—your hobbies, interests, and even how you dress may fascinate them. They may desire things to be more like when they were embodied or enthusiastic about adapting to your life as it is. Curiosity, openness, and creativity are keys for integrating the challenging aspects while embracing the lighter ones.

## Soul Guiding Others

Part of our sacred assignment from Hekate may be to support others, from acting as a medium who connects the bereaved with a departed loved one to doing divinatory readings to cleansing people and places of unwelcome entities to helping souls cross back and forth from the deeper world. We can be soul guides even in small ways—such as sharing our practices.

Hekate is Psychopomp (Mistress of Souls), which has so much more richness to it than just the task of guiding others to the afterlife. As such, our own soul guiding is an offering to Hekate, and our ability to do it should be considered a real gift from her. At times, the awareness that comes with being called to do this work can be wearying. We may run the risk of exposing ourselves to troublesome spirits. Yet to have mystical and shamanic abilities is to be chosen, in a sense, to be an emissary of our beloved goddess. Perhaps you are a natural-born psychopomp, or you may just be realizing your talents as you are reading this. Whatever the case, tend to these gifts well. May you support others and take loving care of yourself.

One way in which almost all of us are called to serve as psychopomp is when someone passes from this life. It may be our own loss, or we may be asked to support another. The encounters we have with the departed can help us both. If a departed being is confused, we may need to help them go to where they belong. I've had the privilege of doing this numerous times, along with performing rituals to help the newly passed transition smoothly.

When doing this work for others, it is important to consider everyone involved. House hauntings are a good example. I've witnessed spirits causing trouble in the home while the occupants were going through periods of change and chaos. While removal of the spirit helps—a thorough walkthrough with khernips involving juniper often does the job—the energy of the living might also need our attention. A ritual may also be in order, such as the following one that can be applied for the newly departed, anytime a spirit seems unsettled, or the bereaved are struggling with their loss.

## Ritual of Hekate for the Dead

Death is a peculiar thing, for while our departed loved ones are no longer physically present in this life, their memory and energy can be overwhelming. We are the ones who remain, sometimes filled with grief and longing. My dad and beloved great-aunt come to me in my dreams. When I am working in the yard, I feel my father's watchful eye. And the spirits of the dead roam the streets of my little village. Death, in its practical sense, is always nearby as well, for there are three cemeteries within short walking distance of my home. This all reminds me that death is but another phase of life, though it is one that can cause us so much pain.

We can call upon Hekate as Mistress of the Dead for the protection of our loved ones as they journey forward and for own our relief from suffering.

Place a photo or other image of your departed beside a white candle. You can add treasures, such as jewelry, that symbolize your relationship to the departed and their beloved objects.

Light the candle. Contemplate your memories of the departed.

Hold the photo while reciting the invocation.

*Hail Hekate, Mighty Eternal Queen,*
*Divine Mediator,*
*She who walks between the worlds,*
*Torchbearer who shines Her light*
*Upon our path.*

*Hear me now,*
*Mistress of Death,*
*Welcome this departed soul.*

*I call upon You,*
*Great Light,*
*Embrace this soul as they pass through*
*The gates of death.*
*Guide my beloved safely*
*To the other side,*
*Offer them comfort,*
*As they cross the threshold*
*From this life to the next.*

*Be with us now in our time of grief.*
*May we know the peace of eternity.*
*Let the light of their memory burn bright,*
*Give us the faith to know that all*
*That dies shall be reborn.*

*Hail Hekate, Mighty Eternal Queen,*
*Divine Mediator,*
*She who walks between the worlds,*
*Torchbearer who shines Her light*
*Upon our path.*
*Hear me now,*
*Mistress of Death,*
*Welcome this departed soul.*

When finished, make an offering to Hekate of fruit, nuts, or dried fish.
Hold up the offering and say:

*May these offerings be in your favor. Hail Hekate, thank you for your guid-*
*ance of the departed and the comfort you bring to me.*

# Chapter 18

## *Rituals—Transcending through Intentional Experiences*

*Hail Hekate, Goddess of the Moon.*
*Unconquerable ruler of land, sea, and sky.*
*I call upon you to attend my rite.*

*Hail Hekate, Goddess of the Moon.*
*Night-wandering Chthonic Queen.*
*I call upon you to attend my rite.*

*Hail Hekate, Goddess of the Moon.*
*Who reigns over all liminal spaces and times.*
*I call upon you to attend my rite.*

*Hail Hekate, Goddess of the Moon.*
*Divine intervener and mediator.*
*I call upon you to attend my rite.*

*Hail Hekate. Three-Formed Goddess.*
*Reflected in the moon's three faces.*
*Hail Hekate. Key Holder of the Mysteries,*
*The secrets of the moon are yours.*
*I call upon the energy of your glorious moon,*
*Seeking your favor,*
*My intention is true,*
*And my will is strong.*

Rituals can be spontaneous occurrences when we intuitively engage in words and movements that connect us to Hekate and her deeper world. The lighting of a candle and calling her name is a ritual. But rituals are primarily intentional experiences that have structure, such as the excerpt from the Whole Moon

Ritual above; they typically feature a protocol, a script, and specific techniques. I refer to these formal ceremonies as "High Rituals," distinguishing them from more relaxed ones, such as meditations and ritual bathing, which I have been referring to as "rituals."

Rituals connect us to Hekate and the deeper world in the same way that magick does; the difference is that rituals focus more on experience, while spells focus on the outcome. Rituals are about connection, meaning, and transcending the ordinary. Rituals are the keystone of my personal craft and my teaching and writing as a priestess.

We may attune to the mystical, basking in the flow of Hekate, or have shamanic cathartic experiences during a ritual. If we go into a ritual with rigid expectations, the sure result is that we shall have neither experience. Preparations are meant to align us with the spirit of ritual; once we begin the performative aspect, it is time to surrender to the process.

During a ritual, we may become intimately connected with our spirits, so much so that we feel sad upon returning to our normal state of being. Or we can emerge drenched in the love of the goddess. Our task is to lean into these states of being, allowing the ritual to work on us. When we open ourselves up to the "medicine" of a ritual, our shadow often roars against the treatment. In particular, the medicine comes to us through dreams, synchronicities, and inner knowings. What is nourishment to the soul is poison to the shadow. Resistance, that weapon of the shadow, is a sign of the ritual's power. Resistance shows up as doubt. Was it merely my imagination? Why didn't I feel more? These are two questions that typically arise. The answer to the first is "No it wasn't" and to the second, "Soul medicine doesn't need to be felt to work." When we experience true transcendence—the separation of the eternal, etheric self from our corporeal being—we come back changed. As we unite back into wholeness, the medicine our spiritual self holds interacts with the corporeal self. Be gentle with yourself during this period.

Recording the ritual experience is vital. Basic record keeping should include the date and time, moon phase, other astrological considerations, the details of your altar, magickal formulary (e.g., incense and oil recipes), your attire, methods used, and your petition or incantation. A brief description of the experience with key features should also be included. I place that information in my Book of Shadows, but when I process the experience, it goes in my Book of Life.

Rituals have specific routines that are general ways for establishing that we are engaging in an intentional transcendent process. It begins with preparation for the ceremony, including the selection of correspondences, designing the altar, choosing offerings, and logistics such as timing and location:

- Correspondences: botanicals, stones, colors, and other essences, such as astrology, to amplify the experience

- Sacred adornment and attire, such as a talismanic necklace or bracelet and clothing that is only worn during rituals

- The sacred name that identifies your deeper self, unlocking the mysteries and connecting you with Hekate

- A personal declaration of your intention for the ritual

- Creating an altar as a portal of connection to Hekate and other spirits evoked during the ritual, including components such as:

  o Offerings that connect to the theme of the ritual

  o Sacred flame: a candle or other representation of the Hieros Pyr

  o A cauldron for sacred smoke

  o Cleansing: A bowl for performing khernips cleansing, along with a suitable botanical

- A ritual script, invocation, or petition that includes specific segments:

  o Cleansing and creation of sacred space

  o A salutation, calling upon Hekate and spirits linked with the ritual, such as "Hail and Welcome"

  o An invocation, such as:

  *I claim this space sacred, protected from all unwanted and unwelcome, entering this ritual with free will, sound mind, and strong spirit*
  *Proclaiming myself a practitioner of witchcraft and devotee of Hekate. I embrace the spirit of this ritual.*

  o Identifying yourself by your sacred name

- Verses describing the aspects of Hekate and other spirits that you are calling upon, sometimes called a "petition"

- Specific intentions for the experience

- An ending that expresses appreciations and relaxes connection, guiding us back into our physical beings, for example:

*With gratitude for your presence. Hail and Fairwell.*

- Cards for conveying messages

- Journal for making notes and sketches afterward

## The Hekatean Cord Activation

Prior to any ritual, awaken and attune the three selves to prepare yourself to transcend the ordinary. The Unifying the Three Selves meditation will accomplish this. But you can go deeper into the process by enhancing the basic version with the following one.

Focus on your lower belly, the area contained within our sitting bones. This is the epicenter of the root, the font of intuition and emotion. Draw your breath into this root, awakening its essence. It uncoils, stretching toward the depths of Chthonia. Direct this cord down through your root, your legs, then your feet—extending your roots deep into the earth. You are grounded below. Release any tension down into the earth. Draw up nourishment.

Turning your focus to the heart center, breathe it open while feeling the strength of your back. Relaxing into the experience and knowing your own power, you are connecting to the spirit of Enodia. The heart unfurls, becoming a blossoming spiral of connection. It naturally slides toward the root, which reaches up to meet it. The two converge, and any heart issues go down into Chthonia; the power of the lower self interacts with that of the middle.

Now shift your energy to the higher self, the crown. With short breaths that stop in the throat, allow each exhale to clear away the clutter of regular consciousness; open the third eye, the sight of the deeper world and the mysteries of Kleidoukhos. Your crown becomes illuminated, growing upward to the celestial. It also reaches down to the heart, linking them, and descends into the root. This brings all three into attunement. Any bothersome thoughts descend into the earth.

All three weave together, creating a powerful cord that extends deep into the earth and high into the Starry Road, forming branches.

From its branches and roots, the cord transforms into a sphere, an encircling shield that keeps unwanted energy out while still connecting to Hekate and her deeper world.

Higher self, the power of mysticism—feel this force throughout your being, permeating each cell. The center of the higher self is the crown. Focus the energy here, unfurling your connection to the Starry Road.

This is the final part of the reconnection to the moon and creates a channel through which the wisdom of the higher self flows.

You are grounded, centered, and connected.

## Ritual of Commitment and Devotion

Committing to being a devotee is serious and should be entered into with sincerity and contemplation. Should you feel called to proclaim your commitment through a ritual, here is a sample that you can follow as written or use as inspiration for your own personalized ceremony.

In my experience, personally and in witnessing real devotion from those I am closest to, making a vow to Hekate liberates and heals; it forms a sacred contract that benefits all involved. In the coven, we do an annual commitment ritual around the autumn equinox on the Libra new moon. Libra is a sign of commitment and dedication, which helps us balance the deeper world with everyday life.

## Declaration of Commitment

Customize this declaration as you feel led, particularly in stating your sacred name and that of your spirit guide and other allies. You can add your primary epithets and describe the meaning of your offerings as well.

*To Hekate,*
*Guardian, Guide, and Gatekeeper,*
*Keeper of Keys.*
*To the Spirits of the Cauldron,*
*And to the eternal Great Wheel,*
*I come to you in truth,*

*My name is my vow.*
*I proclaim my devotion,*
*As I commit myself to this journey.*
*I now walk your crooked road.*
*I abide in your Crossroads.*
*I declare of my own free will that I am*
*A student of your knowledge,*
*Practitioner of your witchcraft,*
*And seeker of your mysteries.*
*May all that would block my way be banished,*
*May I be protected and connected,*
*And may my life be an offering.*
*Hail Hekate,*
*And all the guiding spirits.*

## Performing the Commitment Ritual

Work with the general components of the rituals described previously, adapting them to the nature of this ceremony. A fresh candle, infused with botanicals and adorned with a sigil, is perfect. You can then light it and proceed into your daily ritual, followed by this one.

## Dark Moon Ritual

A High Ritual, this follows the general components of a standard ritual—from offerings to identifying by your sacred name near the beginning—but is more formal and "important." High Rituals are ceremonial, with a specific protocol in comparison to less structured and intuitive rites.

*Great Hekate, Attend me now.*
*On this night when your moon*
*Hides her face out of respect for you.*
*I stand before you,*
*Making sincere offerings.*
*Bestow your wisdom upon me.*
*Limitless, Eternal Hekate.*
*I banish the profane,*
*Speaking only truth.*
*Hear me now.*
*Know my name.*

*Great Mistress who Spins the Wheel.*
*Anima Mundi, World Soul.*
*I seek entrance to your mysteries.*
*Lampadios, Divine Torchbearer,*
*The sacred flame in all,*
*Ignite it within me.*
*Enodia, Queen of Crossroads,*
*Illuminate my way.*
*Kleidoukhos, Keeper of Keys,*
*You hold the knowledge.*
*Propylaia, open your gates for me.*
*May I transcend the ordinary.*
*Ergatis, Energizing Goddess,*
*Awaken my own power.*
*Chthonia, Queen of the Depths,*
*Grant me the keys of witchcraft.*
*Rixipyle, Breaker of Barriers,*
*So I may be liberated from what blocks and binds.*
*Hekate, Psychopomp, Guide of Souls,*
*May I be ever true to mine,*
*And connected to your deeper world.*
*With gratitude, and affection,*
*Hail and Farewell.*

## Noumenia Practices, Ritual, and Invocation

After the dark moon comes the first waxing crescent, which the ancients observed as Noumenia, the beginning of the lunar month. When the moon reappears after observing darkness for Hekate, it is time to set intentions for this new period.

Start by clearing away anything remaining from the Honoring Hekate on the dark moon ritual; clean out cauldrons and remove anything in your sacred space that feels like you need to let go of it. Then reset the cauldrons and create intentions for the coming weeks.

Here are some ideas for establishing cauldrons for the new month:

● *Cauldrons of Land and Sky:* Add botanicals for use as sacred smoke throughout the month.

● *Cauldron of Sea*: Fill a cauldron with pure water and set it overnight under the crescent moon, creating a water to use throughout the month.

● Develop personal "cauldron intentions" for the month:

  ○ *Cauldron of Land*: Intentions relating to your actions and interactions with others in the physical realm, including those focusing on organizations, relationships, work, and home. For example, *"My actions and interactions reflect what is real and true to me, aligning me with my purpose and bringing meaningful experiences."*

  ○ *Cauldron of Sea*: Set the tone of your emotions and attune to your intuition for the month by using an affirmation, such as *"I am in touch with, and guided by, my emotions and intuition. All emotions are sacred."*

  ○ *Cauldron of Sky*: For focusing on the mind and the higher echelons of the mystical, set intentions that concern thoughts, wisdom, and alignment with your own soul and the greater forces. *"I am in right alignment within and with Hekate and my own soul. My thoughts are valuable, yet they are only a small piece of my totality."*

Choose a keyword that emerges from your intention-setting process as a guiding talisman for the month, allowing you to attune to the energy of all your intentions with just one word. This can then be rendered into a sigil that's placed on candles, charms, and so on.

Once your sacred space is refreshed, invoke the new month with the verse below or one of your own.

Ignite a candle, hold your chosen cauldron in both hands, and recite:

*Great Hekate,*
*On this Noumenia,*
*Your Wheel turns again,*
*And the cycle begins anew.*

Circle the cauldron counterclockwise in the left hand:

*On this Noumenia,*
*The past is in the past,*
*All that no longer serves is banished.*

With the cauldron in the right hand, circle clockwise:

*On this Noumenia,*
*I circle myself in protection,*
*Connecting to Hekate and her deeper world,*
*Renewing my truth and power.*

Recite your cauldron intentions, then raise the cauldron high with both hands:

*On this Noumenia,*
*I begin again.*
*Hail Hekate.*

This is an excellent ritual to perform as part of ritual bathing, emerging from the water washed clean for the new month. Follow up this ritual with a card reading (*The Great Goddess Oracle* deck would be perfect) to guide you through the coming weeks.

Part of my personal work for this day is planning for the month ahead by adding the lunar signatures for the entire month to my personal planner. This connects my intentions with the moon's energy; I also add my keyword to the calendar. After the lunar energy has merged with my intentions and keyword, then I do the practical business of operationalizing my intentions through scheduling and planning.

## The Sacred Seven Full Moon Ritual

It is natural for a witch to summon the moon's energy. This is the remembering of what we have always known. The moon is our divine mediator: the merging of the stars, darkness, and earth; our ally in working with the forces and spirits. We rejoin with these forces while summoning lunar energy, calling them forth within our own beings, creating wholeness within ourselves and illuminating our truth.

The moon is a primal force whose currents infuse the earth and us. The changing intersections of the moon, the earth, and the sun result in the different crossroads that are part of the lunar cycle. Each one has dominant energies that we can summon into our witchery. Waning for removals, waxing for attracting, dark for honoring Hekate, new for beginnings. In this ritual, the full moon is summoned for the powers of wholeness and illumination, merging us with the Sacred Seven forces within us and in the external world.

The moon contains the energy of the Starry Road, reflected by the solar influence on her cycle. This is the realm of the sky, connected to our higher selves. The moon is also of the earth, empowering our cycles—both within us and in nature—and even formed from our planet. The material moon represents the active middle self. The moon also contains the shadows, the lower self, the intuition, and the emotional depths of the sea. The moon infuses and influences the four elements of earth, air, fire, and water. The growth cycles, the winds, the tides, and even fires are under the moon's spell. Fire is also reflected by the moon through her entwinement with the sun.

Each part of the lunar cycle carries a unique energy signature. The full moon represents wholeness and illumination. The full moon represents the womb from which all life on earth grows. It is the external embodiment of the core of the planet. Symbolically, the moon sets and rises out of this core. Each night, Selene emerges from Hekate's Cave to share her energy with the world.

**Ritual Preparation**

A talisman with the images of the moon's phases on one side and the four elements and three worlds on the other can be crafted to connect you to the Sacred Seven forces evoked during the ritual.

Sacred Seven moon water comprised of the moon phases, four elements, and three realms can be made in advance for khernips, offering, and anointing. Prepare the water on the night before your ritual. Pour natural water, such as spring or sea, into a clear glass jar. Inscribe the symbols for the elements and realms on the jar. It's fine to cover it if necessary. Let rest overnight under the moonlight.

This is a ritual of the full moon and is an excellent one to do with your own coven or by yourself.

Perform khernips, lighting the sacred flame, adornment with the kroki (a ritual bracelet; see page 223), cleansing with sacred smoke, and anointing prior to the experiential aspects of the ritual.

**Anointing**

Using the moon water, anoint the root in a clockwise manner:

> *I draw your fuel down into the emotional depths of my root,*
> *Seat of intuition and witchcraft,*
> *You illuminate all that no longer serves,*

*Enhancing my truest feelings and gifts.*
*I claim my wholeness under your bright light.*

Using the moon water, anoint the heart in a clockwise manner:

*I draw your energy into the active energy of my middle self,*
*Center of actions and interactions,*
*You illuminate all that no longer serves,*
*Unleashing my truest abilities and powers.*
*I claim my wholeness under your bright light.*

Using the moon water, anoint the crown in a clockwise manner:

*I draw your essence up in the heights of the higher self,*
*Home of intellect and wisdom,*
*You illuminate all that no longer serves,*
*Empowering my truest thoughts and will.*
*I claim my wholeness under your bright light.*

## Ritual Protocol

Once the preparations are completed, stand under the full moon, either out-side or by an open window. If you can do neither, direct your mind's eye to the moon above and hold the image firmly; this can be supported by the talisman. For this ritual, you remain standing and aware. Recite the invocation.

*Moon, I stand in your fullness,*
*I come seeking the wholeness you exude.*
*Drawing down the brilliant light of your illumination,*
*Revealing within me the truth I seek.*
*I draw your powers into me now,*
*Blending them with my own strength,*
*Activating all that which I have denied myself.*
*Shining into the dark corners, revealing wisdom.*
*Emboldening the light of my authentic self.*
*Filling myself up with your wholeness,*
*Reflecting what I now claim as my right.*
*For in your brightest phase, my truth is illuminated.*
*Your shadows, like my own, fully embraced.*
*Never rejected, but part of my wholeness.*
*Brilliant Luna, Selene, Mother Moon Mistress,*

*known by a thousand names,*
*Hekate's domain.*
*My power mirrors yours.*
*I am eternal, illuminated, and justified.*
*Complete. Whole.*
*Deeper you go into me, merging with my will,*
*Healing, revealing,*
*Your essence empowering my own sacredness.*

Ground yourself by connecting your energy to the earth. Envision a cord running throughout your being, permeating each cell. Direct this cord down through your root, your legs, then your feet, extending your roots deep into the earth.

You are grounded below. This is the tether that will enable you to invoke the moon without losing yourself in the energy, while also connecting you to the lunar energy within the earth, land, and Underworld.

Envision another cord running throughout your being, permeating each cell. Extend this cord out from your heart center to your surroundings, anchoring yourself in them. This keeps you centered and protected during the ritual and allows you to invoke the energy of the moon reflected on the earth.

The final cord evokes the power of mysticism. Feel this force throughout your being, permeating each cell. The center of the higher self is the crown. Focus the energy here, unfurling your connection to the moon above.

You are grounded, centered, and connected.

Soak up the lunar energy beneath you through your roots. Feel the moon's power, which pulses throughout the natural world, creating the tides and our body's rhythms.

*I ground myself with the moon-soaked earth,*
*You illuminate all that no longer serves,*
*Cleansing and restoring my body.*
*I claim my wholeness under your bright light.*

*I wash myself with your tides,*
*You illuminate all that no longer serves,*
*Cleansing and restoring my blood.*
*I claim my wholeness under your bright light.*

Pull in the lunar energy around you, reflected in the moon beams, the shadows, and how material objects change under her glow.

> *I inhale your winds into my being,*
> *You illuminate all that no longer serves,*
> *Cleansing and restoring my breath.*
> *I claim my wholeness under your bright light.*
>
> *I draw your fiery light into my being,*
> *You illuminate all that no longer serves,*
> *Cleansing and restoring my spirit.*
> *I claim my wholeness under your bright light.*

Draw the lunar energy directly down from her through your connection into your being.

> *Through your power, Mother Moon Mistress,*
> *And the Sacred Seven forces of the worlds and elements that*
> *You direct through your light,*
> *I am whole this night.*
> *As I speak it, it is so.*

Collect this energy at your heart center until it becomes a beautiful sphere. Place your hands over your heart, letting the spirit-moon spill out into them, creating a new sphere. Using your hands, stretch that sphere all around you until you are completely enveloped in the spirit-moon that is a blending of your three selves and the moon.

Your hands, heart, and body have merged with the lunar energy.

Your spirit-moon protects you from all harmful energies while connecting you to the forces illuminated by the physical moon's energy. Feel the energy of earth soaked in the moon's power, feel how the moon changes the air, see the fiery reflection of the sun in the moon, and sense the energy of the moon's influence on the waters of the earth.

Draw these elemental forces into your spirit-moon: green for earth, yellow for air, orange for fire, and blue for water. Once combined, the spirit-moon is complete—a perfect mirror of the moon above you.

You can evoke deities into your sphere at this point, if you feel led to do so.

Pause here in this space, becoming energized by the forces you've summoned.

Stay in the energy for as long as you feel led. When you are ready to return to everyday consciousness, begin the disconnection process.

Begin by releasing the moon-sphere surrounding you:

*Earth, I release you now, go knowing your energy was well received.*

*Air, I release you now, go knowing your energy was well received.*

*Water, I release you now, go knowing your energy was well received.*

*Fire, I release you now, go knowing your energy was well received.*

*I release the power of the Underworld, go knowing your energy was well received.*

*I release the power of the Middle World, go knowing your energy was well received.*

*I release the power of the Upper World, go knowing your energy was well received.*

*I release my connection to Mother Moon, who infuses and influences all the Sacred Seven Forces, without and within.*

Feel the sphere absorb back into the Sacred Seven forces and your disconnection from the moon. You feel confident that the connection can be restored at will. You gently return to your regular state of mind.

Retract your cord that binds you with the moon and the Starry Road. Relaxing this force within you, return to your regular state of awareness.

Draw in your cord connecting you to the external world. Relaxing this force within you, return to your regular state of awareness.

Pull up your cord linking you to the Underworld. Relaxing this force within you, return to your regular state of awareness.

This ritual often inspires creativity, insights, and the emergence of new allies. It can be very invigorating or leave you ready to venture into the dreamworld. As with all rituals, it will continue to act on and through you.

## Waning Moon Three Keys Ritual

The waning moon evokes the energy of release and removal. Developing a personal ritual that locks up what is burdening you, sending it to the moon as offering, frees you as you move toward honoring Hekate on the dark moon.

Two of the most powerful symbols associated with Hekate are the number three and keys. She has various epithets associated with the number three, such as Triformis. Her dominion over land, sea, and sky offers a framework for our waning-moon release intentions.

This ritual combines the symbolism of three and keys, while attuning to the natural removal energy of the waning moon. Each key is infused with an intention linked to the three selves: root, heart, and crown.

You'll need paper for making keys and string to bind them together.

Spend some time observing your own thoughts, noting the worries that spiral around in your mind. Write a short declaration of release once you've settled on what burdens you.

You can craft keys from plain paper for burning or burying, or cut them from paper impregnated with seeds and then plant them so that what caused pain is transformed into beauty. For a multicolored approach, use hues that evoke the root, heart, and crown—such as black, red, and white.

After the ritual, you will dispose of the physical keys. Burying or burning the keys amplifies the energy of this working.

First cut out three paper keys. Then you'll need to inscribe them. Add intentions specific to the root, heart, and crown—one for each key:

- **Root**: the emotions associated with what you are releasing

- **Heart**: the actions and interpersonal aspects of what you are releasing

- **Crown**: the beliefs and thoughts relating to what is being released

Next, run a cord (use something light, like embroidery floss) through each key, then tie the cords together so that they are all connected. Wrap the bundle of cords around the three keys, binding them together.

Do your normal preparations for a ritual, align to the waning moon, then hold your keys and recite:

> Hekate's Moon,
> As you flee,
> Take these keys far from me.
> As your cycle changes fast,
> Freed am I from all that's past.
> In perfect trust and purest love,
> I call down your energy from above,
> Sending these keys up to you,
> So that the past is finally through.

Recite your intentions of release, then burn or bury the key talisman.

## Hekate's Fire Dancing Ritual

This is a kinetic ecstatic ritual; physical movement and spoken words combine to help you transcend and enter Hekate's Wheel of Fire. It would be excellent if you can do this beside a roaring bonfire, but it is equally powerful in front of a smoldering cauldron on the altar. This ritual was inspired by my own experiences of fire dancing. To add mystery and challenge to this experience, a blindfold can be worn if it is safe to do so.

Anointing with sacred ash is part of this ritual. Make your own from the remnants of the botanicals you burn in your cauldron. You can create finer ash from these remnants by burning them again. Should you have access to a high heat source, such as a wood stove, there is a technique that renders beautiful ash. Put the burned remnants in a container that can withstand high temperatures and keep it in a strong fire for a minimum of a day.

You will also need to create a playlist of music suitable for ecstatic fire dancing. There are lots of choices online.

Conduct your usual ritual preparations before going into the ecstatic component. Then put on any music that will help you enter trance.

Start to gently sway back and forth. Continue to do so while reciting the invocation to maintain your connection to the Wheel of Fire. See it spinning from deep within you; as you move your hips, you swirl it into motion, connecting you to the fire on your altar or at the bonfire. Open up your three selves, letting them dance through you into the altar, creating a dancing flame to welcome Hekate in your sacred space. Recite:

> *I call to you, Queen of the Hieros Pyr,*
> *For you were born of the stars and darkness,*
> *You are the spark,*
> *Giving birth to your sacred flame.*
> *Your fire reigns.*
> *Your fire breathed life into the world,*
> *Descending into your fiery cave at the core,*
> *Fueling your eternal cauldron*
> *Your flames fuel all that is.*
> *From hence you walk the worlds,*
> *Guiding your chosen.*
> *Hail Hieros Pyr, Keeper of the Wheel of Fire,*
> *May I walk in your Wheel of Fire.*

You'll perceive her Wheel of Fire as she deems best for you. Then proclaim:

*I enter your Hieros Pyr,*
*I walk your Wheel of Fire,*
*Dancing in the flames.*
*Let me drink your fire,*
*Fueling my power,*
*Let me carry your fire,*
*Burning all that which no longer serves,*
*Igniting what longs to be born.*
*Revealing to me your mysteries.*
*For your fire is without end or beginning,*
*The flame burns and gives birth,*
*The smoke spreads your power,*
*And I rise from the ashes.*

Anoint the epicenters of your three selves with the ashes.

Resume your dancing if you have stopped. Embrace the flames as you move. Really let go and dance in Hekate's flames.

When you are ready, conclude the experience. Take your time disconnecting from the Wheel of Fire. You may have been given a sumbolon of your unique fire. Stop dancing and steady your breath. End the experience with:

*All gratitude for permitting me to walk your Wheel of Fire.*
*I take my leave now,*
*Returning to my physical being.*
*I honor this flame that can never be dimmed.*
*I bless this smoke, sending forth the power of Her flame,*
*Hail to thee, Hekate, Hieros Pyr.*
*You are the Wheel of Fire.*
*The Star-Fire,*
*The Fire creating all life,*
*The guiding torch,*
*The source of our witch-fire,*
*And the fire of destruction.*
*I am your fire made flesh.*
*I carry your torch,*
*Lighting my way, guiding others, and governing the power of destruction.*
*Hail to thee.*

The firewalking trance can leave you depleted or invigorated. Excess of either is a sign that you need to pull yourself back to the middle world using a centering technique. You can also use a sensory grounding technique by connecting with a taste, smell, touch, sight, and sound.

After you disconnect from the Hieros Pyr, you may become very chilled; prevent this by wrapping up in a blanket as soon as the ritual is complete. Make sure you eat a carb-rich snack while processing your experience.

**Inner Temple Throne Ritual and Journey**
The personal inner temple is our mystical sacred space, connected to the great Hekate's Temple. It may have been some time since you visited to claim your sacred name. Now it is time to return to construct your own throne.

This journey is best done on the dark moon and is especially suitable as an end to a devotional cycle. This is a more elaborate experience that merges a ceremonial aspect with a meditative journey and includes powerful Voces Magicae evocative of Hekate.

This is a very personal ritual; it uses all the components of your craft that will comprise your "throne," from botanicals to aspects of Hekate. Your personal power sigil and sacred name will adorn the throne. Your throne can also include your astrology, characteristics, experiences, and so on. Create an altar of them as an offering to Hekate and the spirit of witchcraft, or craft an actual throne, incorporating these items and spirits.

Purple is an excellent color for wearing during this journey. I also recommend that you use the color as a correspondence for this ritual, as it evokes royalty, empowerment, and personal agency. Your personal power sigil can be held, worn, or applied as a tattoo for this ritual.

Do the usual cleansing of mind, body, spirit, and place, then recite the invocation.

*Hail Hekate,*
*She who is the Anima Mundi,*
*The Soul of the World,*
*Sovereign Queen of Witches.*

*ASKEI KATASKEI ERON OREON OMEGA SAMNI BAUI* [always said three times] *PHOBANTIA SEMNE* [spoken once].

*I have created my own throne,*
*Borne of your blood and mine.*

*I sit here as your sovereign witch.*
*Aligned with the spirits,*
*Practitioner of your craft.*
*I seek to place my throne with my*
*Inner Temple,*
*Guide me as I do so.*

## Entering the Inner Temple

Close your eyes now. Let your physical self rest, safe in the space you've created. See the entrance to your inner temple. You cross into this sacred place, stepping through the entrance to your temple. Take note of the appearance; see how it has changed since you last were here. The objects you've selected for constructing your throne accompany you. Some you carry; others walk with you.

When you are ready, begin to assemble the materials for your throne. As you organize these objects, the necessary tools appear. Begin building your throne; take your time to carefully select what objects to place and where. Rearrange things as necessary. The spirits of the animals, entities, and deities being placed into your throne join in your work. The final element is to add your sigil and sacred name.

Once your throne is finished, you claim your seat as sovereign. Sit down. Feel the power you have created; it matches your own power. Rest for a few moments, taking in the spirits and guides who helped construct your throne, basking in the energy.

From your throne, you hold court with Hekate, your spirits, allies, guides, and other deities who helped with the construction. Your temple shimmers, becomes more majestic, as if you have transcended into a higher realm. Arise from your throne to place your offering at a moon altar. While you stand before the altar, Hekate and her companions come to you with messages and gifts. When this is finished, you return to your throne. As you sit down, it shifts back into your personal temple.

Tend to anything in your temple that calls for your attention. When it is time, make your way out, walking down the path back to the entrance to your physical self. Cross the threshold. Open your eyes and touch your personal power sigil. How has it changed now that you've created your throne?

The process of ascending to your throne invokes greater sovereignty, including the wisdom of the higher self, often resulting in a strengthening of our magickal and mystical abilities. There is much to process within this complex ritual. I highly recommended journaling about the feelings you experienced as you ascended, along with contemplating the spirits who attended. Record your messages from Hekate and your companions.

# Chapter 19

## Initiation—Meaning and Guide

*The energy of your fires burns within me.*
*Your mighty winds are my breath,*
*The waters of your creation run through my veins,*
*And my feet walk your road.*
*Like you, I am the darkest night of the Underworld,*
*The starry heights of the Upper World,*
*And all points in between.*

Initiations are moments of spiritual rebirth, when we cross a threshold between who we were and what we are becoming. After an initiation, we have moments of intense connection to Hekate and her deeper world, of knowing beyond words that we are, indeed, made of her. We know we are sacred and powerful, and have a purpose. There is a paradigm shift that permeates throughout us. There is a death of what no longer serves, and then there is the emergence into our new selves. I call these "Kore" experiences. Like Persephone exiting the Underworld to begin anew, so do we. We are "maidens" all over again, but wiser and attuned to our own power just as she was.

As we evolve, so do our initiations—a form of spiritual "leveling up." With each initiation, we are reborn, beginning a new path toward the next unknown initiation. Hekate lights the way, offers keys, as we step further into her spinning wheel.

There are two broad categories of initiations: the spontaneous ones, where the very essence of our beings evolves into a deeper awareness, and the purposefully planned ceremonies. In the first type, which can occur during meditations, rituals, or when we simply embrace our true nature, there is a spiritual shift in how we connect with Hekate and her deeper world and the way we conduct our lives. The mysteries move into our consciousness, bringing real attunement and awareness. These can be mystical experiences of stepping into the flow of Hekate's Wheel or shamanic soul transformations where we undergo spiritual surgery.

Sometimes, however, it is not until after we understand the significance of an event that a spontaneous initiation will occur—long after we've had the experience. Years ago, I had a profound encounter with two crows and received a message from them: "You will never walk alone." At the time, I thought it referred to romantic relationships. It wasn't until years later that, completely out of the blue, the message that Hekate had spoken through the crows came to me. In that moment, I was initiated, unlocking the knowledge that Hekate had always been with me during a dark time in my life.

After periods of study, we may feel ready for an initiation ceremony to acknowledge our accomplishments. More like a graduation than a soul initiation, these ceremonies are important milestones that we have earned. However, unlike graduation from a formal education setting, self-initiation ceremonies are deeply personal. You'll know when the time has come for one.

## Preparation for Initiation
In the coven, when students in the advanced programs are preparing for their initiation, they craft an acrostic, render a Declaration of Initiation, craft a talisman, and then do a presentation. This is followed by a ceremony with the rest of the coven.

The following process is based on this protocol but adapted for personal use. The new moon, especially the Aries one near the spring equinox, which is the start of the new astrological year, is an ideal time for initiations.

## Devotional Cycle
Beginning on a dark moon, start a devotional cycle that includes daily reflection on the journey that led you to be ready for an initiation ceremony.

## Vox Magica of Initiation
Do a thorough review of your experiences and practices; consolidate this into an acrostic (vox magica). This will become the foundation for the declaration and talisman, which are the initiatory offerings.

## Cauldron of Initiation

As you do your review, add tokens (symbols) of the journey to a cauldron; the cauldron will be featured in the ceremony. You can even temporarily remove items from your Cista Mystica.

## Declaration of Initiation

> *Great Hekate, my allies, and helpmates with me on this crooked path,*
> *I declare that I am initiated into the magick and mystery,*
> *I have claimed the keys offered.*

A Declaration of Initiation is a personal statement reflecting your accomplishments, featuring the primary aspects of Hekate that you are aligned with, and expressing appreciation for your guides and helpmates—the spirits, correspondences, workings, and so on that support your journey.

Begin by calling upon Hekate, with primary epithets, and then state your sacred name: "*I declare that I am* [name], *and am seeking initiation into your mysteries.*" Listing the epithets, along with the keys you have claimed, forms the heart of the declaration. Here's an example:

> *Great Hekate, Enduring Guardian, Gatekeeper, and Guide,*
> *I declare that I am well prepared for*
> *Initiation into Your Mysteries.*
> *I have well tended to the Keys you gave,*
> *And through them, I am initiated:*
> *The Key of Dadophoros, Torchbearer,*
> *I have been devoted to following where you lead.*
> *The Key of Ameibousa, Transformer,*
> *I have been changed for the better by magick.*
> *The Key of Kleidoukhos, Keeper of Keys,*
> *I have witnessed your mystery, and I hold it in reverence.*
> *This declaration is my offering and pledge.*

## Talisman of Initiation: Kore Sigil Egg Knot

This talisman is your offering during the initiation ceremony. It is a talisman of rebirth, for use during initiations and the season of spring. This working connects us to the spirit of Kore, Persephone emerging from her time in the Underworld. An egg is the foundation, symbolizing all that went into the creation of it while also evoking the potential of it. In some ancient references,

Hekate was called Kore, perhaps speaking to her powers relating to emergence, growth, and rebirth as symbolized by the youthful maiden. *Kore* means both an "innocent young woman" and "sprout," the emerging plant from the seed.

Eggs are excellent purifiers, cleansing away all that no longer serves; their shell protects the mystery within, and they were included in ancient Hekate's suppers. Start with a plain one that has no decorations. You can use real a hard-boiled or blown-out egg or a stone one. However, the unfinished wooden ones that are around 2.5 inches in length work perfectly to make a long-lasting talisman.

This is a cording spell, with a "nest" made for holding the egg, in the style of a macrame plant holder. Each of the four cords connects to the primary forces of fire, earth, water, and air. Four evokes the energy of growth and stability. The number eight, signifying completion, is evoked by the number of cords and the number of bay leaves.

This is ideal to do during the spring equinox, as well as during a crescent waxing moon.

## Supplies

- Candle (represents fire)
- Sacred smoke—a mixture of fennel, rose, and lavender works well (represents air)
- Egg
- Personal sigil representing initiation and rebirth
- Paint markers for inscribing the egg
- Oleum Spirita or another enchanting oil
- 8 bay leaves, or charms that you can write on
- Hole punch and scissors
- 10 yards 2 mm cording, such as macrame string or yarn
- 24 small beads with openings large enough to fit on your cord, optional
- Circe's Wash or moon water (represents water)
- Container of soil or botanicals (represents earth)

**Procedure**

When you are ready to create the talisman, light a candle and burn sacred smoke or get the diffuser going.

Inscribe the sigil you created onto the egg. Once it has dried, enchant it with Oleum Spirita.

Punch a hole in each of the bay leaves, if using. Inscribe the leaves or charms with a mixture of remembrances of your journey and keys for manifesting what you are seeking as you emerge. Work with the four forces (fire, earth, water, air) so that there is one remembrance and one manifesting for each. You will end up with four of remembrance and four for manifesting. Once dried, add Oleum Spirita.

Cut eight strings that measure about twenty-four inches each. Unify them with a knot about six inches from the bottom. Say, *"Knot of one, the spell's begun."* At this point, you may want to turn your work upside down to make it easier to handle.

Divide the eight cords into four pairs. Tie each pair together with a knot about half an inch above the bottom knot. Add beads if desired, one on each cord so that there are eight in total. Adding the beads can be a bit tricky. To do it, thread a needle with regular thread. Tie the two ends of the thread into a secure knot. Slide the cording into the loop created by doing this. Insert the needle into the bead and slide the bead down the thread and over the cording. It will be tight, so give it a good tug to get the bead on the cord.

Criss-cross the eight cords into four new pairs so that the two pairs on the left swap partners, and the two pairs on the right do likewise. This is where the egg "nest" starts. Tie these into four new knots, about half an inch from the previous ones so that a diamond design takes form. Add beads.

Next, the two middle pairs swap partners, and the two outer pairs swap. Tie a third set of four grouping knots about half an inch above the last knots. Add beads. This should have formed the little nest into which you can insert the egg. You'll have three rows of knots and diamonds, with a total of twelve knots and twenty-four beads.

Group all the cords together and tie a knot about a third of the way from the top. The part above the knot you can use to tie for hanging. Flip your work the right way up (if you've been working upside down).

Slide the bay leaves or charms onto the eight strands of the tail and then knot all eight together. Say, *"Knot by knot, this spell's complete."*

## Enchanting Incantation

Now that the talisman is made, enchant it with the following incantation.

Hold a lit candle over the talisman and recite:

> *Kore,*
> *Endless One.*
> *Returning.*
> *Emerging.*
> *Growing.*
> *Attend my spell.*

If this talisman is part of your rebirth or initiation process, add some lines to the incantation describing this. Then say:

> *I call upon Sacred Flame, burn away all that no longer serves and illuminate what is real and true, drawing into this talisman.*

Rub the talisman with the water:

> *I call upon Sacred Water, cleanse away all that no longer serves and wash this talisman with what is real and true.*

Pass the talisman through the sacred smoke:

> *I call upon Sacred Smoke, blow away all that no longer serves and infuse this talisman with what is real and true.*

Touch the soil or botanicals:

> *I call upon Sacred Earth, absorb all that no longer serves and nourish this talisman with what is real and true.*

With the Oleum Spirita, anoint the sigil on the egg, rubbing in a clockwise direction, while reciting:

> *Kore, Kore,*
> *I call you to life.*
> *Kore, Kore,*
> *Honoring all that led me here,*
> *And emerging,*
> *Becoming truer, more real,*
> *And growing.*

Anoint the gathering knot at the bottom of the talisman, rubbing in a clockwise direction, and say:

> *Kore, Kore,*
> *These cords I bind*
> *To strengthen the spell,*
> *My knots cannot be undone.*

When finished, hold the Kore talisman at heart center and recite:

> *Kore, Kore.*
> *The spell is done.*
> *As I speak it,*
> *So it becomes.*

Keep your Kore talisman close and connect with it as part of your daily ritual. This talisman has a powerful personality. It will remind you of how far you've come, what you deserve, and so much more.

## Sacred Adornment: Crafting or Choosing a Kroki

A kroki is a ceremonial bracelet worn for High Rituals and other workings. It can be worn daily as a talisman. Craft one to signify your initiation.

There's no one way to craft or choose a kroki. You can make one from simple braids or do complex beadwork. Or you can purchase a bracelet that just *feels* right.

The most basic technique is to braid or knot three cords into a bracelet, adding charms, then infusing it with Oleum Spirita when complete. The kroki should be worn on the left wrist.

## Initiation Ceremony

Since this is your personal initiation, feel free to adapt it so it works best for you.

**Sacred adornment**: Kroki of Initiation

**Offerings**: Declaration of Initiation and Kore Sigil Egg Talisman

**Purification**: Khernips, with a botanical suitable for initiation—such as thyme, rosemary, or lavender. You may want to create moon water suitable for the occasion.

**Sacred Flame**: Inscribe a candle with your Sigil of Initiation and infuse it with Oleum Spirita.

**Sacred smoke**: The above mentioned botanicals work well, as does the Hekate's Cauldron Incense in *Entering Hekate's Garden*.

**Oleum Spirita**: For anointing yourself during the ritual

**Cauldron of Initiation**: Place objects and symbols of your journey, which is the evidence supporting your initiatory status, in a cauldron.

**Altar**: Create an Altar of Initiation with the ceremony accoutrements and other remembrances of your journey, including the Cista Mystica. Imagery evocative of the primary epithets of Hekate you have connected with, your spirit guide, and other objects can also be included.

## Initiation Script

Standing at your altar, light the candle, and perform the three-fold procedure. Moving the candle counterclockwise, say:

> *This space is cleansed from all that is unwelcome.*

Clockwise:

> *This space is protected, and the circle cast.*

Put on your kroki:

> *This connects me to mine own sacredness, to Hekate, and to her deeper world. This ritual has begun.*

Perform khernips, igniting the botanical sprig, immersing it in the water, and reciting:

> *I banish all that harms, I speak only the truth, and shall be heard.*

Ignite the sacred smoke:

> *May this sacred smoke connect me to the mysteries as Hekate reveals.*

Recite your Declaration of Initiation, then make your offerings:

> *Great Hekate and my allies,*
> *I make these offerings as evidence of my devotion and accomplishment.*
> *May they be well received. May you grant entrance into your mysteries.*

Pause here to let them accept the offerings, noting any perceptions that come through. Then with the Oleum Spirita and beginning at the root, anoint in a clockwise direction:

*I anoint my root, seat of emotions and intuition. May mine by worthy of initiation.*

Anoint the heart center:

*I anoint my heart, the crossroads of myself and the world. May my actions be worthy of initiation.*

Now anoint the crown, clockwise in the middle of the forehead—the physical representation of the third eye:

*I claim my crown and awaken my third eye, seeing into your mysteries. May my thoughts be worthy of initiation.*

Get comfortable, close your eyes, and attune your three selves.

With your deeper vision, see yourself entering Hekate's Temple. Inside the temple is a great cauldron in which you immerse yourself; your known allies surround the cauldron. Within the cauldron are allies of plant, animal, and stone. Some will be familiar, some new, signifying your evolution into a deeper connection to the mysteries.

When you are ready, emerge from the cauldron. Hekate calls you to her throne, speaking of this new journey and offering you a new key.

With her torch, she illuminates your way out of the temple. Express gratitude and bid Hekate and your allies "Hail and Farewell."

Take your time coming back into your physical self and returning to regular consciousness. As you contemplate the experiences and sensations, you will find yourself forever changed by the initiation.

Create a talisman based on the new key that Hekate gave you. Wear it as you begin the journey anew.

# Author's Note

*Entering Hekate's Cauldron* is the final book in the trilogy I wrote expanding on my first book about Modern Hekatean Witchcraft, *Keeping Her Keys: An Introduction to Hekate's Modern Witchcraft*. The first part of this series, *Entering Hekate's Garden: The Magick, Medicine, and Mystery of Plant Spirit Witchcraft*, offers readers practical and mystical ways to embrace green witchcraft. The second, *Entering Hekate's Cave: The Journey through Darkness to Wholeness*, is dedicated to healing the shadow. This final installment is a compendium of knowledge, spells, and spirits.

While writing *Entering Hekate's Cauldron*, I made the decision to focus on sharing as much witchery as possible, rather than having a lengthy reference section—which would have greatly reduced the practical content of this book. I value thoughtful analyses of Hekate and magick, from philological sources to psychological approaches, as well as contemporary understanding. I am indebted to the authors whose work inspires me, and they deserve acknowledgement. I call my repository of sources "Hekate's Library," and it currently has over 250 books and articles on its virtual and physical shelves.

Hekate's history, from ancient rituals to her portrayal in art and literature, and her numerous epithets were drawn from dozens of works, including ancient texts, scholarly articles and books, and online databases (such as Perseus). Investigating Hekate's history often leads to transcendent experiences for me. There are moments when I profoundly connect to the words and images on the page or screen. Ancient spells spring to life, descriptions of ancient chthonic altars and magickal boxes inspire me to create versions of them, a priestess of Hekate at Lagina jumps across the centuries to become a special advisor, and a weathered philosopher, Proclus, takes up residency in my thoughts and dreams.

Should you be looking for an excellent source about ancient Hekate, I recommend *Hekate Soteira* by Sarah Iles Johnston; her other publications, such as *The Restless Dead: Encounters between the Living and the Dead in Ancient Greece*, and her numerous peer-reviewed articles, such as the one on "lamp"-bearing goddesses in "Myth and the Getty Hexameters," are also wonderful resources. The *Greek Magical Papyri* (PGM) are inspirational in my work. This ancient compendium of spells and knowledge is a font of inspiration, especially if you are curious about how ancient magick may have been practiced. Although *The Chaldean Oracles* can open us to the greater mysteries, it is a challenging read; however, working through it can be very meaningful. The *Greek English Lexicon* (LSJ), along with the supplements, are fundamental resources on the ancient epithets of Hekate, although there are omissions that have been detailed in subsequent scholarly articles, such as "A List of Epithets from the *Greek Magical Papyri* That Are Not Recorded in the LSJ and LSJ Supplements" by Eleni Pachoumi in *Glotta* 87 (2001): 155–158.

Examining the origin, purpose, and contents of ancient Hekate's suppers has required deep research into ancient texts, several of which are quite obscure, yet very intriguing. For example, The Lucian of Samosata Project, an online database, contains *The Dialogues of the Dead*, which inspired the lustral eggs ritual. I spent a year exploring the ancient recipes that most likely were used to create the components of the meal, from the fresh cheese recipe in this book to the cultural significance of a type of fish (mullet) included in the supper. *A Taste of Ancient Rome* by Ilaria Gozzini Giacosa offers modern takes on ancient recipes and provides insight into how those preparing the ancient suppers may have viewed food and cookery. Seeking Hekate's ancient symbols, and how they were included in ancient magick, led to me discovering the Campbell Bonner Magical Gems Database.

Hekate featured as a character in several stories, myths, and plays—such as Euripides's *Medea* and Ovid's *Metamorphoses*—and in the telling of Persephone's story in *The Homeric Hymn to Demeter*. My collection of academic theses, dissertations, articles, and books is vast. One example of a scholarly article that is worth reviewing is "The Hecate Cult in Anatolia: Rituals and Dedications in Lagina" by Coşkun Daşbacak, in *Anados 6–7/2006–2007 Studies of the Ancient World*, that details how Hekate was worshiped in ancient Anatolia, which was quite different from other areas. The work of Dr. Christopher A. Faraone on a variety of topics related to Hekate and ancient magick has been most helpful. The *Oxford Classical Dictionary* has also been very useful. For an academic treatment on ancient magic, Daniel Ogden's *Magic, Witchcraft, and Ghosts in the Greek and Roman Worlds* gives insight into this topic, while *Daughters of Hecate: Women and Magic in the Ancient World*, an anthology edited by Kimberly B. Stratton and Dayna S. Kalleres, contextualizes gender and magick in antiquity.

My interpretation of the epithets is drawn from English translations and by examining the original context and meaning of the word. In particular, the classic *Greek-English Lexicon* by Henry George Liddell and Robert Scott is invaluable for researching Hekate's epithets, and there are academic articles exploring them further that I drew from. Discovering the epithets compelled me into deeper study, from Johnston's take on Hekate as Kleidoukhos to seeking to better comprehend Enodia (also spelled Ennodia or Einodia) in works such as *Religion and Society in Ancient Thessaly* by Maria Mili.

As a psychologist, I am most appreciative of authors who have explored Hekate from a psychological standpoint, several of whom are cited in *Entering Hekate's Cave*—such as the works of James Hillman; C. G. Jung, including his *Essays on a Science of Mythology: The Myth of the Divine Child and the Mysteries of Eleusis* that he coauthored with C. Kerényi; and the contemporary works of Charlene Spretnak and Jean Shinoda Bolen.

My primary influences for understanding tarot cards include Mary K. Greer and Rachel Pollack. My approach to astrology is "modern traditional," inspired by astrologers such as Demetra George. For decoding symbols, *The Book of Symbols: Reflections on Archetypal Images*, edited by Ami Ronnberg and Kathleen Martin, is one of my favorites. For the symbolism of animals, the modern classic by Ted Andrews, *Animal Speak: The Spiritual and Magical Powers of Creatures Great and Small*, has long been a reliable source.

Regarding sources for correspondences, *Entering Hekate's Garden* contains a comprehensive reference section for plants. For botanicals, stones, colors, and numbers, I merged my personal experience with standard properties as given in works historical and modern. An example of a modern reference guide on correspondences is *Llewellyn's Complete Book of Correspondences* by Sandra Kynes. Nicholas Pearson's many books on stones are highly recommended, and I often use his works as reference material. For exploring the world of spirits, Christopher Penczak has many wonderful books. I am inspired by not only reframing ancient workings but also amazing authors and teachers, particularly Judika Illes, who I am so fortunate to have as my editor.

Covina, your spirit and all those who belong to the coven, is such an immense blessing. To Apphia, Pandeia, and all the others, gratitude for being guides and helpmates. My sons are with me every step of the way, providing insight and support, being sounding boards, and bringing joy. And to Christen, my partner in all things.

# List of Epithets

| Epithet | Meaning |
|---|---|
| Adementos | Unconquered |
| Agia | Sacred |
| Aglaos | Beautiful |
| Agriope | Fierce |
| Aidonaea | Of the Underworld |
| Aizeos | Vigorous |
| Alexeatis | Destroyer of Evil |
| Alkimos | Strong |
| Ambrotos | Eternal |
| Ameibousa | Transformer |
| Amphiphaes | Illuminator |
| Amphiprosopos | Looking Both Ways |
| Anassa | Queen |
| Anassa Eneroi | Queen of the Dead |
| Anima Mundi | World Soul |
| Antaian Theou | Greeter |
| Aoroboros | Devourer of the Dead |
| Apotropaios | Averter |
| Archikos | Royal |
| Aregos | Helper |
| Ariste | Best |
| Arkyia | Entrapper |
| Arrhetos | Indescribable |
| Astrodia | Star Walker |
| Atala | Tender |
| Atala Phroneousa | Kindhearted |
| Atasthalos | Reckless |
| Athanatos | Immortal |
| Autophyes | Self-Begotten |

| Epithet | Meaning |
| --- | --- |
| Azonos | Limitless |
| Azostos | Unleashed |
| Baridoukhos | Guardian of Boats |
| Basileia | Queen |
| Borborophorba | Filth Eater |
| Brimo | Terrifying |
| Bythios | Of the Deep |
| Chthonia | Of the Earth |
| Dadophoros | Torchbearer |
| Daidalos | Cunning |
| Darmasandra | Subduer of Men |
| Daspleti | Frightful |
| Deinos | Terrible |
| Despoina | Lady |
| Doloeis | Astute |
| Drakaina | Serpent-Dragon |
| Eidolios | Ghostly |
| Eileithyia | Midwife |
| Einalia | Of the Sea |
| Ekdotis | Bestower |
| Ekklesia | Of the Assembly |
| Elateira | Charioteer |
| Empylios | At the Gate |
| Enodia | Of the Road |
| Epipurgidia | Of the Tower |
| Episkopos | Guardian |
| Epiteichea | Stronghold |
| Erannos | Lovely |
| Ergatis | Energizer |
| Erigeneia | Setting Moon |
| Erototokos | Bringer of Desire |
| Eukoline | Good Tempered |
| Eupatereia | Noble Born |
| Geneteira | Great Mother |
| Gorgo | Somber |
| Hegemonen | Guide |
| Hieros Pyr | Sacred Fire |
| Iokheaira | Archer |
| Kalligeneia | Mother of Beautiful Children |
| Kalliste | Fairest |
| Kapetoktypos | Tomb Disturber |
| Kardiodaitos | Heart Eater |

| Epithet | Meaning |
| --- | --- |
| Katachthonia | Subterranean |
| Kleidoukhos | Keeper of Keys |
| Klothaie | Spinner of Time |
| Kore | Maiden |
| Kourotrophos | Guardian of Children |
| Kratais | Strong One |
| Kynegetis | Leader of Dogs |
| Kynokephalos | Dog-Headed |
| Kynolygmate | Howling |
| Kyon Melaina | Black Dog |
| Kydimos | Glorious |
| Kyria | Supreme |
| Lampadios | Torchbearer |
| Leaina | Lioness |
| Leontoukhos | Lioness |
| Liparokredemnos | Of Renown |
| Maera | Shining |
| Makairapos | Blessed |
| Mastigophoros | Punisher |
| Medusa | Protector |
| Megiste | Greatest |
| Meisoponeros | Vice Hating |
| Melaneimon | Darkness |
| Mene | Moon |
| Mormo | She Monster |
| Nekyia | Mistress of the Dead |
| Nerterios | Infernal |
| Noeros | Intellectual |
| Nomaios | Pastoral |
| Nykhia | Of the Night |
| Nyktipolos | Night Wanderer |
| Nyktophaneia | Night Shining |
| Nymphen | Bride |
| Nyssa | Beginning |
| Oistroplaneia | Divine Madness |
| Opaon | Follower |
| Ophioplokamos | Dressed in Snakes |
| Oroboros | Tail Eater |
| Ourania | Celestial |
| Ouresiphoites | Mountain Wanderer |
| Paionios | Healer |
| Pammetor | Mother of All |

| Epithet | Meaning |
|---|---|
| Pandamateira | All Powerful |
| Pandoteira | All Giver |
| Pantrophos | All Nurturing |
| Parthenos | Virgin |
| Pasikratea | Universal Queen |
| Pasimedousa | Ruling over All |
| Pege | Source |
| Pege Psychon | Source of Souls |
| Phaenno | Brilliant |
| Phaesimbrotos | Bringer of Light |
| Phileremos | Lover of Solitude |
| Phoberos | Fearful |
| Phoebe | Bright |
| Phos | Light |
| Phosphoros | Light Bearer |
| Photoplex | Lightning Striker |
| Phylake | Guardian |
| Physis | Nature |
| Podarke | Fleet Footed |
| Polyodynos | Sufferer |
| Polyonumos | Many Named |
| Porlykleitos | Renowned |
| Presbeia | Ancient |
| Prodomos | At the Threshold |
| Promethikos | Visionary |
| Propolos | Guide |
| Propolousa | Guide |
| Propylaia | Gatekeeper |
| Prothyraea | Gatekeeper |
| Protistos | Primal |
| Psychopomp | Soul Guide |
| Pyriboulos | Of Fiery Counsel |
| Pyridrakontozonos | Serpent |
| Pyriphoitos | Firewalker |
| Pyripnoa | Fire Breather |
| Pyrphoros | Torchbearer |
| Rexichthon | Earth Shatterer |
| Rixipyle | Breaker of Barriers |
| Sarkophagos | Flesh Eater |
| Skotia | Darkness |
| Soteira | Savior |
| Speirodrakontozonos | Covered in Serpents |

| Epithet | Meaning |
| --- | --- |
| Stratelatis | Leader |
| Tartaroukhos | Ruler |
| Tauropolos | Straightforward |
| Tertraoditis | Of the Crossroads |
| Thanategos | Death Bringer |
| Thea Deinos | Dread Goddess |
| Therobromon | Roaring One |
| Tletos | Patient |
| Triformis | Three-Formed or Triple Goddess |
| Tymbidian | Somber |
| Zatheos | Divine |
| Zonodrakontos | Serpentine |
| Zoogonos | Seed of Life |
| Zootrophos | Nourisher of Life |

Sources include ancient texts such as *Orphic Hymns, Greek Magical Papyri, The Chaldean Oracles*, and others.

# About the Author

Cyndi Brannen, PhD, teaches and writes from the crossroads of the deeper world and modern life. She merges her career as an applied social psychologist with meditation, ritual, and natural magic centered on the goddess Hekate as World Soul. Her work explores the journey through darkness to wholeness using the archetypes of the witch and Hekate. Cyndi's teaching focuses on personal healing through herbalism, rituals, meditations, and exploration of the deeper self. She founded the Covina Institute, a soul school dedicated to the pursuit of wholeness through structured programs of study and transcendent experiences. Find her at *keepingherkeys.com*.

# To Our Readers

Weiser Books, an imprint of Red Wheel/Weiser, publishes books across the entire spectrum of occult, esoteric, speculative, and New Age subjects. Our mission is to publish quality books that will make a difference in people's lives without advocating any one particular path or field of study. We value the integrity, originality, and depth of knowledge of our authors.

Our readers are our most important resource, and we appreciate your input, suggestions, and ideas about what you would like to see published.

Visit our website at *www.redwheelweiser.com*, where you can learn about our upcoming books and free downloads, and also find links to sign up for our newsletter and exclusive offers.

You can also contact us at *info@rwwbooks.com* or at

Red Wheel/Weiser, LLC
65 Parker Street, Suite 7
Newburyport, MA 01950